PALGRAVE STUDIES IN CULTURAL /
Series Editors

Anthony J. La Vopa, North Carolina State University

Suzanne Marchand, Louisiana State University

Javed Majeed, Queen Mary, University of London

The Palgrave Studies in Cultural and Intellectual History series has three primary aims: to close divides between intellectual and cultural approaches, thus bringing them into mutually enriching interactions; to encourage interdisciplinarity in intellectual and cultural history; and to globalize the field, both in geographical scope and in subjects and methods. This series is open to work on a range of modes of intellectual inquiry, including social theory and the social sciences; the natural sciences; economic thought; literature; religion; gender and sexuality; philosophy; political and legal thought; psychology; and music and the arts. It encompasses not just North America but Africa, Asia, Eurasia, Europe, Latin America, and the Middle East. It includes both nationally focused studies and studies of intellectual and cultural exchanges between different nations and regions of the world, and encompasses research monographs, synthetic studies, edited collections, and broad works of reinterpretation. Regardless of methodology or geography, all books in the series are historical in the fundamental sense of undertaking rigorous contextual analysis.

Published by Palgrave Macmillan

Indian Mobilities in the West, 1900–1947: Gender, Performance, Embodiment
By Shompa Lahiri

The Shelley-Byron Circle and the Idea of Europe
By Paul Stock

Culture and Hegemony in the Colonial Middle East
By Yaseen Noorani

Recovering Bishop Berkeley: Virtue and Society in the Anglo-Irish Context
By Scott Breuninger

The Reading of Russian Literature in China: A Moral Example and Manual of Practice
By Mark Gamsa

Rammohun Roy and the Making of Victorian Britain
By Lynn Zastoupil

Carl Gustav Jung: Avant-Garde Conservative
By Jay Sherry

The French Enlightenment and Its Others

The Mandarin, the Savage, and the Invention of the Human Sciences

David Allen Harvey

palgrave
macmillan

THE FRENCH ENLIGHTENMENT AND ITS OTHERS
Copyright © David Allen Harvey, 2012.

Softcover reprint of the hardcover 1st edition 2012 978-1-137-00253-2

First published in 2012 by
PALGRAVE MACMILLAN®
in the United States—a division of St. Martin's Press LLC,
175 Fifth Avenue, New York, NY 10010.

Where this book is distributed in the UK, Europe and the rest of the world,
this is by Palgrave Macmillan, a division of Macmillan Publishers Limited,
registered in England, company number 785998, of Houndmills,
Basingstoke, Hampshire RG21 6XS.

Palgrave Macmillan is the global academic imprint of the above companies
and has companies and representatives throughout the world.

Palgrave® and Macmillan® are registered trademarks in the United States,
the United Kingdom, Europe and other countries.

ISBN 978-1-349-43381-0 ISBN 978-1-137-00254-9 (eBook)

DOI 10.1057/9781137002549

Library of Congress Cataloging-in-Publication Data

Harvey, David Allen, 1971–
    The French Enlightenment and its others : the Mandarin, the savage,
and the invention of the human sciences / David Allen Harvey.
        p. cm.—(Palgrave studies in cultural and intellectual history)
    Includes bibliographical references.

    1. Enlightenment—France. 2. Cultural pluralism. 3. France—
Intellectual life—18th century. I. Title.

B1925.E5H37 2012
9449.034—dc23   2012010442

A catalogue record of the book is available from the British Library.

Design by Newgen Imaging Systems (P) Ltd., Chennai, India.

First edition: August 2012

Contents

Acknowledgments

In writing this book, I have benefited from the feedback, suggestions, and support of a great many friends and colleagues. I would like to thank April Shelford, Matt Matsuda, and Jeremy Popkin for their useful feedback on different parts of this project, and Ray Jonas, Tom Kselman, Michael Wilson, and John Warne Monroe for their continuing support and encouragement. At New College of Florida, I have been fortunate to have had wonderful colleagues—particularly Carrie Benes, Bob Johnson, Thomas McCarthy, and David Rohrbacher—who have helped to create a pleasant and intellectually stimulating work environment. At Palgrave Macmillan, Chris Chappell and Sarah Whalen have helped in many ways, both large and small, to bring this book project to fruition, while series editor Anthony LaVopa and the two anonymous reviewers all offered useful feedback, which has made the final product that much stronger. As always, any remaining weaknesses are my own.

Throughout the writing of this book, New College of Florida provided me with summer research support, including a travel grant for a visit to the Bibliothèque Nationale de France (BNF) in summer 2007, and a sabbatical in fall 2010 that allowed me to complete the first draft of the manuscript. I would especially like to thank Gordon Bauer, my predecessor as chair of the Division of Social Sciences at New College, for extending his term of administrative service for an additional semester to allow me to take my scheduled sabbatical. The American Philosophical Society graciously awarded me a Franklin Research Grant in summer 2010, which allowed me to make a second research trip to France, this time to the Archives Nationales d'Outre-Mer (ANOM) in Aix-en-Provence. The archivists and staff at both the BNF and the ANOM were invariably professional and prompt in providing me with the books, microfilms, and archival cartons I needed to complete this project.

Conducting research at a small liberal arts college located far from major research collections presents unique challenges, and so I would like to make two additional acknowledgments. The interlibrary loan staff at Jane Bancroft Cook Library in Sarasota, particularly Barbara Dubreuil and Ed Foster, were invariably helpful and courteous, promptly and cheerfully processing literally hundreds of requests for loan materials over the six years I have worked on this project. Second, though we have never met and they have no idea how much they have helped me, I would like to thank everyone affiliated with the Gallica digitalization project at the BNF, which has made over a million books, periodicals, and images available online for free download. Technological advances and institutional leadership have made possible an unprecedented *démocratisation du savoir*, which I am sure would have pleased the eighteenth-century Republic of Letters.

Parts of chapter 3 were previously published in "The Noble Savage and the Savage Noble: Philosophy and Ethnography in the *Voyages* of the Baron de Lahontan" (*French Colonial History* 11 (2010), 161–191), and "Living Antiquity: Lafitau's *Moeurs des sauvages amériquains* and the Religious Roots of the Enlightenment Science of Man" (*Proceedings of the Western Society for French History* 36 (2008), 75–92). I am grateful to the publishers of both journals for allowing me to reproduce material from these articles in the present volume.

Most of all, I would like to thank my family, particularly my wife Alicia and son Victor James, for their constant love and support. This book is dedicated to them.

Introduction

The collective imaginary of eighteenth-century France was populated—one might even say haunted—by a vast array of exotic Others. Throughout the literature of the period, foreign characters, including a Huron chief (Lahontan), Persian gentlemen (Montesquieu), Chinese mandarins (d'Argens), an Incan princess (Mme. de Graffigny), and a Tahitian elder (Diderot), drew contrasts between French Old Regime society and the customs and mores of their supposed homelands, usually to the detriment of the former. Political theorists used cross-cultural comparisons, invoking Oriental despotism (Montesquieu again), the noble savage (Rousseau), or the Confucian bureaucratic order (Quesnay and the Physiocrats) to make broader points about government, natural law, and human nature. French readers avidly devoured published narratives of travels to distant lands, and men of letters compiled, recycled, and commented on such texts in a growing corpus of cross-cultural discourse.[1] In addition to these textual representations, French learned society and the broader public alike marveled at exotic visitors to France, such as the Ottoman ambassador Mehmed Efendi, the albino African child identified only as the *nègre blanc*, and perhaps most of all, the Tahitian Aotourou, brought to France by Louis-Antoine de Bougainville in the course of his voyage around the world.

This book examines the French Enlightenment's interest in human diversity, broadly defined, and its quest for a unified science of man, which would link all of the peoples of the world, both past and present, into a common panorama of humanity across space and time. It looks not only at the grand theorists, such as Voltaire, Rousseau, Montesquieu, and Buffon, but also at the range of other eighteenth-century authors who helped to gather and publicize the information out of which the former built their syntheses. Explorers, travelers, missionaries, and government officials set out from eighteenth-century France to the most remote corners of the globe, recording detailed information on remote peoples and cultures, which the philosophers, scientists, and scholars of the metropole brought together in novel ways to support their arguments regarding human

1

nature, natural law, and the course of universal history. In their quest to uncover the underlying principles governing human society, Enlightenment thinkers invented new fields of inquiry, which over the following centuries would evolve into the disciplines of political economy, sociology, comparative religion, and both physical and cultural anthropology, and transformed existing fields such as history and political theory.[2]

My central aim in this book is to recast and contextualize contemporary scholarly debates on "Enlightenment universalism" and an alleged "Enlightenment project" through a close historical examination of the French Enlightenment's engagement with the issue of human diversity, and to challenge several prevailing but, in my view, misguided interpretations of that engagement. One widespread interpretation, first articulated by Romantic critics at the end of the eighteenth century, maintains that the Enlightenment failed to appreciate the significance of cultural diversity, assuming that those "barbaric" customs that deviated from European norms would disappear as the result of the civilizing process.[3] A second interpretation, derived largely from the work of Edward Said, acknowledges Enlightenment Europe's interest in exotic Others but denies its ability to derive any meaningful information about them, arguing instead that its "Orientalism" was a projection of European concerns, linked organically to projects of colonial domination, which allowed Westerners "to manage—and even produce—the Orient," constituting a "system of truths" that limited what could be said about the non-European world.[4] A third interpretation, developed by postmodernist critics under the influence of Horkheimer and Adorno's *Dialectic of Enlightenment* as well as that of Foucault's equation of knowledge and power and Lyotard's diagnosis of the "postmodern condition," postulates that a monolithic, totalizing "Enlightenment project" represents the culmination of an amorphously defined, but pervasive (and perverse) "modernity," the failure of which, they maintain, is amply demonstrated by the catastrophes of the mid-twentieth century.[5]

For reasons that I hope will become evident throughout this book, I believe that these interpretations fail to do justice to the French Enlightenment's engagement with human diversity. The first argument—that the Enlightenment was ahistorical and uninterested in diversity—is easily refuted by the quality and quantity of eighteenth-century French writings on the diverse peoples and customs of the past and present, though it continues to surface periodically in contemporary cultural debates.[6] The second—that

Western discourse about the Orient (and by extension, other non-Western peoples and cultures) is a closed, self-referential system that tells us a great deal about the West, and very little about the actually existing Orient—is not so much incorrect as incomplete. It is certainly true, as Kathleen Roberts has written, that "alterity construction is typically much more pertinent to Self than Other" and that "the Other that is created through narratives of alterity is imaginary, stereotypical, and biased."[7] Indeed, I will argue throughout this book that French scholars and literati frequently referenced exotic characters, locales, and institutions to substantiate arguments within intra-European political or philosophical debates, and that these self-referential purposes often compromised the accuracy of their representations of non-Western cultures (as, e.g., with the concepts of "Oriental despotism" or the "noble savage," heuristic devices with limited value for understanding actual Middle Eastern or Native American society).

Nevertheless, as I hope to demonstrate, many of these thinkers aimed to develop a science of society that would be truly universal in scope, and were acutely aware that, if such a science were limited to contemporary Europe, it would remain necessarily incomplete and parochial in character. Cross-cultural comparisons, the primary topic of this book, were central to this quest for knowledge, and served as the foundation for the elaboration of the *sciences humaines* in eighteenth-century France. The comparative method of the Enlightenment, which formed the core of the emerging "human sciences," involved collecting, assembling, and comparing the most accurate evidence available regarding the human experience across both space and time. In a famous footnote to the *Discourse on the Origins of Inequality*, Rousseau lamented the uncertain status of much of the information on non-Western societies, and advocated a more systematic collection of evidence by a community of philosophic travelers.[8] The idea that the gathering of data on the customs of specific exotic peoples could offer insights into the nature of humanity writ large was a founding impulse toward the subsequent development of anthropology, and served as one of the guiding principles of the scientific voyages of the late eighteenth century, of which the Bougainville expedition was the most prominent French example. Such cross-cultural comparisons could, and often did, inspire sentiments of European superiority, but they could also lead to an urbane cultural relativism and respect for human diversity. The future philosopher and statesman Anne-Robert-Jacques Turgot wrote as a young student in 1746 that "travels inspire a spirit of tolerance. We become accustomed to view heretics and infidels as people built like ourselves."[9]

The third argument—that Enlightenment theories of man and society formed part of a monolithic "Enlightenment project" that largely defined the nature and course of "modernity"—is a philosophical rather than a historical question, and such ethereal levels of abstraction are difficult for the earth-bound, empirical historian either to confirm or to refute. The notion that there exists a unitary "Enlightenment project," formulated in the eighteenth century and still unfolding in the present, has been shared both by those, such as Jürgen Habermas, who seek to defend such a project, and by the greater number of contemporary theorists, such as the British cultural geographer David Harvey (no relation), who denounce it.[10] At its worst, such sweeping, ahistorical generalization leads to the offhand condemnation of an entire epoch of the Western past; Richard Wolin has observed that "in the standard postmodernist demonology, the Enlightenment bears direct historical responsibility for the Gulag and Auschwitz...(and) modern totalitarianism is merely the upshot of the universalizing impetus of Enlightenment reason."[11] In response to such claims, James Schmidt has argued that "the Enlightenment project is largely a projection of the Enlightenment's critics, a projection that fastens onto a few thinkers or tendencies within a broader period and, having offered an account of what it sees as the failings of these thinkers or these tendencies, prides itself on having demonstrated the failure of the entire age."[12]

The problem with defining a reductionist, one-dimensional "Enlightenment project," of course, is that it collapses important differences between major thinkers and glosses over the contradictions, ambiguities, and self-critical doubts present in their works. It is a fact worth contemplation that, while most Western European languages have adopted a singular noun to refer to the most prominent period in the intellectual history of the eighteenth century—"the Enlightenment," *"die Aufklärung,"* *"la Ilustración,"* and so on—the French language has not. Both eighteenth-century contemporaries and subsequent French commentators have spoken instead of *"le siècle des Lumières"* (the century of lights) or *"un siècle éclairé"* (an enlightened century), terms that indicate the importance of the central metaphor of light, signifying the triumph of reason and knowledge over superstition and ignorance, to the culture of the age, but which also implicitly acknowledge the impossibility of reducing its multiplicity and many contradictions to a single definition. Recognizing this, some historians have begun to distinguish between different national contexts (the French and Scottish Enlightenments, for example), to contrast the better-known "moderate" Enlightenment of Newtonian Deists with a "radical" Enlightenment of pantheists, atheists, and freethinkers, and to speak of a distinctive "colonial Enlightenment" related to that of the metropole, but sharply opposed to it on certain points (notably issues of race and slavery).[13] All of these distinctions are valid, and most will surface in one way or another in the pages that follow, but it should also be stressed that even the moderate, metropolitan French Enlightenment, with which this book is primarily concerned, was far from speaking with a single voice.

Daniel Gordon argues that postmodern critics of a reified "Enlightenment project" fail to appreciate the difference between what Ernst Cassirer called the *esprit de système* of seventeenth-century metaphysical philosophers such as Descartes and Leibniz, who sought to construct all-encompassing philosophical systems by deduction from first principles, and the *esprit systématique* of the eighteenth century, which rejected such abstract formulations, and instead sought to advance knowledge through empirical observation of the (natural and social) world.[14] Indeed, as we shall see, eighteenth-century French theorists, explorers, and scientists regularly berated one another for constructing "systems," which, they claimed, obscured rather than facilitated the interpretation of nature and of human society alike. It is this "systematic spirit" that best accounts for both the diversity of Enlightenment interpretations and their underlying family resemblance, for while many of the figures we will consider in this study shared certain basic assumptions, their empirical observations and the interpretations they developed to explain them led them in different directions and gave rise to frequent, sometimes acrimonious debates.

It is my argument that, as eighteenth-century French thinkers sought to come to terms with human diversity across time and space, they did not band together behind a single and unitary "Enlightenment project" that twenty-first-century readers might choose to defend or to combat, but rather jostled against one another in a broad "discursive field," in which *philosophes*, antiquarians, literati, scientists, travelers, missionaries, and officials participated in lively debates on topics such as human origins, racial difference, the power of customs, laws, and climate to shape societies, and the possibility for and meaning of progress. I borrow the term "discursive field" from Robert Wuthnow, who has defined it as a "symbolic space" that "provides the fundamental categories in which thinking can take place ... establishes the limits of discussion and defines the range of problems that can be addressed."[15] The spatial metaphor reflected in the term "discursive field" is particularly relevant to my purposes, in that it accounts for both commonalities and differences, allowing the historian to refer to "the Enlightenment" as a reasonably cohesive intellectual community (or, to use the term preferred at the time, a "republic of letters") without suggesting that all Enlightenment thinkers were in agreement on all issues of importance. In fact, as we shall see throughout this book, their differences were fundamental and far reaching. Did the rapid social and cultural change that Western Europe had experienced since the Renaissance constitute progress or decadence? What was the proper relationship between Europeans and the non-European peoples they encountered in their travels? Should (and could) slavery be abolished in France's Caribbean colonies, and should the French monarchy seek to maintain and expand its colonial empire? Should (and could) non-European "primitives" be remade in Europe's image, or was the lot of the "savage" happier than that of man in civilization?

Underlying nearly all of these questions is a creative tension between the Enlightenment's universalism and its recognition of and desire to explain human difference. Sankar Muthu has observed that "the idea of a deep tension between what might be called the universal and particular elements of human life, society, and thought informs a variety of contemporary philosophical debates ... about the meaning, distinctiveness, and significance of 'the Enlightenment.'"[16] Whatever Eurocentric blind spots the *philosophes* may have had (and they undoubtedly had many), most of them consciously attempted (though not always successfully) to avoid projecting their own "systems" onto non-Western societies. On the contrary, their empiricist "systematic spirit" inspired them to seek out the most accurate information available about peoples and cultures very different from their own, for only through such a comprehensive and comparative approach could the *sciences humaines* aspire to true universality. Ursula Vogel has observed that the epistemological assumptions of Enlightenment proto-anthropology demanded such an inductive approach, writing, "Given that neither the certainties of religious faith nor the *a priori* constructions of metaphysical systems could any longer provide reliable guidance ... questions about the nature of man and society could only be answered by observing human existence in all its diverse manifestations."[17]

This desire to derive general principles from particular cases best explains the eighteenth century's fascination with travel narratives and tales of distant, exotic lands. Seeking to discover an underlying unity amid such great diversity, Enlightenment authors argued whether there existed a common underlying human nature, whether this nature derived from divine creation and "innate ideas" or from human physiology and purely natural causes, whether visible differences between human beings, such as skin color, hair type, and the formation of facial features, reflected innate differences in physical or mental capacity, and whether climate, customs, or forms of government were most instrumental in defining the unique character of different peoples. No consensus emerged out of these debates, in which, contrary to twenty-first-century assumptions, the "universalist" side was more often than not the "progressive" side. Opponents of slavery and colonialism, such as Condorcet and Diderot, justified their positions by appealing to the common humanity that Africans, Native Americans, and Pacific islanders shared with Europeans, while the critics of universalism, such as Pierre-Victor Malouet and Cornelius de Pauw, were less likely to defend a multiculturalist "right to be different" than they were to assert the innate inferiority of non-European peoples. Certainly, the defenders of the Caribbean plantation complex had no illusions as to which side the "philosophers of Paris" were on, and their complaints regarding the naïve humanitarianism and utopian egalitarianism of Enlightenment thinkers abound in the French colonial archives.

Things understandably look quite different from our present vantage point. It is a sad but incontestable truth that most of the leading figures of the Enlightenment were, by twenty-first-century standards, racist, sexist, classist, and Eurocentric, sometimes shockingly so. It is also true, however, that this somewhat anachronistic observation misses the point, and fails to capture the range of Enlightenment debates regarding the causes and significance of racial and cultural diversity, debates whose echoes in many ways continue to reverberate down to the present. Rather than establishing a genealogy of contemporary prejudices and summarily perp-walking the *philosophes* before the tribunal of posterity, I have sought to explore the ambivalences and ambiguities of eighteenth-century discourses on human difference, in order to understand how and why Enlightenment-era France began to think about issues of race, diversity, hybridization, cultural assimilation, and human progress.

If we suspend our impulse to rush to judgment and look at eighteenth-century France with fresh eyes, we will find a society, though different from our own in many ways, which struggled to come to terms with many of the same issues and processes with which we continue to grapple even today. While it has become fashionable to refer to our own times as the "information age," and to reflect upon the meaning and consequences of contemporary "globalization," we sometimes forget that such concerns are by no means new. The eighteenth century was, in its own way, an information age. It witnessed a dramatic expansion of print culture—the appearance of newspapers and journals, the expansion of book publishing, both legally licensed and clandestine, the spread of a lively subculture of pamphlets, placards, and published legal briefs, and the harder to measure, but no less significant, person-to-person circulation of unpublished treatises, polemics, and satires in manuscript form.[18] The eighteenth century was also an age of globalization.[19] Spain, Portugal, and the Netherlands sought to consolidate their far-flung colonial empires and to expand effective control from the coastline into the hinterlands, while the dominant powers of the age, Britain and France, fought for empire and influence in North America, the Caribbean, South Asia, Africa, and (in the form of rival voyages of exploration) even in the uncharted zones of the Pacific and the far south. These twin developments created an ever-broadening stream of information regarding distant lands and peoples, a vast body of data to be mined by a new generation of thinkers seeking to elaborate the new *sciences humaines*. Writing at the dawn of the global capitalist order rather than at its apogee, the cultural differences and barriers to mutual understanding with which eighteenth-century observers were confronted were even greater than those that we encounter in the increasingly interconnected world of the twenty-first century.

The first four chapters of this book examine the importance of encounters, both actual and textual, with the Islamic world, China, the Americas, and Africa and the Pacific, respectively, to the development of the Enlightenment science of man and society. The fifth chapter surveys the differing theories of race and human difference developed in Enlightenment France, while the sixth chapter considers Enlightenment responses to the moral challenge of slavery. Finally, the seventh chapter discusses the emergence of stadial, evolutionary narratives of sociocultural development, which furnished the emerging *sciences humaines* with a flexible and powerful toolkit for cross-cultural analysis and philosophical contemplation, and concludes with an examination of how eighteenth-century French observers' awareness of Europe's growing technical and economic superiority over the non-European world led to new debates about the ethics of colonization and acculturation.

While I reject the notion of a unitary "Enlightenment project" and an overly teleological and tautological definition of "modernity," I believe that the critics who invoke these concepts are correct to believe that eighteenth-century learned discourse has had a major impact in shaping how the modern West has defined itself, its relationship to the wider world, and the course of historical development. Eighteenth-century debates between French scholars, travelers, and philosophers (both those whose works have been incorporated into the canon of "great books" and those who are all but forgotten today) still matter in the twenty-first-century world, because the issues of progress, alterity, and the ethics of cross-cultural encounters that they debated remain as relevant as ever.[20] Our contemporary discourse will be greatly impoverished if we neglect or dismiss the complex, self-critical, and multifaceted legacy of the Enlightenment, which, I believe, can redirect debate away from a false choice between monolithic universalism and absolute cultural relativism, toward old/new approaches that seek to understand *both* the unity *and* the diversity of humankind.

1

Philosophy in the Seraglio: Orientalism and the Enlightenment

Facing Europe along the southern and eastern shores of the Mediterranean and at times reaching into the corners of Europe itself, the Islamic Orient has long been the West's most enduring Other and its most persistent point of reference for meditation upon the meaning of cultural difference. Relations between Christendom and the Islamic world have often been characterized by mutual hostility, as Muslim control over the Christian holy places outraged devout believers, while Muslim domination of the Iberian and Balkan peninsulas was perceived by some Europeans as a mortal threat to Western Christian civilization. It would, of course, be a gross error to suggest that relations between Christian Europeans and Near Eastern Muslims have always been marked by hostility and warfare; on the contrary, important patterns of cultural interchange and maritime commerce arose in the late medieval and early modern periods, integrating the seafaring Italian republics of Venice and Genoa as well as French Mediterranean ports such as Marseille and Toulon into an emerging world economic system. As a result of these contacts, Near Eastern Muslims were far more familiar to early modern Europeans than were Chinese, Native Americans, Pacific islanders, or other peoples who, as we shall see in the following chapters, offered grist for the mill of Enlightenment theories on the nature of man and the fundamental principles of human society.

As a result of this familiarity, Enlightenment thinkers and authors who imagined and depicted the "Orient" did not paint upon a blank canvas. Rather, they drew upon preexisting images and representations of the great Islamic empires of the early modern era—Ottoman Turkey, Safavid Persia, and Mughal India—and on historical accounts of the life of Mohammed, the early caliphates, and the medieval

Crusades. France's connections to the Islamic world intensified in the sixteenth century, when shared fears of universal empire under the Austrian and Spanish Habsburgs led François I to seek an alliance with the Ottoman Empire, then at the height of its power under Suleiman the Magnificent. As Thomas Kaiser has noted, the Ottoman Empire "played a direct, major role in contemporary European power politics and thus remained a concern of the French state and the French public at large throughout the early modern period."[1] Over the following centuries, diplomatic envoys traveled back and forth across the Mediterranean, polyglot merchant communities and bustling commercial emporia developed in port cities from Marseille to Smyrna, and a small but growing community of French scholars and learned travelers began to take an interest in Oriental languages and cultures.[2] These contacts and the wealth of information they supplied led by the late seventeenth and early eighteenth centuries to a cultural vogue for "Orientalism" in France. French Enlightenment authors, informed by travel narratives and translations of ancient and modern texts, were fascinated by the possibilities the mysterious Orient offered for political and social critique, particularly with regard to the model of "Oriental despotism," the question of religious fanaticism, and the differing role and status of women in society. In this sense, the Islamic Orient proved "good for thinking" (as Robert Darnton has said of cats in early modern folklore[3]), even if most of the thinking it inspired was, in the final analysis, more about contemporary Europe than the classical or modern Near East.

Exploring Cultural Difference: The Orient as Mirror

By its very existence in close proximity to Christian Europe and by its close similarities and striking differences to familiar norms, the Islamic Orient forced early modern Europeans to recognize the broad range of customs, beliefs, and practices that constituted the human experience. Constantin-François de Chasseboeuf, comte de Volney, one of the last of the prerevolutionary French observers of the Near East, remarked that, for European travelers to the Orient, "what is most striking... is the almost total opposition of their customs to our own; one would say that a premeditated design sought to establish a mass of contrasts between the men of Asia and those of Europe."[4] While some Christian polemicists used this difference to highlight the contrast between the true religion and the perfidy of Islam (and had done so since the first contact between Christians and Muslims in the seventh century), numerous early modern travelers and scholars drew contrasts that were not invariably in favor of the West. Rather, they were as apt to praise the early modern Islamic empires in order to critique their own societies, or to highlight the artificiality of all cultural conventions.

Early modern French travelers to the Orient did not write of their experiences from a vantage point of colonial superiority. On the contrary, many of them were struck by the vastness of the eastern empires and the pomp and splendor of their imperial courts. The jeweler and merchant Jean Chardin, who visited Persia from 1666 to 1667 and again from 1672 to 1677, called it "the greatest empire in the world," while the physician François Bernier, who resided for a decade at the Mughal court, expressed amazement at the vast extent and fabulous riches of the Indian ruler, remarking, "I believe that he alone possesses more than the Grand Seigneur [i.e., the Ottoman emperor] and the king of Persia together."[5]

One of the most influential figures in defining and depicting the Orient as a foil to the contemporary West was Antoine Galland. Though best known as the translator of the *Thousand and One Nights*, Galland was also instrumental in collecting rare Oriental manuscripts for the Bibliothèque du Roi and in securing the posthumous publication of Barthélemy d'Herbelot's *Bibliothèque orientale*. Introducing this work with a preface that Henry Laurens describes as a "veritable manifesto of Orientalism,"[6] Galland lamented that "general History as we possess it, in combining sacred history with profane, has until now been defective, in that that of which we speak, which forms part of it, has been lacking."[7] Arguing that the history and literature of the Islamic and pre-Islamic world formed an integral part of the cultural legacy of humanity, Galland praised d'Herbelot's vast erudition, noting his mastery of Arabic, Persian, and Turkish as well as of Latin, Greek, and Hebrew, and stressed the utility of his compilation in introducing the vast body of Oriental literature to the French public. Arguing against the attribution of barbarism to the Orient, Galland observed that "the scholars of the Oriental nations have a great field for acquiring in their country what we call erudition, in reading all the good books which they have in great number...That being so, one should not be astonished, as many people are, that they neglect to learn our languages or to study our books and histories...as they have so much of their own with which to occupy themselves."[8] In contrast to Macaulay's famous dismissal of the whole of Oriental learning in his *Minute on Education* a century and a half later, Galland argued that the societies of the Islamic East had their own erudite traditions, which were in no way inferior to those of the West, and with which Western scholars might fruitfully occupy themselves.

Similarly, in the introduction to his biography of the prophet Mohammed (one of the first Western works to depict the founder of Islam in a favorable light), Count Henri de Boulainvilliers lamented that so little was known in the Europe of his time about his subject, despite the fact that Mohammed was "the founder of a larger, more powerful empire than that of the Macedonians and Romans." He attributed this ignorance to "the little usage we have of still-living Oriental languages, even as we ardently cultivate the languages that perpetuate the memory of the ancient Greeks and Romans." Boulainvilliers expressed regret that few French men of letters (himself included) were able to read the ancient Arabic and Persian manuscripts in the Bibliothèque du Roi, and credited Herbelot with demonstrating "how much we could extend our knowledge, and stimulate our lazy sentiments by the faithful translation of so many remaining monuments of the virtue of these Arabs, whom distance and religious difference make us regard as barbarians."[9]

Both Galland and Boulainvilliers invoked the example of the Islamic world in order to jolt their European readers out of their own narrow provincialism, to demonstrate that the world was far larger and the range of human beliefs and customs far broader than those circumscribed by the classical and Christian traditions. In the case of Boulainvilliers in particular, as we shall see later in this chapter, praise of Islam and of its prophet was a rhetorical strategy in an intellectual struggle against Christian dogmatism in favor of a broad-minded cosmopolitanism. A generation after Boulainvilliers, Voltaire would take a similar approach in his *Essai sur les moeurs et l'esprit des nations*, which aimed to be the first truly universal history of world civilizations. Voltaire criticized Bossuet's *Discours sur l'histoire universelle* for its exclusive focus on the history of the Jews, and wrote, "It would have been desirable that he not have entirely forgotten the ancient peoples of the Orient, such as the Indians and the Chinese, who were so considerable even before the other nations were formed," and observed that such "supposedly universal histories...forget three fourths of the world."[10] Through much of the first volume of the *Essai sur les moeurs* and the *Philosophie de l'histoire* subsequently written as a preface to it, Voltaire favorably contrasted the Arabs to the ancient Israelites, dismissing the latter so caustically that many subsequent scholars have labeled him an anti-Semite.[11] I would argue instead, following Peter Gay, that Voltaire's attacks on the Jews, however bigoted and gratuitous they appear to today's readers, form part of a rhetorical strategy to deprivilege the narrative of the Old Testament in favor of a more global, polycentric universal history.

These examples and others like them, which we will examine in greater detail in the remainder of the chapter, should suffice to demonstrate that if, as Edward Said has suggested, the West has "gained in strength and identity by setting itself off against the Orient as a sort of surrogate and even underground self,"[12] the dialogic relationship between the two was far more complex and ambiguous than one of simple domination and subjugation. While in the nineteenth and twentieth centuries, the period with which Said is primarily concerned, Orientalism was often (though not always) complicit in the Western project of imperialism, which it both informed and justified, the power relations between East and West were quite different in the early modern period, and remained in flux for much of the eighteenth century. Henry Laurens has observed that "it is evident that their situation is not the same when the Turks threatened Central Europe as when the European powers colonized the entirety of the Mediterranean basin."[13] Nicholas Dew concurs with this assessment, adding that "this is not to say that the making of Orientalist knowledge in (the seventeenth century) occurred in an absence of power relations, but rather that the power relations in those specific situations need to be studied on their own terms."[14] This chapter seeks to situate eighteenth-century French writing about the Islamic Orient within its original discursive context, the better to understand how the French Enlightenment perceived the Near East and its inhabitants and how it invoked the Orient within the context of political and cultural debates that were largely intra-European in character.

If, in my view, Said errs in depicting Western Orientalism as a monolithic bloc, conflating bookish antiquarian scholars, aesthetically minded poets and novelists, dashing romantic adventurers, and the policy wonks of contemporary think tanks in a way that fails to account for their specificities and frequent disagreements with one another, he is, I believe, correct to argue that the Orient that Western authors observed, imagined, and depicted was as much a projection of their own hopes, fears, and predilections as it was a faithful recreation of actually existing Islamic society. Even the most sympathetic of Western observers were often guilty of oversimplifying and essentializing the Orient, arguing for continuities across time and space that failed to account for the specificities of particular societies or to recognize in the East a dynamic of historical change analogous to that which they correctly identified in their own national histories.

For example, Galland wrote that the manners of the Mongols and Tartars were "not...different from those described by Quintus Curcius in speaking of the Scythians, who were the same people."[15] Similarly, Montesquieu wrote in the *Esprit des lois* that the "laziness of the spirit" of the peoples of Asia precluded change, declaring that "this is why laws, mores, and manners...remain in the East today as they were a thousand years ago."[16] As Said correctly notes, therefore, the Orient was often simultaneously dehistoricized and essentialized, with allegedly unchanging characteristics that could be explained by the timeless effects of climate, religion, or governing institutions.

Along with this tendency to essentialize the Orient was a marked preference for the region's past as opposed to its present. Describing his travels in Egypt, Volney lamented that "the majority of travelers occupied themselves with researching its antiquity rather than its modern state."[17] Such preference was not accidental, but rather reflected the professional background of most eighteenth-century Orientalists and the intellectual concerns that motivated their researches. As Robert Irwin has noted, early modern Orientalism emerged as a subfield of classical studies (due in no small part to the expertise and interest of classicists in deciphering arcane languages), and many of the scholars most active in the field were affiliated with the Académie des Inscriptions et Belles-Lettres, one of the learned societies chartered under the reign of Louis XIV. Perhaps for this reason, Irwin continues, these early Orientalists "tended to be somewhat detached from worldly affairs and their approach to Islam and the Arabs was usually scholarly and antiquarian rather than utilitarian," so that "living languages such as Arabic, Persian, and Chinese were studied as if they were dead languages."[18] Henry Laurens concurs with this assessment, writing that early modern Orientalists "studied the Orient as the *érudits* studied antiquity; that is, from a distance. Its present did not interest them."[19]

In the preface to his tragedy *Bajazet* (1672), set in the Ottoman Empire, Jean Racine (who in addition to his role as one of the greatest dramatists of French classicism also held the post of royal historiographer), wrote, "The distance of space in some ways offsets the too-great proximity of time, for people make hardly any distinction between that which is, if I may so speak, a thousand years away, and that which is at a thousand leagues' distance...both have entirely different manners and customs. We have so little contact with the princes and the other residents of the seraglio that we consider them, so to speak, as people who inhabit a different century from our own."[20] This approach also contributed to the tendency, which we have already noted, of placing a greater emphasis on the Orient's past than on its present, and of likening the alleged "decadence" of the contemporary Islamic world with that of the later Roman Empire. Laurens concludes that "the habit of considering the Orient as another antiquity led to the treatment of Oriental languages and culture as if they belonged to a vanished society."[21]

The early stages of Western scholarly study of the Near East were also framed by the prevailing religious and historical concerns of post-Reformation Europe. Laurens notes that "the first contact with the Semitic Orient came by way of the Bible. Therefore, the Orientalists, whatever the sincerity of their faith, were always forced to confront religious issues."[22] Interest in ancient Egypt, Palestine, Syria, and Mesopotamia was fueled by their centrality to the Old Testament narrative and the field of "sacred geography," which sought to situate and study the locations in which key biblical events took place. Initially knowledge of these ancient civilizations was limited to the information that could be gleaned indirectly from the Bible or from classical Greek sources, and most of the (few) early modern scholars who learned Arabic approached it by way of Hebrew. Most of these early Orientalist researchers sought to examine ancient Egyptian and Mesopotamian civilizations through a Judeo-Christian prism and to reconcile the information thus recovered with people, places, and events mentioned in the Bible. Anthony Grafton has shown that the field of "sacred chronology" emerged in the Renaissance era as an effort to create a new, more truly universal, timeline for history from both sacred and pagan sources. Joseph Scaliger, the most eminent of the sixteenth century chronologists, focused primarily on the civilizations of the ancient Mediterranean, beginning with the relatively well-known histories of Greece and Rome, and proceeding from there to the Egyptians, Phoenicians, and Mesopotamian civilizations, at that time known primarily through Greek intermediaries. While Scaliger, Grafton argues, scrupulously followed his sources wherever they led and made no efforts to make his dense and arcane works accessible to nonspecialist readers, many of his seventeenth-century heirs wrote "to prove . . . points in theology or in the comparative history of religions."[23] Most prominent among such motives was the desire to prove or to disprove the historical truth of the sacred chronology of the Bible through comparison with the records of other ancient civilizations, an approach that inevitably distorted their depictions of the latter. As we shall now see, these theological concerns also colored Western narratives of the origins and spread of Islam, which was far from a purely academic concern to *dévots* and *philosophes* alike.

Perceptions of Islam between Reason and Fanaticism

The *Bibliothèque orientale*, an encyclopedic compilation of Islamic and pre-Islamic history and culture, was the crowning achievement of the "baroque Orientalism" of seventeenth-century France and one of the Enlightenment's most important sources of information and inspiration on the Near East. Its author, Barthélemy d'Herbelot, born in Paris in 1625 into the nobility of the robe, never traveled to the Orient, but developed an interest in Near Eastern cultures as a result of his travels to Italy, where he met with Jewish, Greek, and Armenian merchants from the Ottoman Empire, studied Arabic and Turkish, consulted the collections of the Vatican Library, and began to collect eastern manuscripts. His dedication to this pursuit won him a series of official honors, as he was appointed an interpreter for Oriental languages to the French court, and later as a royal professor of Oriental languages at the Collège de France. The *Bibliothèque orientale*, which included 8,158 entries running over a thousand pages, was the product of a lifetime of collection, translation, and study, and did not appear until after his death in 1695. Many of these entries consisted of passages translated directly from Arabic or Persian sources mixed in with tendentious editorial commentary, particularly with regard to religion. A devout Catholic, Herbelot dismissed Mohammed as a false prophet, allegedly inspired by Jewish and Christian heretics, calling him "the famous impostor Mohammed, author and founder of a heresy that took the name of the religion which we call Mohammedan." The holy book of Islam fared no better, as Herbelot called the Koran "a tissue of vulgar impostures that disprove themselves" that "could make no impression on the spirit of a man who wishes to use the lights of his reason."[24]

While reporting that Muslims believed the Koran to be of divine origin and "have a respect for this book which approaches idolatry," Herbelot stated his own theory that Christian heretics expelled to the Arabian desert "provided Mohammed with unfaithful and ill-conceived memoirs on the Old and New Testaments with which he presumed to cover his impostures," and further argued that "the Jews ... contributed their part, and it is not without reason that they boast today that twelve of their principal doctors were the authors of this detestable book, with the purpose of confusing the Christians with regard to the scope and universality of their religion." Herbelot concluded, "One should also note that the Koran is full of the erroneous sentiments of the heretics mentioned above, which strengthens the conjecture made regarding the composition of this book."[25]

The *Bibliothèque orientale* would go on to exercise a broad influence over the Western imagination of the Orient in the Enlightenment and Romantic eras, as generations of poets and philosophers would mine it for exotic subject matter to rework in their own literary creations. Nicholas Dew notes, however, that the initial reaction to the work's publication in 1697 was "muted incomprehension," and contemporaries remarked that booksellers, having acquired copies of the massive tome at great expense, were unable even to give it away.[26] Part of the problem was stylistic, for Dew observes that the *Bibliothèque* was composed as a reference tool for fellow *érudits*, of whom there were simply too few at the end of the seventeenth century to constitute a viable market. Alphabetized according to Arabic and Persian, rather than French or Latin spelling (for example, Christ appears as "Issa ebn Miriam," or "Jesus son of Mary"), and referring readers to manuscripts in those languages stored in the Bibliothèque du Roi (which Herbelot himself had catalogued), which most of them would be unable to read, contemporaries found the *Bibliothèque orientale* an impenetrable jumble. Calling the text "something resembling the labyrinthine libraries imagined by Borges," Dew concludes, "If the *Bibliothèque orientale* was a scientific instrument, it was one that did not work very well. It was unable to impose meaning on the reader; it was instead a place of possibility, a place for readers to lose themselves."[27]

If erudite classical scholars found that religious concerns inevitably encroached on their academic work regarding the Orient, many gentleman amateurs and philosophical polemicists were drawn to the subject precisely because of its relevance to the heated religious and philosophical debates of the age. One of these was Henri de Boulainvilliers, best remembered today as the most prominent and extreme exponent of the "Gothic" theory of French medieval history, which held that the French nobility, descended from the Frankish warriors who conquered the Roman province of Gaul as the empire collapsed, constituted a separate "race" from the commoners, and enjoyed a privileged status by right of conquest.[28] Boulainvilliers's final work, left incomplete at the time of his death and published posthumously in 1730, was the *Vie de Mahomed*. Boulainvilliers's biography differed sharply from traditional Christian polemics, which portrayed Mohammed as an impostor and a false prophet, driven by ambition and lust, and instead presented Mohammed as a great man, the founder of a mighty empire, and the bearer of a rationalized religion, which Robert Irwin describes as "a pastoral Arab anticipation of eighteenth-century Deism," [29] clearly superior to the decadent Eastern Christianity that it overturned. Boulainvilliers rejected Herbelot's accusation, which had a long history in Christian anti-Muslim polemic, that Mohammed had adopted his false system through the influence of a heretical Christian monk, and instead presented Mohammed as preaching "a religion stripped of all controversies, which proposed no mysteries that could offend reason…which cannot be attributed to the suggestion of some ignorant monk…but rather which appears as the result of a long and deep meditation on the nature of things, on the state and disposition of the world at that time, and on the compatibility of religion with reason." [30]

While Boulainvilliers's depiction of Mohammed is favorable, specifically rejecting centuries of slander by Christian polemicists, it would hardly meet with the approval of orthodox Muslims. Islam according to Boulainvilliers is not divinely revealed truth, but the conscious creation of a remarkable man, a system of belief intended to mobilize the Arab people in order to unite them into a vast and powerful empire. Boulainvilliers compared Mohammed favorably to the greatest conquerors of classical antiquity, declaring that "he directed his enterprise with all the skill, delicacy, constancy, and great ambitions of which Alexander and Caesar would have been capable in his place." Boulainvilliers, in fact, argued that Mohammed was greater than these conquering heroes of the West, observing that "he knew less of self-interest, greed, luxury, and prodigality…Neither did he subjugate his country; on the contrary, he wished to govern it only to make it mistress of the world, and he and his successors made such disinterested use of its riches that they should be admired in this respect even by their greatest enemies." [31] Boulainvilliers's Mohammed is more philosopher-king than prophet.

Voltaire engaged intellectually with Islam and the Orient on numerous occasions throughout his long career, though in an inconsistent and idiosyncratic way. The contradictions within his vision of Islam are best explained by the fact that Voltaire was rarely interested in Islam in and of itself, but returned regularly to it to score points in his ongoing struggle against religious intolerance and dogmatism within Christian Europe. Two of his early dramatic works, *Zaïre* and *Le fanatisme, ou Mahomet le prophète*, are set in the historical Orient (Jerusalem during the Crusades and sixth-century Arabia, respectively), and depict Islam in a negative light, indicative of Voltaire's hostility to religious dogmatism more generally. The title character of *Zaïre* was born a French noblewoman, but raised as a Muslim since childhood and is betrothed to the Muslim prince Orosmane. Zaïre discovers her true identity when her brother returns from France to ransom their father from Orosmane's dungeons, and is forced to choose between her beloved and her family. When she attempts to escape from the harem to receive religious instruction from a priest, Orosmane, suspecting her of infidelity, follows her, stabs her to death, and commits suicide once he has realized his error. Rather than a polemic against Islam, *Zaïre* appears as an appeal for tolerance and humanity against both Christian and Islamic dogmatism.[32]

Le fanatisme, however, takes a much more negative stance, depicting Mohammed as a sinister and cynical fanatic, driven by ambition and cruelty, who coldly manipulates a son to unknowingly murder his own father, a virtuous pagan who remains loyal to the old gods. In one of the key dialogues of the play, Mohammed proudly boasts, "A new God is needed for the blind universe...I bring a more noble yoke to entire nations."[33] The pagan Zopire, the victim of Mohammed's intrigues, reproaches him for seeking to spread religion by force: "You wish, by bringing carnage and terror, to command all humans to think as you do. You ravage the world, and you pretend to instruct it?" When his own son arrives to murder him, Zopire asks him, "Can you believe in a God who commands hatred?" Ultimately, Seide overcomes his doubts and commits the crime, only later learning that Zopire was his father. Mohammed's manipulation of Seide becomes clear at the end of the play, when his servant Omar poisons the youth so that the prophet can seduce his beloved (and sister) Palmire, who kills herself at the end of the final act after publically condemning Mohammed's treachery.[34] *Le fanatisme* is not, it should be noted, a historically accurate work.[35] In a dedicatory letter to Frederick the Great, Voltaire acknowledged that he had taken liberties with the life of the prophet, excusing himself by arguing that his intention was not "to depict a true action on the stage" but rather "to represent the most frightful inventions of trickery, and the most awful actions of fanaticism. Mohammed here is but Tartuffe with arms in hand."[36] Voltaire's real target is not the historical Mohammed, but the spirit of religious intolerance, whether Muslim or Christian, which he is made to represent. Many of Voltaire's contemporaries saw through this ruse, and the play was suppressed soon after its premiere due to opposition from the clergy.[37]

By contrast, in the *Essai sur les moeurs*, Voltaire followed Boulainvilliers in presenting Mohammed not as a vulgar impostor, but as an inspired statesman and lawgiver and the advocate of a purified religion strikingly similar to enlightened Deism, though like his predecessor, he represented Mohammed's mission as human rather than divine in origin. "Having well understood the character of his compatriots, their ignorance, credulity, and susceptibility to enthusiasm," Voltaire wrote, "he saw that he could make himself a prophet. He conceived the design of abolishing Sabianism in his country, which consisted of a mix of the cult of God and that of the stars." In its place, "he planned to restore the simple cult of Abraham or Ibrahim, from whom he claimed descent, and to recall men to the unity of God, a dogma which he believed to be disguised beneath all religions." Voltaire further argued, "It is to be believed that Mohammed, like all enthusiasts, violently struck by his ideas, first presented them in good faith, strengthened them with fantasy, fooled himself in fooling others, and supported through necessary deceptions a doctrine which he considered good." Though he regarded Islam as a purely human creation, Voltaire nonetheless compared it favorably to both Judaism and Christianity, writing that "the legislator of the Muslims, a powerful and terrible man, established his dogmas through courage and force of arms, but his religion became indulgent and tolerant. The divine founder of Christianity, living in humility and peace, preached forgiveness of offenses, and his holy, mild religion has become, through our fury, the most intolerant of all, and the most barbarous."[38]

Given Voltaire's lifelong crusade against *l'Infame*, it is not surprising that this contrast between Muslim tolerance and Christian fanaticism runs throughout the *Essai sur les moeurs*. Voltaire sharply condemned the Crusades, whose death toll he estimated at two million souls, writing, "Never did antiquity see these emigrations from one part of the world to another due to religious enthusiasm. This epidemic fury appeared for the first time, so that there would be no plague which did not afflict the human race." After discussing the Turkish capture of Constantinople in 1453 under Mehmet II, Voltaire remarked that "the Turks do not always treat the Christians as barbarously as we imagine. No Christian nation permits the Turks to have a mosque among them, while the Turks permit the Greeks to have churches."[39]

While the later Voltaire contrasted Ottoman religious tolerance with the intolerance of Christians, Montesquieu used reports of growing religious intolerance in the Orient to comment obliquely on recent acts of religious persecution in France. In Montesquieu's *Lettres persanes*, a letter from Usbek to Mirza made a most thinly veiled allusion to the revocation of the Edict of Nantes and subsequent expulsion of the Huguenots from France, noting that the current shah, Soliman, intended to expel the Armenians from Persia. Usbek warned that "in outlawing the Armenians, one may in a single day destroy all the merchants and almost all the artisans of the kingdom. I am certain that the great Shah Abbas would have preferred to cut off his two arms rather than to sign such an order, and that in sending to the Mogol and the other kings of the Indies his most industrious subjects, he would have thought himself giving over half of his estates." Montesquieu's source for this discussion appears to have been the traveler Jean Chardin, who had praised the Persian emperor Abbas for his religious tolerance, noting that "he brought into the capital city a colony of Armenians, who were a laborious and industrious people," who quickly came to dominate a flourishing trade between Persia and its neighbors, a role that no doubt recalled to him the role of both Huguenot and Jewish merchant diasporas in Europe at the time.[40] Montesquieu's Persians further noted that "the persecutions that our zealous Mohammedans have made against the Guebres have forced them to move together to the Indies, and have deprived Persia of this nation, so gifted in farming, and which alone, by its labor, was suited to overcome the sterility of our lands."[41]

Montesquieu's depiction of Islam and the Orient was even more negative in the *Esprit des lois*. He wrote that "in Mohammedan empires the people derive from religion a part of the astonishing respect they have for their prince," and argued that while Christianity tended toward moderate government, Islam was uniquely conducive to despotism. "From the character of the Christian religion and that of the Mohammedan religion, one should, without further examination, embrace the one and reject the other," he wrote. "The Mohammedan religion, which speaks only with a sword, continues to act on men with the destructive spirit that founded it."[42] We will now examine the theory of "Oriental despotism," as articulated by Montesquieu from his reading of seventeenth-century travel narratives.

Oriental Despotism

One of the most persistent and pervasive discursive prisms through which Western scholars and philosophers perceived the Orient was the concept of "Oriental despotism." Although the contrast between liberty-loving Westerners and eastern tyrants is as old as the Greek chronicles of the Persian War, Oriental despotism in its modern form derives largely from the works of Montesquieu, who in turn drew much of his information about Islamic societies from the narratives of learned seventeenth-century travelers such as Jean Chardin, François Bernier, and Antoine Galland.[43] Chardin blamed the "arbitrary government" of the rulers of Persia and India for the increasing desolation and depopulation of their realms, citing "the dreadful effects of this kind of politics, for in proportion as the Great Mogul extends his empire...the people, and at the same time plenty and riches, decrease." Chardin also argued that despotism corrupted ruler and ruled alike, writing that the Persians "never act out of generosity...they do nothing but out of a principle of interest, that is to say, out of hope or fear. And they cannot conceive that there should be such a country where people will do their duty from a motive of virtue only, without any other recompense."[44] Similarly, Galland's preface to the *Bibliothèque orientale* associated the Islamic faith with despotism, as he wrote that Islamic rulers established their laws in conformity with the Koran "so that their infraction would be regarded as an attack upon religion, the principle maxim by which the perverse doctrine of Mohammed, which has caused such great harm to Christianity, has been followed over so many centuries by this great number of sectarians."[45]

One of the most important sources for the Enlightenment image of Oriental despotism was the physician François Bernier, a disciple of the philosopher and scientist Pierre Gassendi and an urbane denizen of Parisian salons and erudite libertine circles who spent 12 years at the court of the Mughal emperor Aurengzeb. Although he praised the Mughal ruler as "a great and rare genius, as a great statesman, and as a great king," Bernier also described Aurengzeb's brutal elimination of rival claimants to the throne, though he blamed these atrocities on the absence of an established order of succession by primogeniture, which "obligates all the princes born to the royal family by condition of their birth to the cruel necessity to conquer and reign by causing all of the others to perish to ensure their own power and survival, or to perish themselves to ensure that of another." Bernier also favorably contrasted Aurengzeb's ruthless energy with the lethargy that he claimed characterized most of the monarchies of Asia. "One of the primary causes of the misery, bad government, depopulation, and decadence of the empires of Asia," Bernier wrote, "is that the children of kings, raised among women and eunuchs...are stunned when they emerge from the harem as if they came from another world, or emerged out of some subterranean cavern where they had spent their entire lives." Even after assuming power, Bernier argued that these despots lived in ignorance and isolation, "surrounded by their slaves, their mothers, their eunuchs, who know only how to manage cruel intrigues, having one another strangled, or pursuing one another, or even the viziers and great lords, while no one who possesses anything can be sure of his life."[46] This portrait of a sensual, debased Oriental court would have a great impact on the eighteenth century's imagination of "Oriental despotism."

Bernier's sociological observations would also influence the ways in which Montesquieu drew the distinction between despotism and legitimate monarchy, as he highlighted the absence of a hereditary nobility and of secure private property rights as among the most important differences between East and West. Bernier observed that the Mughal courtiers were not "sons of great families, as in France. All the lands of the kingdom belonging to him [the emperor], it follows that there are neither dukes nor margraves, nor any rich land-owning families subsisting from their rents and patrimony, they are often not even sons of Omrahs, for as the king is the heir to all their goods, it follows that these houses cannot long maintain themselves in grandeur; on the contrary, they fall often and suddenly . . . These Omrahs are ordinarily but adventurers and foreigners of all nations . . . whom the Mogol raises to whatever dignities he chooses, and breaks them at his will."[47] Similarly, Chardin blamed the despot's ability to seize the lands and possession of his subjects for Persia's decline from its past glories, writing that, while in the past, "the rights of proprietors to their lands and goods were inviolably sure and sacred . . . at present the government is despotic and absolutely arbitrary."[48] Montesquieu concurred with this assessment, asserting that the absence of private property rights in the Orient ensured that "nothing is repaired, nothing improved . . . One draws all from the land, and returns nothing to it; all is fallow, all is deserted."[49]

The role of private property in defining citizenship and limiting the power of rulers became so engrained in the tradition of aristocratic liberalism, as elaborated by Locke and Montesquieu, that the alleged absence of secure property rights in the Orient was taken as a characteristic mark of despotism, and would subsequently inspire Karl Marx's concept of the "Asiatic mode of production."[50] Bernier argued that this system invariably gave rise to the same social ills: arbitrary abuse of power by viziers and provincial governors, and fields left fallow or cultivated only through the use of force, as landowners have no incentive to undertake costly investments to improve their property, nor peasants to labor in the fields, as the arbitrary system of governance denies them the security of enjoying the fruits of their efforts. Bernier concluded that the absence of private property rights, "the foundation of all that is good and beautiful in the world," would necessarily lead the Islamic empires to "tyranny, ruin, and desolation." He further argued that the rulers of Europe should learn from the example of the Orient, warning them that, if they were to infringe upon the sanctity of the property rights of their subjects, "they would soon find themselves kings of abandoned deserts, of beggars and barbarians." If private citizens could not be secure in enjoying the fruits of their own labors, Bernier asked, "Where would be these infinite towns and villages, these lovely country houses and fields cultivated and maintained with so much industry, care and labor? And where, consequently, would be the revenues drawn from there, which enrich both subjects and the sovereign?"[51]

In the eighteenth century, as we have noted, it was Montesquieu who developed the insights from seventeenth-century travel narratives into a coherent theory of Oriental despotism as a distinct form of government. Concerned with the need to defend the ancient feudal institutions of the French kingdom from the encroachments of Bourbon absolutism, Montesquieu famously distinguished between legitimate monarchy, based upon the principle of honor, the rule of law and tradition, and a highly complex and differentiated social structure of "intermediary bodies" between the sovereign and his subjects, and despotism, whose principle was fear and in which the caprice of the despot was unlimited by the power of the law, the sanctity of property rights, or the countervailing force of an independent hereditary nobility. Asli Çirakman observes that "depicting the Ottoman government... was a safe way to demonstrate the absurdities of absolutism and arbitrary government."[52] Montesquieu's representation of the Islamic Orient remains a shadowy reflection of French society under absolutism. In the *Lettres persanes*, Montesquieu's Persian protagonist Usbek Orientalizes the dying Louis XIV, writing, "He has often been heard to say that, of all the governments of the world, that of the Turks, or that of our august sultan, pleases him the most, so highly does he regard Oriental politics."[53]

While Montesquieu's analytical categories are fundamentally based upon systems of government, his work also reflected a tendency to essentialize the differences between societies and to attribute these differences to natural rather than cultural causes, thereby reifying the divide between the free West and the enslaved East. "The empire of climate," Montesquieu declared in the *Esprit des lois*, "is the first of all empires." More specifically, he declared that "great heat enervates the strength and courage of men and there is in cold climates a certain strength of body and spirit... The cowardice of the peoples of hot climates has almost always made them slaves and the courage of the peoples of cold climates has kept them free."[54] Arguments for cultural difference based on the causality of climate are as old as Aristotle, and had also been used by the early modern travel writers on whom Montesquieu relied.[55] Chardin wrote, "that the hot climates enervate the mind as well as the body... 'Tis by the same reason likewise, that the knowledge of the Asiatics is so restrained that it consists only in learning and repeating what is contained in the books of the Ancients, and that their industry lies fallow and untilled... 'Tis in the North only we must look for the highest improvement and the greatest perfection of the Arts and Sciences."[56] As we shall see later in this and subsequent chapters, Montesquieu's attribution of cultural differences to the forces of climate gave rise to a great deal of debate among his contemporaries and successors, who would argue at length over the relative impact of environment, heredity, and systems of government in shaping human societies.

The concept of Oriental despotism, elaborated by Montesquieu out of seventeenth-century narratives of travel to the Near East, quickly became an *idée reçue* of the Enlightenment, in which religious fanaticism, tyranny, and moral degeneration combined to corrupt and degrade ruler and ruled alike. In a 1749 draft of an essay for the Académie de Soissons, the young Anne-Robert-Jacques Turgot wrote that "raised in the seraglio, home of softness and cruelty, the Turks have no industry and know only violence."[57] The authors of the *Histoire des deux Indes* wrote in 1770, "Under the yoke of a religion which consecrates tyranny in placing the throne upon the altar, which forbids ambition while permitting sensuality, which favors natural laziness in prohibiting the exercise of the mind, there is no hope for great revolutions. Therefore the Turks, who so often slaughter their masters, have never dreamed of changing their government."[58] While a few eighteenth-century authors challenged this stereotype by questioning its foundations, as we shall see below, the greater number took Oriental despotism as a given and a point of departure for their reflections on the differences in customs between East and West.

Gender and Cultural Difference

Of the various contrasts between the Christian West and the Islamic Orient, few captured the interest of French observers more than the status of women. Chardin's account of Persia described the seclusion and veiling of Persian women, though he hesitated on whether to attribute this to "pride, vainglory, or modesty... [or] the jealousy of their husbands."[59] Unlike many of his fellow Westerners, Boulainvilliers gave preference to Oriental customs, praising the physical strength, endurance, and bravery of Arab tribesmen and contrasting their "virile firmness" with the "lively, feminine passions" of Westerners.[60] Boulainvilliers also praised the seclusion of women in the Orient, declaring that "the separation of women, as it is practiced throughout the Orient, is a sure means of excluding them from the intrigues of government, and of preventing the storms which they have too often provoked in the world. When they occupy themselves only with the care of pleasing their husbands, domestic peace will be preserved in their households, as it will be throughout the universe when their immoderate passions no longer increase its troubles." Boulainvilliers further argued that Christian monogamy was preferable in theory to Islamic polygamy, but argued that the former, contrary to human nature, drove Western men to infidelity and socially harmful illicit affairs. "Our maxims are preferable," he wrote, "but we exempt ourselves from following them, and it is in vain that purity and fidelity present themselves to us in the most gracious forms; the maxims of the Muslims are simpler and more natural."[61]

As is the case with many other matters, Voltaire's position on the differences in gender norms between East and West was inconsistent and contradictory. In *Zaïre*, Voltaire contrasts the seclusion of women unfavorably with their greater freedom and status in French society. In the sultan's harem in Jerusalem, Fatime tells Zaïre, "You speak to me no more of those lovely countries, where the women, adored by a civilized people, receive that tribute which your eyes deserve. Companions of a spouse and queens everywhere, free without dishonor and wise without restraints, never owing their virtues to fear." Zaïre's betrothed, the sultan Orosmane, becomes intransigent once his suspicions of infidelity are awakened, declaring, "Let us follow the ancient ways of the kings of the Orient...It is too shameful to fear one's mistress. Let us leave that baseness to the West. This dangerous sex, which wishes to dominate everything; if it reigns in Europe, here it must obey."[62] In the *Essai sur les moeurs*, however, Voltaire took a more equivocal stance, defending the practice of polygamy, writing, "Nature is in agreement with the Orientals, for in almost all animal species multiple females have only one male," adding that "women in hot climates soon cease to be beautiful and fertile." "The laws of the West," he went on, "seem more favorable to women; those of the Orient, to men and to the state."[63] Voltaire returned to this issue in the conclusion to the *Essai*, writing that "the greatest difference between the Orientals and ourselves is the manner in which we treat women."[64] Here, however, he implicitly presented Europe's greater esteem for women as a mark of its more advanced civilization.

The French Enlightenment's most extensive treatment of the differences in gender roles between France and the Islamic Orient is, of course, Montesquieu's *Lettres persanes.* Montesquieu's Persian visitors are shocked by the licentious freedom enjoyed by Parisian *mondaines* who "have lost all restraint...instead of that noble simplicity and lovely modesty...one sees a brutal impudence to which it is impossible to grow accustomed."[65] Rica described the court of Louis XIV as a sort of gynocracy, dominated by the intrigues of women, writing:

> When I arrived in France, I found the late king absolutely governed by women, despite that, at his age, I think he was the ruler of the earth who had the least need of them...There is no one employed at the Court, in Paris, or in the province, who does not have a woman through whose hands pass all the graces and sometimes the injustices that he can bestow. These women are all in relation to one another, and form a sort of republic whose members, always active, assist and make use of one another, it is like a new state within the state, and he who is at court, in Paris, in the provinces, and sees the actions of ministers, magistrates, prelates, if he does not know the women who govern them, he is like a man who sees a machine in operation, but is unaware of its mainsprings.[66]

Though noting that such liberty is contrary to Persian norms, Rica approaches the matter in philosophic fashion, musing that "among the most civilized peoples, women have always had authority over their husbands. This was established by law among the Egyptians, in honor of Isis, and among the Babylonians, in honor of Semiramis. It was said of the Romans that they commanded all nations, but they obeyed their wives."[67] Diana Schaub notes that the harem functions discursively in the novel as a symbol of despotic rule, which carries within itself the seeds of its own destruction, writing, "There are in the *Persian Letters* essentially three levels of despotism: the sexual despotism of Usbek's harem, the political despotism of Louis XIV's increasingly Orientalized France, and the spiritual despotism of the biblical God and his earthly viziers."[68] The novel's dramatic conclusion, in which Usbek's favorite wife Roxane reveals that she has been deceiving him all along and kills herself, her suicide a defiant challenge to the laws of patriarchy, serves to highlight Montesquieu's message that despotism is an inherently unstable system, corrupting master and slave alike. Montesquieu made this point even more explicitly in the *Esprit des lois*, arguing that "each man follows the spirit of the government and brings to his home what he sees established outside it," with the result that "in Asia domestic servitude and despotic government have been seen to go hand in hand in every age." Praising the role of women in cultivating sociability and refined manners in France, he concluded that "one is fortunate to live in these climates that allow communication between people, where the sex with the most charms seems to adorn society and where women, keeping themselves for the pleasures of one man, yet serve for the diversion of all."[69]

The contrasts in the status and role of women between France and the Orient not only provided fodder for fictional Muslims in French literary works, but also attracted the attention of real-life Islamic observers of French society under the Bourbons. At almost exactly the same time that Usbek and Rica were supposed to have resided in France, an Ottoman ambassador, Mehmed Efendi, paid an official state visit to the young Louis XV. Much like Montesquieu's fictional Persians, Mehmed Efendi commented on the cultural differences between East and West and expressed bemused frustration at the tendency of the French to gawk and stare at foreign visitors. The Ottoman dignitary was particularly struck by the prominent public role of women at the French court and in polite society, and later wrote, "In France, esteem for women prevails among men. The women can do what they want and go where they desire. To the lowest, the best gentleman would show more regard and respect than necessary. In these lands, women's commands are enforced. So much so that France is the paradise of women."[70] Efendi's reaction was not unusual; Fatma Göçek writes, "One feature of European society that constantly startled the Ottomans was the participation of women in social life. Public deference shown to women in this participation was especially noted. All Ottomans as well as other Muslim visitors who had visited Europe made almost similar remarks about it."[71]

As the eighteenth century drew toward its close, French assessments of Oriental gender norms became increasingly negative. The baron François de Tott, a Hungarian nobleman in the service of France, commented critically on the jealousy of Turkish husbands and the seclusion of their wives. He reported that a Turkish official he met was scandalized that he allowed his wife to converse freely with other men at a diplomatic reception, and described a visit that his wife and mother-in-law were invited to make to a woman of the Turkish elite, who expressed surprise that European women were allowed to meet their husbands prior to marriage, and "complained of the barbarity, which at thirteen years of age, united her to a decrepit old man, who treating her like a child, had inspired her with nothing but disgust."[72] He also expressed pity for the plight of Turkish women who fell victim to seduction and were subsequently murdered by their husbands or lovers, writing that "their bodies, striptd and mangled, are frequently seen floating in the Port, under the very windows of their murderers."[73] Similarly, Volney condemned the subordination and seclusion of women in Islamic societies, writing that "this Mohammed, so passionate for women, did not however give them the honor of treating them in his Koran as a part of the human race," and argued that polygamy led to "a continuous civil war" within the household, leading men to scorn their wives and women to resent their husbands.[74] He contrasted this with the prominent public role of women in the court society and salon culture of Old Regime France, which he credited with developing the "spirit of conversation, gentility, and light-heartedness, which has become the distinctive character of our nation in Europe."[75] In an age in which many of his contemporaries, most famously Rousseau, criticized the prominent role of women in French society, Volney thus praised them as civilizing agents, and cited greater equality between genders as a measure of progress.

Anquetil-Duperron and the Critique of "Oriental Despotism"

We have seen thus far that the eighteenth-century French discourse on the Orient was produced both by travelers who reported their experiences of voyages to the East and by learned scholars who pored over arcane Oriental manuscripts in the royal archives. Only a few men combined both of these roles, one of the most prominent and prolific of whom was Abraham-Hyacinthe Anquetil-Duperron. Like the majority of French Orientalists, Anquetil-Duperron's interests were primarily antiquarian. Fascinated by ancient manuscripts in the Bibliothèque du Roi that no one in France was able to read, he resolved to travel to India, where he studied for a number of years with Parsi *destours* to learn ancient Persian and to study the teachings of Zoroastrianism, which the Parsis had brought with them into exile in India following the Islamic conquest of Iran, the ancestral homeland of Zoroaster. Anquetil-Duperron's journey was a perilous one, coinciding with the Seven Years' War and the dramatic shifts it brought to the balance of power in the Indian subcontinent. He was captured by the English on his return voyage home, and the precious manuscripts he brought back with him were temporarily confiscated. Eventually, Anquetil-Duperron was able to return to France, and his translation of the *Zend-Avesta*, published in 1771, secured his reputation as the leading French Orientalist of his time, making available a system of belief previously accessible to Europeans only indirectly through Greek sources.[76]

While Anquetil-Duperron's interest lay primarily with South Asia's distant, pre-Islamic past, his voyages gave him ample opportunity to become acquainted with its present state. His firsthand familiarity with the three great modern Islamic empires led him to reject the formulation of "Oriental despotism" articulated by Montesquieu and his many imitators. "Until now," he wrote, "the princes of the Orient have scarcely been known but through qualities destructive to humanity. Excessive pomp, absolute despotism, cruelty, arbitrary conquests, bloody regimes, it seems, according to the majority of European writers, that the history of these vast countries is but that of several great brigands, who take turns destroying all that which nature, between devastations, vainly produces."[77] Believing that the French study of the Near East had been distorted by a false paradigm, Anquetil-Duperron composed a massive treatise, *Législation orientale*, to refute it.

Anquetil-Duperron specifically rejected several of the main tenets of the theory of Oriental despotism as untrue. While Montesquieu had contrasted legitimate monarchy governed by laws and traditions to despotism governed only by the caprice of the despot, Anquetil-Duperron observed that the Koran contained a system of law and codes of conduct that the sultans could not abrogate at will, and that this system was safeguarded by the *ulama* (assemblies of Islamic scholars) and *qadis* (Islamic judges), who thereby functioned much like the "intermediary bodies" that Montesquieu insisted were necessary to limit the power of kings.[78] Anquetil-Duperron also argued that the oft-made assertion (reported by Bernier and repeated by Montesquieu) that there were no secure private property rights in the Orient was likewise false.[79] He rejected the contention that Asian empires were as poorly governed as Montesquieu suggested, citing as proof to the contrary the riches that drew European merchants to India in the first place, and argued that European authors applied a double standard in their analysis of society and government in East and West. "What is bad in Asia is always a consequence of the government," he remarked of such biased accounts, while "in his own country, he would attribute the same inconveniences to the soil, the heavens, the malice of men, for there it is reason which has dictated the laws." He found a similar double standard in discussions of state-craft in accounts of the recent revolutions in Persia and India, declaring, "Europeans, when they speak of Orientals, call this trickery; in Europe, it is political skill."[80] Anquetil-Duperron chided his compatriots for their ethnocentrism, writing, "Educated in the knowledge of four or five hundred leagues of land, the rest of the globe is foreign to us...What could we learn from foreigners who drink, eat, dress, marry, raise their children, and live in society! We know everything that the Greeks and Romans have taught us. We understand the languages of these two peoples. Do we need further enlightenment?" He lamented that the peoples of Asia, America, and Africa had thus far attracted only the attention of merchants and adventurers seeking profit, rather than that of scholars and philosophers (we shall see in the following chapters that this objection is somewhat overstated), and condemned the widely held belief that "barbaric peoples, without manners or laws, can present us opportunities for profit, but the spirit cannot be enriched among them."[81] Anquetil-Duperron reminded his compatriots that "with all our knowledge, our politeness, our civilization, if the ancient Greeks would return, they would treat us as barbarians. Let us reject these words, and believe that any people can, even differently from us, have a real value, laws, customs, and reasonable opinions."[82] He suggested that the frustrations and difficulties that Europeans faced in establishing themselves in the Indies led them to produced biased, unduly negative reports on Asian societies, writing:

> A private citizen, a merchant, statesman, soldier, even a man of letters, full of belief in the excellence of European government, travels to India, always to make his fortune, that is to earn in four years what in his own country he would not earn in twenty. The difficulties he encounters in arriving embitter him. The officer is impeded in his conquests by what he calls "a troop of blacks." What scandal! The least of his soldiers believes himself greater then their chief. The merchant, the statesman finds other Europeans in the country in competition with the natives, always over money; the latter have the effrontery not to allow themselves to be swindled without protest.[83]

Anquetil-Duperron concluded: "The study of the languages and history of Asia is not a matter of mere words or of simple curiosity, for it allows us to understand countries more extensive than Europe, and presents us a tableau suitable to perfect our knowledge of man, and especially to ensure the inalienable rights of humanity." "The Orient," he continued, "has more important objects to engage our curiosity than the tales of the *Thousand and One Nights*. It is readers who are lacking, and not books. But nothing can be learned without effort. Man with difficulty abandons his native country, the diet to which he is accustomed. It is simpler to say, 'There is neither history, nor geography, nor sciences in these barbaric countries. What good is it to plunge oneself into nonsense which can teach us nothing?' As if nonsense wasn't to be found everywhere! Read at least, to be sure of the judgment you wish to render."[84]

Henry Laurens notes, however, that Anquetil-Duperron's efforts to refute Montesquieu's false assumptions regarding the political and economic structures of the Islamic empires had little impact on the theoretical model of Oriental despotism, writing, "The theory of despotism, the purpose of which was direct criticism of the political regime in power [in France], was not greatly affected by the objections of the Orientalists. At most, it was recognized that the situation of the Orient was more complex than previously imagined."[85] Since "Oriental despotism" was not really about the Orient itself, but rather was a rhetorical tool in the arsenal of the opponents of French absolute monarchy, it could not be overturned through the accumulation of empirical information about Islamic societies. Furthermore, by the time that Anquetil-Duperron published his refutation of the theory of Oriental despotism, the balance of power between the Western powers and the Islamic empires of the East had already shifted decisively in favor of the former. The middle decades of the eighteenth century were a traumatic period for the Ottoman, Persian, and Mughal empires, in which both internal strife and decay and increasing threats and encroachments from outside came together in a pattern of irreversible decline. At the same time, France's setbacks in other fields of colonial endeavor, particularly the loss of the Seven Years' War that drove the French out of the North American mainland, led French statesmen such as Choiseul and Sartine to seek other theatres for the expansion of French power and influence. From the late 1770s onward, Laurens writes, French attitudes toward the Orient reflected a "climate of pre-intervention."[86]

The Decline of the East and Perceptions of Decadence

As we have already had occasion to note, the middle decades of the eighteenth century mark a decisive turning point in the balance of power between the European states and the Islamic empires of west and south Asia. This shift began with the overthrow of the Safavids, arguably the weakest of the three great Islamic empires, in 1722, inaugurating a period of political instability and endemic violence in Persia that would last the rest of the eighteenth century. The sacking of Delhi by the Persian conqueror Nader Shah in 1739 fatally weakened the Mughal Empire, which increasingly was unable to resist British encroachments in Bengal, and would in a century's time fall under British colonial rule. The Ottoman Empire, which as late as 1683 was able to strike deep into the heart of Europe, suffered a series of reverses over the following decades, as the expansion of Habsburg and Romanov power toward the east and south began to reverse centuries of Turkish advances in the Balkans and the Black Sea littoral. While in the sixteenth century, a defeated François I had appealed to the mighty Ottoman Empire in an effort to stave off Habsburg universal imperium, in the eighteenth, French statesmen began to worry that the crumbling of Ottoman power in the Balkans would tilt the balance of power in Europe to the benefit of France's rivals. This shift became increasingly clear after the Russo-Turkish War of 1768–1774, which ended Turkish control over the Crimea and placed the "eastern question" on the European diplomatic agenda.[87]

One consequence of this growing instability was the appointment of baron François de Tott as a French military attaché to the Ottoman Empire during the Russo-Turkish War, and his subsequent mission to inspect the state of French merchant outposts throughout the Levant. Tott's role was an ambiguous one, and the ambiguities in his appointment reflected real differences of opinion among France's governing elite; the French minister of war, the comte de Vergennes, wanted France to assist in the modernization of Ottoman military and naval forces to restore stability to the region, whereas the minister for the navy and colonies, Antoine de Sartine, favored abandoning the Turks to claim a share of the spoils from the declining empire.[88] Throughout his travels, Tott assumed an attitude of superiority that anticipated the imperial proconsuls of the following century. Charged by the duc de Choiseul with assisting the Ottoman defense against Russian attacks, he repeatedly complained of Turkish ignorance of modern military science and stubbornness in clinging to old customs, blaming "the cowardice, disorder, and habitual negligence of the Turks." He spoke dismissively of the geometric knowledge of the Ottoman court mathematicians, reporting that they were unable even to calculate the angles of a triangle, and complained of how his pragmatic measures for maintaining defenses were undermined by religious scruples, recounting the horror that an Ottoman official expressed at his insistence on using rammers with bristles of pig's hair to clear and reload the barrels of cannon.[89]

Tott's commentary on Ottoman society drew upon classically inspired notions of the decadence of declining empires. He reported that Constantinople had degenerated from its ancient splendor, writing, "Placed between two seas, this city would be at once the center of agriculture, commerce, arts, and sciences, did not the infatuated hand of Despotism break every instrument of culture and industry for twenty leagues round. Constantinople, inclosed within the circle of its ancient walls, presents the traveler with nothing on the land side, but an appearance of desolation, while towards the sea, a thousand vessels in the center of an immense ampitheatre, seem continually arriving from all nations, to bring the tribute which the whole world owes its Metropolis." He found the very topography of the city to be evidence of this decadence, observing, "The richest ruins, confounded with the most vile materials, present, at every step, the affecting picture of ignorance and barbarity, confusedly mingled with the precious remains of the learning of the ancient Greeks."[90] Tott also lamented the licentiousness of public festivals in Constantinople, in which one beheld "all that was customary in ancient Rome, at the time of the Saturnalia. The slaves enjoy a respite, and are permitted to be merry in presence of their masters...It is plain, that a government, which seems by its own nature destructive of joy, can no otherways produce its appearance," as the downtrodden people "takes advantage of the opportunity to enjoy the feeble and transitory semblance of its felicity."[91]

Tott's critique of Ottoman institutions also drew upon the rhetoric of Oriental despotism as framed by Bernier and Montesquieu. He wrote that "under a despotic government, the existence of any person is necessarily precarious. No one can be ambitious without despising his own life, and what regard can he have for the lives of others?" He lamented that "according to the laws of war in Turkey...any province which revolts shall be given up to pillage, and the inhabitants reduced to slavery. This is the universal practice of all Asia, and on such savage principles is half the world still governed."[92] Even the sultan himself was not free of fear, for Tott observed that "the arbitrary monarch cannot lose his power for a moment, but it is immediately seized on by the multitude." Tott acknowledged, as Anquetil-Duperron had noted in response to Montesquieu, that the power of the Turkish sultan was limited by Islamic law. Noting that "the Ulema can interpret the law as they please," Tott nonetheless observed that the sultan "disposes of all the riches, the employments, and the lives of his subjects, and has terrible means to make himself obeyed."[93] Frédéric-Melchior Grimm's *Correspondance littéraire*, though faulting Tott's "negligent" and "pretentious" style, praised his contributions to Western knowledge of Ottoman society, writing that "we have read nothing that offers a truer idea of the government and manners of the Turkish nation" than Tott's "precious anecdotes which bear the stamp of careful observation" and which "bring forth the dominant character of the nation."[94]

Tott appealed to the memory of the first great Western conqueror of the Orient to hint at the desirability of such a conquest in the present. Describing the harbor of Alexandria, which he called the project of "a genius bold and sublime," Tott suggested that enlightened European rule could restore the city to what it had been under Alexander, when "it became the city of all nations, and the metropolis of commerce." "His name honours these ashes, which barbarous ages have heaped up, and which only wait to be tempered by some beneficient hand, to form a cement for the reconstruction of the most noble edifice the human mind has ever conceived."[95] As we shall see in the final chapter, such appeals would become increasingly frequent in the final years of the eighteenth century, and would eventually lead to the Napoleonic expedition to Egypt in 1798.

Constantin-François de Chasseboeuf, comte de Volney, who traveled throughout the Middle East in the years prior to the French Revolution, offered one of the Enlightenment's final meditations upon the contrast between European dynamism and Asian decadence. While still a very young man, an unexpected inheritance gave Volney the means to spend three years traveling through Egypt, Syria, Lebanon, and Palestine. Volney later recorded his observations in a two-volume study, *Voyage en Syrie et en Egypte, pendant les années 1783, 1784, et 1785*, as well as a more literary and poetic work, *Les Ruines, ou méditations sur les Révolutions des Empires*. Although Volney discussed the traces of the region's past, he was primarily concerned with its present, and his account of his travels offered a thick description of the peoples, cultures, and contemporary history of the Middle East.

Volney joined Bernier and Montesquieu in denouncing the alleged absence of secure property rights in the Orient. He argued that free institutions, which preserved order and guaranteed the property rights of citizens without restricting their autonomy, encouraged social progress, while despotism, which constrained the actions of subjects while leaving their belongings, even their very lives, subject to the whim of the despot or his agents, discouraged it. Volney wrote, "To awaken activity, there must be objects to meet desires; to maintain it, there must be the hope of achieving their enjoyment. If these two circumstances are lacking, there will be no activity, neither for private citizens nor for the nation, and this is the case with Orientals in general, and particularly for those with whom we are concerned. Who could engage them to act, if no movement offered them the hope of enjoying the fruits of their efforts?" Volney argued, therefore, that it was government and religion, and not climate, which determined the character and dynamism of peoples, a theme to which we will return. He concluded, "It is because their influence acts despite the differences of soil and climates, that Tyre, Carthage, and Alexandria once had the same industriousness as London, Paris, and Amsterdam...(and) that Russian and Polish peasants have the apathy and indifference of the Hindus and Negroes."[96]

Volney thereby reversed the direction of causality posited by Montesquieu: rather than the weakness and inertia of peoples, itself the product of climate, giving rise to despotism, it was despotism that caused its subjects to become weak and indifferent by depriving them of freedom and preventing them from the secure enjoyment of the fruits of their labor. In making this distinction, Volney historicized the Islamic world, attributing its contemporary state not to essentialist, intrinsic features of the "Oriental" character, but rather to the contingent outcome of specific historical events. He observed that the major empires of eighteenth-century Asia were all the products of relatively recent foreign conquest: the Ottoman Turks over the Middle East, the Central Asian Mughals over India, and the Manchus over China. While the history of Europe certainly bore witness to similar episodes of conquest (Volney's French readers would undoubtedly have thought of the conquest of Celtic Gaul first by the Romans under Caesar, and later by the Germanic Franks, the topic of a great deal of presentist-oriented historical debate in Old Regime France), Volney argued that such episodes were sufficiently remote in Europe's past that "the traces of the ancient revolutions disappear each day, the foreign conquerors have drawn nearer to the conquered natives, and their mixture has produced identical national bodies, which now share the same interests." In the Orient, by contrast, "the native peoples, subjugated by still recent revolutions to foreign conquerors, have formed mixed bodies, in which the interests are mutually opposed." Volney attributed the despotic rule of Asian empires to the legacy of conquest, under which "according to the law of barbaric peoples, the vanquished is entirely at the disposition of the victor; he becomes his slave; his life, his goods belong to him." Significantly, however, Volney did not define despotism as an essentially "Oriental" characteristic, writing instead that "such was the law of the Romans, the Greeks, and of all the societies of brigands that have been honored with the name of conquerors."[97] We shall return to Volney's meditations on the decadence of the empires of Asia in the final chapter, where we will argue that these observations contributed to the progressive, evolutionary interpretation of universal history that would be one of the most distinctive (though not universally accepted) aspects of Enlightenment thought. In this formulation, the decadence of Asia and the dynamism of Europe were not features intrinsic to climate, religion, or unchanging natural character, but rather were the natural consequences of good or bad government and of the imposition or release of fetters on human creativity, the cultivation of the arts and sciences, and the pursuit of enlightened self-interest. Before that synthesis could emerge, however, Enlightenment observers would cast a broader net, examining more distant and unfamiliar societies in their quest to elaborate a truly universal science of man.

Conclusions

As we have seen in this chapter, the Islamic Orient served a number of related discursive functions for the scholars, literati, and learned travelers of Enlightenment France. As the West's most enduring Other, it served as a constant reminder that Western Christendom was not the only possible model for human civilization, and forced both *dévots* and *philosophes* to come to terms with the diversity of the human experience across space and time. Most often, the Islamic Orient was invoked as a negative example, although the traits that were attributed to it, such as religious fanaticism, despotic rule, and the subjugation of women, were projections of aspects of European society that commentators wished to challenge. The Enlightenment's perception of the Islamic Orient was not unambiguously negative, however, and it would not be linked to a colonialist agenda until the final quarter of the eighteenth century, when the visible shift in the balance of power between East and West created an opening that the competing imperial powers of the age sought to enter.

The heyday of "baroque Orientalism," to use Nicholas Dew's term, was relatively brief, and was already coming to a close at the dawn of the Enlightenment. As a result of their relative decline *vis-à-vis* the West over the course of the eighteenth century, Asli Çirakman observes, "the Ottomans lost their image as formidable and eventually ceased to provoke curiosity in the European public."[98] The ongoing expansion of Europe's horizons also contributed to this shift, as other peoples and cultures began to exert a more powerful pull on Europe's collective imagination. Robert Irwin writes that "the short-lived craze for Arabic was succeeded by an equally transient fashion for Chinese studies and Chinoiserie...A literary cult of the Chinese sage developed, English landowners had their gardens landscaped in the Chinese manner, French *philosophes* brooded on the supposed merits of Chinese imperial despotism, and the German philosopher Leibniz studied the *I Ching*."[99] We will now turn to examine the Enlightenment's encounter with Confucian Chinese civilization and the uses to which it was put in the political and philosophic debates of the age.

2
The Wisdom of the East: Enlightenment Perspectives on China

Unlike the Islamic Near East, which had been known to the West for centuries, China constituted a "new world" for early modern Europe, which had been only dimly aware of its existence before the sixteenth-century voyages of exploration. In the seventeenth and eighteenth centuries, China came to be admired by many Westerners in a way that the Islamic world never was. Respected for its great antiquity, the stability of its institutions and customs, and the urbane wisdom and tolerance of its ruling elite, China was embraced as a model of "enlightened despotism," which some *philosophes* saw as the solution to the chronic instability and conflict of their own societies, and the Chinese mandarin became one of the favored stock characters for Enlightenment authors seeking to criticize the European status quo. For Enlightenment Sinophiles, China represented a rationalist utopia, a place where meticulous organization and the refinement of manners ensured a harmonious and prosperous society.

Much like Western representations of the Islamic Orient, Enlightenment discourse on China had far more to do with France itself than with the Middle Kingdom. Michael Keevak has written that "the vogue for Chinese things was based on a distinct *lack* of knowledge about the empire ... This was a *rêve chinoise*, not a modern ethnography, and Western ideas about China remained thoroughly Eurocentric fantasies filtered through long-standing prejudices and stereotypes about the fabled Middle Kingdom."[1] China was not exactly a blank screen on which European observers could project whatever they wanted—the ethnographic information provided by the Jesuits and other observers was too extensive and too specific for that—but it did serve as a sort of Rorschach test in which those Europeans who contemplated it (Jesuits, Deists, philosophers, and political economists) could see what they wanted to see. Whatever the specific image of China a particular Western observer came away with, the very fact of China's existence, and the great antiquity and refinement of its civilization, posed a challenge to Europe's sense of its identity and place in the world. Imperial China would prove both seductive and disconcerting to early modern European observers, forcing them to balance the merits of competing forms of civilized society as they theorized new concepts of natural law, the diversity of customs, and the course of human progress.

The Chinese Model

French Enlightenment Sinophiles, of whom Voltaire was the most prominent example, praised the Middle Kingdom as a model of an enlightened and well-ordered society, which they contrasted with the tumultuous, irrational state of France from medieval feudalism to the sixteenth-century wars of religion. In the *Essai sur les moeurs,* Voltaire praised imperial China as a model for a rationally administered and highly cultivated society, writing that "in general, the spirit of order and moderation, the taste for science, the cultivation of all the arts useful for life, a prodigious number of inventions that make these arts easier, composed the wisdom of the Chinese."[2] He further remarked that "the human spirit can certainly not imagine a better government than that where everything is decided by great tribunals, subordinated one to the other, whose members are only selected after several severe examinations...If there was ever a state in which life, honor, and property were protected by the laws, it is the empire of China."[3]

Given the consistent hostility of Voltaire and other Enlightenment authors toward the Jesuit order, it is richly ironic that the Enlightenment's celebration of China as an enlightened despotism governed according to natural law by a wise elite of mandarin scholar-administrators was borrowed lock, stock, and barrel from the Jesuit relations of the late seventeenth century. The Jesuit mission to Asia began with the travels of St. Francis Xavier in the sixteenth century and the subsequent establishment of a Jesuit mission at Peking under the direction of Matteo Ricci, who set the tone for subsequent efforts at winning over the mandarin elite by learning the Chinese language and adopting Chinese dress and customs. The Jesuit foothold in China was threatened on several occasions in the early seventeenth century, first by a wave of persecutions aimed at preventing religious proselytization, and subsequently by the invasions from the

north that led to the overthrow of the Ming dynasty and its replace-
ment by the Qing in 1644. Thereafter, however, the Jesuits enjoyed a
long period of protection and favor at the imperial court under the
protection of the Kangxi emperor, who valued their knowledge of
science and technology. [4]

One of the first Jesuit histories of China, written by the Portuguese
missionary Alvarez Semedo, established the image of China as
a well-ordered society governed by a learned elite of mandarin
scholar-bureaucrats. Semedo praised the wisdom and virtue of Hun
Vu, the fourteenth-century founder of the Ming dynasty, who hum-
bled the great warlords, excluded members of his own family from
holding office, and entrusted the government to the mandarins.
Semedo wrote that this wise ruler "placed the whole government in
the Literati, who are created such by way of concurrence... without
any dependence at all on the Magistrates, or the King himself, but
only by the merit of their learning, good parts, and virtues. He did
not annul those ancient laws which concerned good government."
Semedo described the virtue of the emperors, who sought to lead by
moral example, and reflected, "Who seeth not how much reason we
have to envy these heathens, who, although they are exceeded by
us in the knowledge of things belonging to faith, do yet oftentimes
surpass us in the practice of moral virtues?"[5]

Most Enlightenment-era French readers encountered the Jesuit
construction of China through Jean-Baptiste du Halde's *Description
géographique, historique, chronologique, politique, et physique de l'Empire
de la Chine et de la Tartarie chinoise,* published in 1735 in four massive tomes.[6] Though du Halde himself never visited China, he drew
extensively from the travel narratives and treatises of his fellow
Jesuits and corresponded with many of the long-serving missionaries at the court of Peking, and his highly positive account served
to crystallize a number of themes that would be echoed repeatedly
by Enlightenment Sinophiles. Du Halde stressed the rationality
and benevolence of imperial governance, writing that wise pater-
nalism and filial piety were the bonds that united the emperor to
his subjects as members of an extended and interdependent family. He praised the bureaucratic system of administration through
a corps of mandarins who were selected by rigorous examinations,
repeatedly observed by imperial representatives, and who could be
removed for bad conduct. He condemned Chinese popular religion,
particularly Taoism and Buddhism, as superstition and idolatry, but
greatly admired the ethical doctrines of Confucius, insisting that
these in no way contradicted the teachings of Christ. In du Halde's

presentation, popular "superstitions" represented corruptions of the pure natural wisdom of ancient Confucianism, so that the Jesuits, by preaching the Gospels, were in a sense helping the Chinese to recover their true selves. As we shall see, however, the secular and skeptical authors of the eighteenth century would use the evidence that the Jesuit scholar compiled to plead a very different case.

The favorable portrait of China produced by the Jesuit relations and treatises of the seventeenth century and synthesized in du Halde's magnum opus appealed to eighteenth-century French observers for a variety of reasons. Certainly the idea of a government administered through the agency of men of letters was tremendously attractive to French writers and intellectuals who, despite the respect with which they were usually (though not always) treated by the court and by their noble patrons, had few opportunities to shape or enact policy directly. The sixteenth-century wars of religion and the civil war of the Fronde in the seventeenth century were not long distant, and events such as the expulsion of the Huguenots in 1685 and the destruction of the Jansenist convent of Port-Royal in 1709 remained within living memory. As a model of enlightened and tolerant rule, the Kangxi emperor of China compared favorably to Louis XIV on a number of counts.[7] In the early eighteenth century, therefore, critics of religious intolerance and advocates of a rationally ordered society under enlightened absolutism looked to the East for inspiration. One of the most prominent of these Enlightenment Sinophiles was the marquis d'Argens, whose *Lettres chinoises* used imperial China as a mirror with which to reflect the faults of contemporary French society.

Jean-Baptiste du Boyer, marquis d'Argens, was a novelist, pamphleteer, and courtier who produced a great number of works modeled on Montesquieu's *Lettres persanes*, notably the *Lettres juives*, *Lettres cabalistiques*, and the *Lettres chinoises*, with which we will concern ourselves here. Written from 1738 to 1742 and published in serial form, the *Lettres chinoises* are structured as the correspondence between a half dozen Chinese mandarins scattered across the globe. The most prolific contributors are Sioeu-Tcheou, in Paris, and his friend Yn-Che-Chan, who remained behind in Peking, but d'Argens created additional travelers as needed in order to include reports from Persia, Japan, Siam, Russia, Germany, and Scandinavia. Rather than a simple duality between East and West, d'Argens thus offered a broad panorama for his readers to reflect philosophically upon the variety of customs and conventions of mankind. Like the *Lettres persanes*, the *Lettres chinoises* compared the manners, morals, and gender relations of the East to those of the West. Sioeu-Tcheou described the people of Paris as obsessed with novelties, commenting that "the empire of fashion is as powerful over the French spirit as that of jealousy among the Turks and Tartars," and criticized the overuse of powder and makeup by French women, which "made their faces resemble the skin of a tiger."[8] The traveling mandarin further lamented that the French, unlike the Chinese, showed no respect toward their elders, and faulted French court society for its tacit approval of adulterous liaisons as "gallantry."[9]

Like the Jesuits who preceded him, d'Argens held up the Chinese imperial system as a model of wise and benevolent governance. Sioeu-Tcheou praised the examination system for the selection of mandarins, noting that by contrast, "In France...all judicial positions are sold, and held by families as patrimonial goods. One purchases here the right to judge men like a merchant in China purchases a bundle of merchandise."[10] D'Argens's correspondents also criticized the social pretensions of the clergy and nobility, stressing that the wiser Chinese instead honored peasants and merchants as useful, productive members of society.[11] Criticizing the recent French kings Henri III and Louis XIII for being led astray by corrupt courtiers, d'Argens's narrator Sioeu-Tcheou laments that truly great kings, such as Augustus, Henri IV, or Frederick the Great, are rare, and finds it extraordinary that so few rulers recognize that their true interest lies in being useful to their subjects and thereby ensuring the enduring admiration of subsequent generations.[12]

D'Argens's celebration of Frederick the Great, his patron at the time, as one of the rare great kings of history was evidently self-interested, while his selection of Augustus reflects the predominant classicism of Enlightenment culture. His praise of Henri IV, however, reflects one of the underlying motifs of Enlightenment Sinophilia—the contrast between the religious fanaticism that had torn European society apart in the two centuries since the Reformation and the ecumenical tolerance that appeared to reign at the Chinese imperial court. Here as well, as we shall now see, the intrepid Jesuit missionary-scholars served as the unwitting sources of Enlightenment anticlericalism.

Confucius between Jesuits and Philosophes

In their efforts to win Chinese converts, the Jesuits were careful not to offend Chinese sensibilities by attacking rituals and customs at the heart of Chinese social life, such as the rites performed to honor the emperor and the spirits of deceased ancestors. Indeed, as

Liam Brockey has observed, the position of the missionaries, a small group of Westerners far from home and living on the margins of a vast and powerful empire, was always precarious, and depended on the indulgence of the imperial authorities. Therefore, while their counterparts in the Americas were free to attack "pagan superstitions and idolatry," using coercion if necessary, the Jesuit mission to China had to proceed more carefully. Consequently, they argued that the "Chinese rites" were purely secular rituals in which Chinese Christian converts could participate without dishonoring their new faith. They also took care not to condemn traditional Confucian values and beliefs, nor to suggest that venerable ancestors who had not heard the word of the Gospels were condemned to eternal damnation. Instead, Ricci argued in his memoirs, "One can confidently hope that in the mercy of God, many of the ancient Chinese found salvation in the natural law."[13]

Just as they sought to make Christianity appear less alien and threatening to the Chinese mandarins, the Jesuits also sought to make China appear less foreign and heretical to European audiences. In 1687, members of the Jesuit order published an anthology of Confucian texts and maxims, translated into Latin as *Confucius sinarum philosophus*, representing the Chinese philosopher as a virtuous sage whose teachings reflected the truth of an original "natural religion" and were in no way contradictory to Christianity. Basil Guy writes that the Jesuits created "an image of the Middle Kingdom less in accordance with reality than with the needs of the moment...In the kingdom of the Son of Heaven, there dwelt a virtuous people, civilized from time immemorial, whose moral attitude was perfection itself." Observing that the Enlightenment *philosophes* adopted this characterization and used it for their own ends, Guy further remarks: "It is thus amusing to note that in European minds at least Confucius still owes his renown as a sublime sage to the chicanery which accompanied this crisis in western intellectual history."[14] The Jesuit celebration of the wisdom of Confucius bordered on heresy, and critics of the order would argue that it crossed the line entirely. Colin Mackerras writes that "the translator was in fact imputing to the Chinese a knowledge of truth irrespective of Christian revelation. Indeed the introduction to the translation asserts specifically that the ancient Chinese must have had knowledge of the true God and worshipped him."[15]

As they sought to approximate China to Europe, the seventeenth-century Jesuits also benefited from a fortunate accident. In 1625, workmen in the western Chinese city of Xi'an accidentally discovered a stone stele with inscriptions in both Chinese and Syriac, bearing a cross and preaching a new doctrine called *jingjiao*, or "luminous teaching." A Chinese convert and scholar named Li Zhijao read the inscription and published it with commentary, suggesting that *jingjiao* might be "the same holy religion of the West that has been preached by Matteo Ricci," and the stele was indeed subsequently proven to be the work of Nestorian Christians who had traveled to China from the Near East in the eighth century. Though of only minor interest in China itself, the stele was celebrated by Jesuits as proof that the gospel of Christ had indeed been preached to the far ends of the earth, and that the Chinese, having already been exposed to the true religion in the past, would be uniquely receptive to their missionary outreach in the present. Although in fact, as Michael Keevak notes, "the 'luminous religion' was little more than a marginal creed in an ancient dynasty that had tolerated a wide variety of foreign philosophies," it soon became central to seventeenth-century Jesuit accounts of Chinese civilization, and was seized upon by the seventeenth-century Jesuit scholar Athanasius Kircher as proof of his theory of the Egyptian origins of Chinese civilization.[16]

The Jesuits' enthusiastic and optimistic representations of Chinese civilization and Confucian philosophy were not universally accepted, and many of the sharpest criticisms of their views came from rival Catholic orders, particularly the Dominicans and members of the French Société des Missions Etrangères. These groups, envious of the Jesuits' successes and suspicious of their close ties to the mandarin elite, lobbied the Vatican against Jesuit indulgence, accusing the rival order of diluting the truth of Christianity and seasoning it with pagan elements in order to make it more appealing to idolatrous palates. These polemics, which escalated in intensity over the latter decades of the seventeenth century, exploded into the "Chinese rites" controversy of the turn of the century. Ironically, a Chinese imperial edict of 1692 that explicitly tolerated Christian missionary activity worsened the dispute by encouraging rival religious orders, which were less accommodating to Chinese tradition than were the Jesuits, to enter the empire, where they soon condemned its customary rituals. After a decade of debate and consideration, in which the Propaganda Fide and the Roman Inquisition weighed in on the side of the doctrinaires, Pope Clement XI condemned the Jesuit interpretation of the Chinese rites in 1704. Relations between the Catholic establishment and the Chinese imperial court deteriorated rapidly thereafter. Maillard de Tournon, a papal legate appointed to announce the Vatican's decision in China, was expelled by the Kangxi emperor two years later, and a Chinese imperial edict subsequently required all Catholic missionaries to accept the emperor's secular interpretation of the Confucian rites—and thereby deny that of the pope—in order to continue to preach in China. Caught between these irreconcilable positions, the Jesuit mission to China withered in the following years, until the subsequent emperor expelled most foreign missionaries from China in 1724.[17]

European critics of Counter-Reformation orthodoxy were quick to seize upon the contrast between the tolerant Chinese emperor Kangxi, who allowed Christian clergy to proselytize in his empire even though he did not share their faith, and the inflexible Vatican, which condemned all beliefs and customs different from its own. Pierre Bayle wrote, "I do not know why the Christians make so few reflections on the spirit of tolerance that reigns among these pagan kings whom we loudly condemn as ferocious barbarians. Here is a Chinese emperor, entirely persuaded that the religion of the Jesuits is false and totally opposed to that which he and all of his subjects profess, who nonetheless suffers these missionaries and treats them quite humanely."[18] The German philosopher and mathematician Gottfried Wilhelm Leibniz suggested that China should "send missionaries to us to teach us the purpose and use of natural theology, in the same way as we send missionaries to them to instruct them in revealed theology."[19]

Voltaire condemned "the miserable disputes that we have seen in Europe over the Chinese rites," and wrote that the Vatican's attempt to decide the issue "could not have been more absurd had the republic of San Marino set itself up as mediator between the Grand Turk and the Persian Empire."[20] He further argued that the conflicts between the Jesuits and their Dominican and Franciscan critics weakened the cause of Christianity in China, and wrote that "the Chinese were astonished to see sages who were in disagreement over what they should teach, who reciprocally persecuted and anathematized one another, who instigated criminal prosecutions in Rome, and who deferred to congregations of cardinals to decide whether the emperor of China knew his own language as well as the missionaries sent from Italy or France."[21] Voltaire contrasted the dogmatic squabbling of the Catholic religious orders to what he represented as the pure, natural religiosity of Confucian China, writing, "Never was the religion of the emperors and courts dishonored by imposture, never disturbed by quarrels between the empire and the priesthood... Their Kung Fu-tze, whom we call Confucius, imagined neither new opinions nor new rites; he was neither medium nor prophet; he was a wise magistrate who taught the ancient laws...He recommended only virtue, he preached no mysteries."[22]

Much as Voltaire would do across his many works, the marquis d'Argens contrasted the urbane tolerance and world-weary wisdom of his Chinese observers to the religious bigotry and superstition of European society in the *Lettres chinoises*. Sioeu-Tcheou condemned the religious wars that had devastated Germany in the previous century, calling them "as ridiculous as sacrilegious," and lamented that, despite "the extravagances, cruelties, and barbarities that fanaticism has inspired...men have not become wiser or more sensible." Contrasting the madness of holy war with the tranquility of China, where "we mortally hate persecutions...and abhor wars of religion," the mandarin asserted that "missionaries would never have been tolerated there, if it had been known that the opinions which they taught could one day be harmful to the state."[23] In the later sections of the work, d'Argens became increasingly strident and explicit in his attacks on the Jesuit order, discussing in detail both the "Chinese rites" controversy and the Nestorian monument of Xi'an, which he repeatedly denounced as a forgery. D'Argens used these sections to paint the Jesuits as duplicitous and deceitful, enforcing religious orthodoxy at home while blending Christian and Chinese elements in the Peking mission. Yn-Che-Chan wrote that these missionaries had initially sought "to make us Christians, but after they had spent a few years among us, they seemed to forget the purpose of their voyage, and they themselves became Chinese," and noted that their "mixture of Christian and Chinese ceremonies" had been condemned by the Vatican.[24] By attacking the Jesuits, virtually the only source of reliable information on Chinese civilization in early modern Europe, d'Argens sought to detach the Jesuit image of a rational, tolerant, well-ordered Chinese society from its theological moorings, the better to use it as a mirror with which to reveal the faults of Christian European society.

In addition to condemning religious conflict within Christendom, d'Argens, speaking through his Chinese observers, offered a passionate defense of the Jews and a stinging critique of anti-Semitism, both medieval and modern. Sioeu-Tcheou declared: "I tremble with horror when I think of the barbarities that men who are considered cultured and civilized commit against unfortunates who are all the more to be pitied because they are only miserable because they follow the dictates of their conscience," and exclaimed, "what barbarity...to kill a man who is guilty of no crime but refusing to lie!" He further concluded: "There is no people who has been so barbaric as the

Europeans, who dare to speak of the ferocity of other nations, who, compared to them, have the most gentle and generous manners," and went on to note that the Turkish sultan Mehmet II, condemned as a despot by Westerners, had granted asylum to the Jews expelled from Portugal.[25] In subsequent letters, he cited and refuted charges of ritual murder and of the profanation of the host, noting the lack of credible evidence, the fabrication of similar false charges against the Templars, and the fact that the Jews, not believing in transubstantiation, would have no reason to destroy "a piece of bread."[26] The wise governance of the mandarins, d'Argens suggested, would never tolerate such barbaric acts.

Eternal China

Of all of the revelations made by the Jesuits regarding imperial China, the one most disconcerting to European intellectual circles was that of the unparalleled antiquity of Chinese civilization. The Italian Jesuit Martino Martini set off a bombshell in European intellectual circles when he revealed that unbroken Chinese chronologies stretched back nearly five thousand years, and that the putative founder of Chinese civilization, the first emperor Fo-Hi, lived around 2950 BC, or about six hundred years prior to the date commonly given for the Biblical Deluge. Virgile Pinot observes that "for the men of the seventeenth century... the antiquity of a nation... was a title of glory still greater perhaps than its sophistication. If for the individual it was a sign of nobility to have ancestors who had participated in the Crusades, for a nation, nobility was to have as founders people who went back to the Deluge." [27] Furthermore, given the monogenist and diffusionist assumptions of the age, it was assumed that whichever civilization could be proven to be the eldest had surely given rise to all the others. This was far from a purely academic question. If this root civilization was not that of the Biblical patriarchs, what was to become of sacred chronology and the story of human origins and the dispersion of peoples narrated in the book of Genesis?

Efforts to reconcile Chinese chronologies with the accepted timelines of (sacred) universal history led to some elaborate, and ultimately unconvincing, intellectual gymnastics. The seventeenth-century Jesuit Athanasius Kircher argued in *Oedipus Aegyptiacus* and *China Illustrata* that China had been colonized centuries after the Deluge by the ancient Egyptians under the conquering pharoah Sesostris (who was in fact a composite of several different historical pharaohs invented by Herodotus[28]). This implausible theory, which required the dismissal of the ancient Chinese annals, was also endorsed by Pierre-Daniel Huet and was revived during the high Enlightenment by the antiquarian Joseph de Guignes.[29] With equal improbability, observing that the Chinese annals spoke of a great flood around 2337 BC, the classicist Etienne Fourmont argued in 1747 that the first emperors of China were in fact the antediluvian patriarchs of Genesis, and that Fo-Hi, the legendary founder of Chinese civilization, was Noah himself, a conclusion that his English contemporary Samuel Shuckford had already reached in 1728.[30] Fourmont argued that "the times of Noah fall with precision in accordance with the times of Fo-Hi, and with regard to the regions of the Ark and of Babel, it can be remarked that the Caucasus is not so far from China, and according to the Annals themselves, Fohi arrived from Xensi [that is, from the west]."[31] Fourmont further argued that, if the Chinese were not descended from Noah, "what are we to think of such a race of men unknown to the rest of the universe?"[32]

Other European scholars resolved the challenge of Chinese antiquity by moving back the date of the Biblical Deluge. Paul-Yves Pezron, a Benedictine monk and antiquarian scholar at the abbey of Saint-Maur, noted in his 1687 treatise *L'Antiquité des Temps rétablie et défendue,* that the Septuagint, the Greek version of the Old Testament, placed the date of creation around 5500 BC, rather than 4000 BC, the date suggested by the Latin Vulgate. Pezron further argued that this chronology "accords perfectly well with the antiquities of the oriental nations, such as the Chaldeans, the Egyptians, and the Chinese." Pezron acknowledged that the civilizations of the East, particularly China, were older than those of Greece or Rome, and wrote that "the Orient began to be settled three or four centuries after the Deluge, and there were already kingdoms in this part of the world, perhaps even before Greece and Italy were inhabited. Asia was the cradle of humanity."[33] Similarly, Nicolas Fréret, the most prominent of the early eighteenth-century French érudits, also favored the longer chronology of the Septuagint over the shorter timetable of the Latin Vulgate version, and observed that the Vatican had never made the Vulgate chronology an article of faith, whereas the Greek Orthodox Church had consistently followed the Septuagint. He argued that "the advantages of the extended calculation to reconcile all the authentic histories of the nations with the chronology of Moses, should lead us to favor the chronology of the Septuagint. There are many of these authentic histories that cannot be rejected without destroying all the rules of criticism and opening the door to an absolute historical Pyrrhonism."[34]

The introduction of the Septuagint chronology to resolve the contradictions between sacred and profane histories resolved the immediate issue at hand, but set a potentially dangerous precedent for Biblical orthodoxy. Martini, Pezron, and the other *dévots*, even as they sought to defend the literal truth of the book of Genesis, removed the Bible from its pedestal and effectively placed it on the same level as the annals of China, the dynastic tables of Egypt, and the astronomical charts of Babylon. Anthony Grafton notes that the discipline of chronology "is based on a philological method which applies equally to Hebrews and to Greeks, to the Bible and to the ancient historians."[35] One orthodox critic, the abbé de Vallemont, recognized the danger and asked: "What will the unbelievers and libertines say about us if, on the authority of memoirs from China, we will change our beliefs and abandon a Bible consecrated by the Church for its antiquity and by the decrees of the Council of Trent?"[36]

If devout scholars were troubled by new revelations regarding the great antiquity of Chinese civilization, their skeptical contemporaries seized upon them as additional weapons in their struggles against religious orthodoxy. Voltaire wrote in the *Essai sur les moeurs* that "it is incontestable that the oldest annals of the world are those of China. These annals flow without interruption. Almost all detailed, entirely wise, without any magical elements, always supported by astronomical observations over four thousand one hundred fifty two years, they extend several centuries beyond, without precise dates, to be sure, but with that plausibility that approaches certitude."[37] Citing the Jesuit astronomer Antoine Gaubil to observe that the Chinese had accurately recorded a solar eclipse in the year 2155 BC, and further noting that China's historical records went back even farther, to the first king Fo-Hi who reigned more than 25 centuries before Christ, Voltaire wrote in the *Essai sur les moeurs* that "their vast and populous empire was already governed as a family in which the monarch was the father, and in which forty legislative tribunals were considered as older brothers, while we were a small band of nomads in the forest of the Ardennes," and wrote in a 1760 letter to the Orientalist Michel-Ange André Leroux-Deshauterayes that China was a well-governed, civilized society at a time when the ancient Gauls were "illiterate barbarians who slaughtered little girls and boys to the honor of Teutates, as we slaughtered them in 1572 in honor of St. Bartholomew."[38]

As these comments suggest, the longevity, continuity, and apparent harmony of Chinese civilization recommended it to French observers distressed by the conflict and upheaval of their own place and time. The marquis d'Argens contrasted the ephemeral rise and fall of the nations of the West with the eternal glory of China, which he attributed to its good governance and to the spirit of tolerance that prevailed in the Middle Kingdom. Reflecting upon the ruins of the Roman forum, I-Tuly, a new correspondent introduced in the fifth volume to discuss the denouement of the "Chinese rites" controversy at the Vatican, likened the causes of the decline and fall of civilizations to the diseases and accidents that shorten the lives of individual human beings:

> [Societies] have a fixed duration which they cannot exceed; one may say that they are born, grow, live, and finally die, just as living creatures do... Of all the peoples of the universe whose histories I have read, I know of none whose situation has been more durable than our own. How many centuries has it endured, without experiencing any of these deadly revolutions?... To what may we attribute this... but to the goodness of our government? I hope that it will long preserve the state of health which it now enjoys.[39]

Like d'Argens's mandarin, Voltaire praised the great antiquity and endurance of China as proof of the wisdom of its fundamental laws, and stressed that the superiority of the Chinese imperial system was proven by the fact that the foreign Mongol and Manchu conquerors had seen fit to adopt it, calling it "a great example of the natural superiority of reason and genius over blind and barbaric force."[40] This process of acculturation of the victors by the vanquished formed the theme of one of Voltaire's dramas in verse, *L'Orphelin de la Chine*, based loosely on a Chinese tale included in du Halde's compendium, in which the devotion of the mandarin Zamti to the dethroned imperial family, which leads him to offer the sacrifice of his own son in the place of the last surviving royal heir, overcomes the wrath of the conqueror Genghis Khan, and moves the latter to offer clemency.[41]

As both Basil Guy and J. H. Brumfitt have noted, Voltaire made use of China as a discursive tool with which to present arguments that were primarily about Europe. Guy writes, "The Chinese ideal became for him simply one more weapon with which to tilt at 'l'infâme'...useful to him only insofar as he could criticize with it contemporary abuse."[42] J. H. Brumfitt concurs, observing that Voltaire projected his own concerns onto Asia, and thereby "discovers the *philosophe* beneath the robes of the Chinese mandarin or the Indian

Brahman."[43] The same would be the case for the Physiocrats in subsequent years, whose celebration of China as a model of bureaucratic and economic rationalization we will now consider.

China and the Physiocrats

In the 1760s, imperial China found a new set of French admirers among the Physiocrats, a group of free market economic reformers who hoped to revitalize the declining and deeply indebted French monarchy by removing restrictions on the trade in grain and other staple commodities. Similar in many ways to their British counterparts Smith, Malthus, and Ricardo, the French Physiocrats remained more traditional in their relative disdain for manufactures and their insistence that agriculture was the source of all wealth. The Physiocrats saw the privileges of the landed nobility, the restrictions placed by urban guilds on the production of goods, and the strict regulation of prices for bread by royal and municipal authorities as so many fetters that prevented the French economy from functioning at an optimal level. Most of them, perceiving the nobility, clergy, and merchant and artisan guilds alike as atavistic forces hindering progress, looked to a revitalized, enlightened absolutism as the best hope for France's economic resurgence.[44] For this reason, a number of Physiocratic reformers held up an idealized vision of China as a model for the French monarchy to emulate.

The most enthusiastic endorsement of China as a model for the West was François Quesnay's *Le despotisme de la Chine*, published in several installments in the Physiocratic journal *Ephémerides du Citoyen* from March to June 1767. Quesnay wrote to defend China against charges of despotism by arguing that the term had been misunderstood. "If one believes the English authors of the universal history," he wrote, "there is no power on earth more despotic than the emperor of China. If by despotism they understand the absolute power to enforce obedience to the laws and fundamental maxims of government, it is true that there is no other human power in China capable of weakening that of the emperor." However, he argued, these historians are unaware "that the constitution of the Chinese government is founded on natural law in such an unshakable manner that it prevents the sovereign from doing evil, and ensures him in his legitimate administration the supreme power to do good, such that this authority is a beatitude for the prince, and a pleasant dominion for his subjects." Quesnay argued that China's stability and prosperity derived from its recognition of natural law, which he defined as "the very physical laws of the perpetual reproduction of the goods necessary to the subsistence, preservation, and comfort of men." In this formulation, the primary purpose of government was to maximize the total economic utility of society, "to cultivate the land with the greatest possible success, and to defend society against thieves and scoundrels."[45]

Quesnay praised the Chinese system of governance by an enlightened elite of mandarins, educated in the principles of government and selected through a system of competitive examinations. He wrote, "The first law should be that which ordered the study of the science of making laws; the first political establishment should be the creation of schools for the teaching of this science. Except for China, all kingdoms have ignored the necessity of this establishment which is the foundation of government." He further declared that "men cannot perceive natural law but by the light of reason which distinguishes them from beasts. The primary object of the administration of a prosperous and durable government should thus be, as in the empire of China, the profound study and continuous and general instruction of natural laws, which constitute the social order."[46] As Basil Guy has observed, Quesnay considers that "the art of government is...the creation and maintenance of a condition in which the laws of nature can best be supported by an absolute monarchy...To this end, the monarch needed wise and good counselors, mandarins, or, as the author would prefer, Physiocrats. With their aid, he should be able to rule as the most benevolent of enlightened despots."[47] Imperial China thus furnished a model for the renewal of the increasingly sclerotic French monarchy.

Quesnay further wrote that "ignorance is the primary cause of the most harmful errors of government, of the ruin of nations and the decadence of empires, from which China has always been so securely protected through the ministry of its mandarins, who form the first order of the nation, who take care to lead the people through the light of reason, and to submit the government to the natural and immutable laws which constitute the essential order of societies." Quesnay then asked: "Are not the endurance, the extent, and the permanent prosperity ensured in the empire of China through the observance of natural laws? Does not this so populous nation with good reason regard those other peoples governed by human will and constrained to obedience by the force of arms as barbarous nations?" In keeping with Physiocratic concerns, Quesnay praised the importance granted to agriculture in China, and wrote, "there are some kingdoms in Europe where one has not yet sensed the importance of agriculture, nor the riches necessary for agricultural enterprises, which can only be pursued by inhabitants noteworthy for their capacities and their wealth, and their rank has been fixed below the common people of the towns."[48]

Quesnay's view of Confucian doctrines was heavily influenced by du Halde, from whom he drew most of his information on Chinese culture. Quesnay thus presented Confucius as a wise and benevolent sage, writing, "All the doctrine of this philosopher tended to reestablish human nature in its ancient splendor and primitive beauty, as granted by heaven, but which has been disfigured by the shadows of ignorance and the contagion of vice."[49] Like the Jesuits, Quesnay represented the Confucian belief system as a rationalized religion, which recognized the existence of a supreme being, and saw Taoism and Buddhism as subsequent corruptions of this original truth. "It is remarkable," Quesnay wrote, "that for more than two thousand years, the Chinese nation has known, respected, and honored a supreme being, the sovereign master of the universe, under the name Chang-ti, without any vestiges of idolatry to be seen. It was not until several centuries after Confucius that the statue of Fo was brought from the Indies, and that a quantity of errors began to infect the empire. But the mandarins, unshakably attached to the doctrine of their ancestors, were never affected by this contagion."[50]

Another Enlightenment Sinophile was the colonial administrator Pierre Poivre, who had traveled extensively in South and East Asia in the 1740s and 1750s as an employee of the Compagnie des Indes, a career that culminated in a stint as intendant of the Isle de France from 1767 to 1773. Doing honor to his name, Poivre dedicated much of his career to the ultimately successful transplantation of cloves, nutmeg, and other spice plants from the East Indies to the Isle de France. Described by the biographical reference in his personnel file as "a good man and a practical philosopher" whose "wise and active administration, after the disasters of the war, returned these fine colonies to a new prosperity," Poivre was, like Quesnay, an adherent of the Physiocratic school, and shared with him the belief that agriculture was the key to all wealth.[51] He often quarreled with the military administrators of the Isle de France, whom he accused of neglecting long-term economic interests in favor of military priorities, engaging in illegal smuggling for personal gain, and exercising arbitrary, despotic authority over the local administration. During the period between his initial return from South Asia to France in 1757 and his designation as intendant a decade later, Poivre wrote a series of short memoirs on his travels, which were subsequently published in 1768 as *Voyages d'un philosophe.*

Poivre's *Voyages* are not a straightforward travel narrative, but rather a didactic parable regarding politics, economics, and the conditions that create the prosperity and poverty of nations. He dismissed Africa as "uncultivated lands, inhabited by unfortunate Negroes," and criticized the government of Siam as a despotic tyranny that sapped the vitality and resources of a potentially productive land, writing, "In this earthly paradise, amidst so many riches, who would believe that the Siamese are perhaps the most miserable of peoples?"[52] The culmination of Poivre's philosophical travels, however, is his enthusiastic description of China. Arriving in Canton, he was amazed by the great size and population of the city, and wondered how the Chinese were able to feed so many people. In his subsequent travels to the countryside, he noted approvingly that the Chinese practiced an extremely intensive form of agriculture, leaving no fields uncultivated, and renewing lands through the use of multiple fertilizers. He wrote that the Chinese system was "followed from one end of the empire to the other since the origin of the monarchy, confirmed by the experience of more than forty centuries, in the nation of the world most attentive to its interests." "The Chinese nation," Poivre continued, "is capable of the greatest works; I have seen no more industrious people in the world. Every day of the year is a workday, except for the first, designated for the exchange of visits, and the last, consecrated to the ceremony of duties rendered to the ancestors. A lazy man would surely be scorned; he would be regarded as a paralytic member burdening the body of which he formed part."[53] In an imaginative reversal of the ethnographic gaze, Poivre remarked that "a Chinese farmer could not keep himself from laughing" if he were to witness the lamentable state of agriculture in eighteenth-century France, "part of our fields left uncultivated, another part dedicated to useless crops, the rest poorly labored...the extreme misery and the barbarity of those who cultivate it."[54]

Elsewhere in his *Voyages*, Poivre used a utopian parable to make the case for the importance of agriculture to the prosperity and happiness of humankind, describing the colonization and transformation of a Southeast Asian country by a wise Chinese mandarin named Kiang-tse. Poivre wrote that Kiang-tse, unlike his French seigneurial counterparts, "distributed his lands to his farmers as pure gifts, without reserving the rights known under the names of *service, lods, and ventes,* rights which...are the most terrible scourge of agriculture, and the idea of which has never touched the common sense of wise peoples." Kiang-tse also led by "providing an example of simplicity, of labor, of frugality, of good faith, and of humanity. He thereby formed no laws; he did far more: he established customs." Poivre then declared: "May I be allowed to state here in passing: what a difference between such men, and those famous conquerors who have stunned, desolated the earth, and who, abusing the right of conquest, have established laws which, even after the human race was freed of them, have perpetuated human misery over the course of centuries!"[55] Poivre concluded his text with the assertion that it was agriculture and the laws, customs, and property rights governing it that determined the prosperity and happiness of peoples, and encouraged the rulers of Europe to emulate the emperor of China, whom he described as the greatest and richest of all the sovereigns of the world.

Poivre credited China's enduring prosperity to the virtue of its founders and their perpetuation of the natural laws of mankind, which had been lost to other peoples. He wrote that "the Empire was founded by farmers in those happy times in which the memory of the laws of the Creator had not yet been lost." Declaring that in China "the cultivation of the land was the most noble occupation, the one most worthy of men and the occupation of all," Poivre argued that "since Fo-Hi, who was the first leader of the nation . . . all the emperors without exception, down to this day, have taken pride in being the first farmers of their empire. One of the most memorable passages in Poivre's description of imperial China is his account of the annual plowing ceremony with which the emperor opened the new agricultural season. Poivre described how the emperor, accompanied by the royal court, would pray to heaven (T'ien) for divine blessing upon his people, perform sacrifices and time-honored rites, and would then "seize the handle of the plow, and open several furrows across the full width of the field." While Poivre had not been present in the imperial capital of Peking to witness the emperor perform the ceremony in person, he had seen the emperor's viceroy perform the same acts in Canton. He wrote, "I cannot recall having ever witnessed any ceremony invented by man with such pleasure and satisfaction as I felt in considering this one."[56] Poivre's description of the annual plowing ceremony, also described by du Halde, Quesnay, and several other Western writers on China, was perhaps the part of his text that most inspired the imagination of his readers, and in 1768 the French dauphin imitated the emperor of China by plowing a small plot of land to set a good example for his subjects.[57]

However, Grimm and Diderot's *Correspondance littéraire* remained skeptical regarding the significance of this ceremony. In their review of Poivre's *Voyages d'un philosophe*, they argued that it held no deeper importance than did many of the ritualistic observances of the Christian monarchies of Europe:

This ceremony is held in the first days of our month of March; each viceroy observes it in his province. M. Poivre saw it in Canton, and one may imagine all that a European philosopher might find noble, emotional, and touching in this spectacle! It remains to be determined whether the emperor attaches to it any of the noble and touching ideas of the European philosopher. Let us be sent a Chinese Poivre, may he arrive at Versailles on the morning of Holy Thursday, and there he will see one of the most powerful kings of Europe washing the feet of twelve paupers. Soon thereafter he will see this monarch, accompanied by all the royal household, serving these twelve paupers at his table. What great and touching ideas will this ceremony inspire in our Chinese philosopher, when he learns that this ceremony is repeated every year to honor the Confucius of Europe who washed the feet of his disciples! He will find it one of the most beautiful human institutions in the world. What greater wisdom, in fact, than to remind once a year the rulers of the earth of the primitive equality and the bonds of brotherhood that unite all men? If this Chinese philosopher returns home, as our travelers do, he will give so touching a description of this ceremony that no one will read it without tenderness. What would be the astonishment of our foreign philosopher if he is told that this ceremony is but a vain formality consecrated by habit, that the prince who observes it has never made a single reflection on the good of humanity at the conclusion of this touching ceremony, and that the philosopher who would dare to address such sentiments to him during the ceremony would soon be imprisoned in the Bastille, where the warden would not wash his feet, and that for centuries all the princes of the Roman faith have practiced this ceremony every year without doing any good for anyone, except for the money and food that is given to twelve paupers?[58]

As it turned out, the Physiocratic writings of the 1760s were a last hurrah of sorts for the Sinophilia of the Enlightenment. The intellectual climate within France was shifting, as both the legacy of Montesquieu and the growing influence of Rousseau led an increasing number of French observers to reject despotism, whether enlightened or not, as a political model, whereas a constellation of factors, including wounded national pride resulting from defeat in the Seven Years' War, the intensification of French colonial activity in the Caribbean, and an increasing sense of European superiority over the non-Western world (which will be discussed at greater length in the following chapters), began to darken China's reputation in French eyes. Colin Mackerras notes, "For a variety of domestic reasons, which had little to do with China, opinion both in France and England moved strongly against China in the second half of the eighteenth century...On the whole, the newly industrializing and supremely confident West now observed a declining China with eyes totally different from those with which their predecessors of not long before had viewed an empire that appeared to be at the height of its glory."[59] We will now consider the reasons for this shift in French Enlightenment perceptions of the Middle Kingdom.

Downgrading China

Even in the middle decades of the eighteenth century, when Enlightenment Sinophilia was at its apex, there was no shortage of discordant voices who questioned the idealized portrait presented by the Jesuits and their secular imitators. Not surprisingly, the baron de Montesquieu, the early Enlightenment's most prominent critic of royal absolutism, was skeptical of the praises then being lavished upon China by Jesuits and philosophes alike. "Our missionaries speak of the vast empire of China as an admirable government," he wrote, but then asked: "Could it not be that the missionaries were deceived by an appearance of order, that they were struck by that continuous exercise of the will of one alone by which they themselves are governed?" For his part, Montesquieu noted dismissively, "I do not know how one can speak of honor among peoples who can be made to do nothing without beatings," and observed, "Our men of commerce, far from giving us an idea of the same kind of virtue of which our missionaries speak, can rather be consulted about the banditry of the mandarins." He concluded that, much like the Islamic empires of the Near East and South Asia, "China is a despotic state whose principle is fear."[60]

While Voltaire was a great admirer of imperial China, his praise was not unqualified, but rather rested on a distinction between an elite Confucian society which he greatly admired and a superstitious popular culture that he often ridiculed. "When we speak of the wisdom that has presided for four thousand years over the constitution of China," he wrote, "we do not presume to speak of the common people: it is in all countries uniquely occupied with manual labor." [61] While Voltaire's admiration of the Chinese sage was such that a portrait of Confucius decorated the walls of Voltaire's residence at Ferney,[62] he dismissed both Taoism and Buddhism as superstitions of the ignorant masses, blasting the latter as "the most ridiculous cult, and consequently that most suited to the ignorant," and described it as having "infected East Asia" from its origins in India. He mocked the belief that the Dalai Lama was a living god as "the triumph of human superstition," and noted with ridicule that the holy man's devotees conserved pieces of his excrement as sacred relics.[63] Voltaire's class biases contributed to his disdain for popular religion, as he wrote that "these sects are tolerated in China for the use of the vulgar, like simple victuals prepared to nourish them, while the magistrates and literati, separated from the people, feed upon a more pure diet."[64] Voltaire also condemned the widespread practice of infanticide among the poor, which he rationalized as the consequence of overpopulation. He suggested that, had the Mongol emperors been truly wise, they could have settled the surplus population on the uninhabited deserts of Tartary, though he recognized that European nations had only recently created foundling hospitals and other means of social assistance, and concluded, "it takes many centuries for human society to perfect itself."[65]

Quesnay's admiration for China was such that he was willing to excuse or downplay those aspects of Chinese society that his contemporaries found most distasteful. After noting Montesquieu's critical assessment of the brutal penal procedures in China, Quesnay responded: "Beatings with a staff are in China a punishment reserved for the guilty, as the whip, the galley, etc., are punishments in other kingdoms. Is there any government without penal laws?"[66] Similarly, Quesnay recognized the practice of infanticide, writing that "the excess of population in China forces the indigent sometimes to commit acts of inhumanity which cause horror," but he argued that "one should not impute this calamity to the very constitution of a good government," and noted that "everywhere there are men in indigence."[67]

The great irony in the Enlightenment's romance with China is the fact that, during the period of greatest philosophical interest in the Middle Kingdom, commercial and cultural interaction between China and the West was minimal. The expulsion of most of the foreign missionaries from China in 1724 and the restrictions placed on

Western merchants, who were confined to a few coastal ports such as Canton, limited opportunities for interaction, and ensured that the information on China that the French philosophes debated was increasingly out of date. One rare exception—the visit of Captain George Anson in the course of his voyage around the world in the 1740s—offered a much more negative assessment, though French admirers of China found it easy to discount as biased and ignorant the opinions of an English naval officer. Four decades later, however, the French explorer Jean-François de La Pérouse came away with a similarly negative impression of the Chinese from a brief stopover in Portuguese Macao in January 1787. La Pérouse wrote that "this people, whose laws are so praised in Europe, is perhaps the most unhappy, the most vexed, and the most arbitrarily governed that exists on earth," and added, lamenting the treatment of European merchants on the Chinese coast, that "not a cup of tea is drunk in Europe which has not cost a humiliation to he who purchased it in Canton."[68] By that point, La Pérouse was not alone in forming a negative view of the Chinese. Chrétien-Joseph de Guignes, son of the Orientalist Joseph de Guignes, served as a French representative in China in the final years of the eighteenth century, and echoed this same paradigm of an ancient, but static and superstitious China. He condemned Chinese society as despotic and corrupt, writing, "I traveled this vast empire from end to end, and everywhere I saw the strong oppress the weak, and every man having a share of authority made use of it to vex, bother, and crush the common people."[69] Guignes was dismissive of claims of China's astronomical knowledge, noting that the sage Mencius himself stated that the Chinese of ancient times were barbarians. Guignes concluded that it was only around the time of Confucius that the Chinese were able to record eclipses with precision, and remarked: "One may affirm that the Chinese have only made use of astronomy in relation to astrology; that is to say, to predict fortunate or unhappy events, in order to guide them in their actions, which they still do at present. They are still more astrologers than astronomers."[70]

The Enlightenment's reassessment of Chinese civilization began even as the Physiocrats continued to sing its praises during the last years of the reign of Louis XV. Grimm and Diderot's *Correspondance littéraire* observed in 1766 that contemporary Europeans in fact knew very little that was certain regarding China. They noted that first the Jesuits, and later the philosophers, were able to look to China and find in it what they wished to see, producing "marvelous relations of a very distant land which could neither confirm their veracity, nor dispute their lies." The result of such varied praise was that China became "the asylum of virtue, wisdom, and happiness; its government, the best possible and the oldest; its morals, the purest and most beautiful that were known; its laws and administration, its arts and industry, so many models for the rest of the peoples of the world."[71] The reviewer noted, nonetheless, that the wise reader would not be "seduced" by such mirages, but would reserve judgment, as "he would want to spend twenty years in China and see these things for himself prior to taking a definite position." Even as it acknowledged the wisdom and benevolence of Confucian ethics, the *Correspondance littéraire* expressed skepticism that China was truly governed by these maxims, remarking: "Read the edicts of all of the emperors and kings of the world, and you will find that they are all fathers of their peoples, only preoccupied with the happiness of their children. Nevertheless, injustice and misfortune cover the entire earth."[72]

The end of the Enlightenment's romance with China, I would argue, resulted primarily from two factors: the adoption of a progressive, evolutionary vision of world history that contrasted Western dynamism to Oriental decadence, and the rejection of enlightened despotism in favor of classical republicanism as a model for political reform. As French observers became more self-confident in Europe's ability to overcome the legacy of its past, they contrasted the rapid technological change and economic expansion of early modern Europe with the supposed stagnation of China during the same period. In its review of Mairan's published correspondence with the missionary-scholar Parennin, the *Histoire de l'Académie des Sciences* celebrated the superior dynamism of Europe in relation to China:

> All of these considerations...lead M. de Mairan to state, with reason, that the genius of the Chinese, though very admirable, is greatly inferior to that of the Europeans, and that they know little how to invent or perfect anything, and this judgment of the Chinese is furthermore confirmed by P. Parrenin. The genius of invention, which leads to such rapid progress in our knowledge, is given to few nations. Most of them know only how to imitate; this is a talent which nature gives even to the simplest of men. But this strength of spirit through which, by launching oneself above the sphere of ordinary ideas, one rises to new and unknown ideas, is almost the unique heritage of Europeans.[73]

Even as it painted a generally laudatory portrait of Chinese civilization, the *Histoire des deux Indes* of Raynal and Diderot drew the same contrast between Western dynamism and the supposed rigidity and stasis of the Orient. It noted that while China had preceded the peoples of Europe in reaching a civilized state, it had made little progress in recent years, and concluded that the Chinese lacked the "spirit of innovation." The *Histoire* also observed that the Chinese were deficient in the arts of war, as demonstrated by the repeated conquest of China by barbarian invaders from the north and west.[74]

As China was most admired by the advocates of enlightened despotism, it is not surprising that the Enlightenment's most outspoken critics of despotism were the most critical of the Chinese model as well. Rousseau sharply criticized China in his *Discourse on the Sciences and Arts*, writing, "In Asia there is an immense country where honors for learning lead to the highest offices of the State. If the sciences purified morals, if they taught men to shed their blood for their country, if they aroused courage, the peoples of China would be wise, free, and invincible." The fact that this was not the case, in Rousseau's view, indicated the emptiness and moral bankruptcy of China's renowned cultural refinement. "There is no vice that does not dominate them," he wrote, "no crime with which they are not familiar."[75] Rousseau also cited the conquest of Ming dynasty China by the Manchus, asking: "If neither the enlightenment of government officials, nor the supposed wisdom of laws, nor the multitude of inhabitants of that vast empire were able to save it from the yoke of the ignorant and coarse Tartar, what purpose did all its learned men serve? What benefit has resulted from the honors bestowed on them?"[76] The baron d'Holbach condemned and dismissed China and Confucianism for reasons similar to those of Rousseau, dismissing Confucian wisdom as "common and trivial maxims that can in no way be compared with those of the Greeks and Romans," and declaring that the sage's teachings, "so praised by some moderns, are favorable to despotism; that is to say, to the most unjust of governments, to paternal tyranny, which they confuse with reasonable authority, to polygamy and to the tyranny exercised over women; finally, they have no object but to produce slaves." D'Holbach concluded "that this sage of the Orient or those who have adopted his maxims have not had the slightest notion of true morality or of natural law."[77]

Perhaps the most negative depiction of China produced by the later Enlightenment came from Cornelius de Pauw, a Dutch polemicist who formed part of Frederick the Great's intellectual entourage at Potsdam. De Pauw's denunciation of China is inseparable from his critique of despotism, as he wrote that "the principal mainsprings of the government [of China] are the whip and the rod; there are no

Chinese, there are no Tartars who can escape it."[78] De Pauw rejected
the notion that Confucianism had led to the perfection of morals,
and offered lurid descriptions of such horrors as infanticide, castra-
tion, polygamy, and slavery in China, writing, "The Chinese can, just
as the Negroes, sell their children, and their legislators have never
had the slightest idea of the limits of parental authority," whereas
Europeans "have destroyed slavery in their lands and have discovered the true limits of parental power, which is the masterpiece of
legislation." He returned repeatedly to the theme of infanticide, and
wrote that "I have not found examples of such atrocity, even among
the cannibals of America."[79] Echoing Montesquieu's description of
despotism, he declared that "the servile fear which directs the actions
of the Chinese is a consequence of their institutions. In effect, who
would not fear, if innocence itself is not secure?" After enumerating
the shameful customs of the Chinese, de Pauw declared: "Such has
been the incorrigible madness of a people whom the Jesuits have
tried to represent to the eyes of Europe as a society of philosophers,
but it is apparent that the Jesuits have never known of what true
philosophy consists."[80]

Diderot was dismissive of the cultural achievements of China in
the *Encyclopédie*, writing that "it is worth noting that the sciences
and the fine arts have made no progress in China, and that this
nation has had neither grand buildings, nor beautiful statues, nor
poetry, nor music, nor painting."[81] In a letter to Sophie Volland in
1760, Diderot criticized Chinese codes of etiquette for "destroying
frankness and making hypocrites of an entire nation."[82] Similarly,
the abbé Mably questioned Quesnay's idealization of China in his
Doutes proposés aux philosophes économistes, writing that "the government of China, lazy by its nature and little industrious, has not had
the wisdom to profit from the fecundity of its lands and the multitude of its citizens to banish poverty and misery."[83] Like Diderot and
de Pauw, Mably criticized the Chinese for unquestioning devotion to
"the puerile minutiae of their ceremonies, rites, and routines," which
prevented them from making progress. Mably concluded, "Two thousand years ago the Chinese had the same amount of knowledge that
they have today."[84]

By the 1770s, French commentators on China increasingly concurred that the despotism of the Chinese empire, far from serving
as a force for progress and rationalization, as Quesnay and Poivre
maintained, had instead frozen it in time and caused its growing
decadence. The progress of the arts and sciences, the proponents of
this view maintained, could only be sustained by free peoples, an

argument that we will examine in greater detail in the final chapter. Revisiting the question of Chinese origins in August 1773 the *Correspondance littéraire* offered a negative assessment of Chinese civilization as both static and despotic:

> What seems to me to be clearly demonstrated regarding the Chinese is that they are one of the oldest peoples of the world, but that they are still at the first stages of the arts and sciences, because they live under the yoke of the most terrible form of despotism, that which governs the customs, manners, and beliefs of private citizens as well as the public administration. It seems to me also demonstrated that the isolation of this people from its neighbors has preserved its industriousness and its ignorance, its laws and its chains. This people, it seems to me, has all the characteristics of the great number of old men: cold and hard prudence, weakness, mistrust, and stubbornness.[85]

Even Voltaire, among the French Enlightenment's most enthusiastic advocates for the greatness of imperial China, drew a similar contrast between Western dynamism and Eastern decadence. Karen O'Brien remarks that for Voltaire, "China is a particularly curious case, representing both a utopia and—since it is a society which has advanced as far as it can go—a haunting image of cultural atrophy."[86] In the dedication to his drama *L'Orphelin de la Chine,* dedicated to the duc de Richelieu, Voltaire wrote, "The Chinese, like the other Asiatics, have remained at the first elements of poetry, eloquence, physics, astronomy, and painting, known to them long before they were known to us. They were destined to begin everything before other peoples, only to make no further progress. They have resembled the ancient Egyptians, who having taught the Greeks, were in the end incapable of being their disciples."[87] Despite his great admiration for the longevity, harmony, and stability of the Middle Kingdom, Voltaire concluded in the *Essai sur les moeurs,* "Finally, with regard to any civilized people of Asia of which we speak, we may say of it, 'It preceded us, and we have surpassed it.'"[88]

Conclusions

In a 1773 review of a "Lettre sur les caractères chinois" by an unnamed Jesuit, the *Correspondance littéraire* remarked that the work's author "bitterly laments the malicious usage that has been made in this century of the memoirs that missionaries have provided, with the best of intentions, regarding the history of the Indies and especially that of China. One must admit that in general the discovery of this country has not been terribly useful to the Church. The resources that philosophy has drawn from it have damned more souls in Europe than the Jesuits have saved in the two Indies."[89] As the reviewer noted, the eighteenth-century encounter with Chinese civilization allowed French observers to draw contrasts between the faults of contemporary Europe and the allegedly superior organization of the Chinese empire. In contrast to a Europe still struggling with religious conflict and a social order in which medieval and modern elements were uneasily blended, China served as a model for a meritocratic, bureaucratic state governed according to reason and natural law. It also served as an example for secular philosophers to argue against religious authorities that the Chinese had perfected virtue and morality without knowledge of the gospel of Christ.

There was never a single French Enlightenment view of China over the course of the eighteenth century, but rather competing discourses, based primarily on what the speaker wanted to see in China, and the point that he wished to make regarding the lessons that contemporary Europe could draw from the Chinese example. Keevak writes that French and other European observers of China were blinded by "the Great Wall of Europe, a kind of mental limit that prevented not only armchair travelers but even real ones from being able in any true sense to compare cultures," which led them to perceive in China those features that they expected to find there.[90] As J. J. Clarke has argued, this admiration does not fit into Edward Said's paradigm of Orientalism as colonialist knowledge, for "it is implausible to suggest that the interest of the Enlightenment philosophes in Confucianism was motivated, even unconsciously, by the desire to dominate China in anything but the most attenuated meaning of that term."[91] Instead, the European admirers of China, from the Jesuit missionary-scholars of the seventeenth century to the Physiocrats in the late eighteenth, presented an idealized representation of China as a model for Europe to follow. This model was closely linked to a worldview that posited enlightened despotism as an ideal form of government, believed that the cultivation of manners and cultural refinement were essential to the civilizing process, was attracted to the notion of a rationally ordered society administered by humanistic philosophers, and valued stability and social peace over the potentially disruptive forces of dynamic change.

Once the value system within France had shifted toward a democratic civic culture, a dynamic and expansive society, and a belief in historical progress in which the leading powers of the West were the principal protagonists, China was no longer valued as a model of good order, but increasingly derided as a static, decadent power frozen in time, a majestic and imposing relic, to be sure, but a relic nonetheless. Keevak observes that by the end of the eighteenth century, "Confucian codes of politeness and morality were increasingly being turned into symbols of oriental duplicity and treacherousness, and the unparalleled antiquity that had once fascinated and challenged the Western world was now a sign of China's backwardness, stagnation, and decay."[92] Similarly, Clarke notes that after the Enlightenment, "China indeed faded almost completely from serious Western philosophical interest and throughout the nineteenth century became instead largely an object of contempt and racist condescension in the West."[93] The flawed but seductive *rêve chinoise* had evaporated, to be replaced by a smug and facile contrast between the dynamic West and the decadent East.

3
The New World and the Noble Savage

As eighteenth-century Europeans looked to the Orient to debate the relative merits of Eastern and Western civilizations, they also looked across the Atlantic to consider the benefits and drawbacks of civilization itself, as weighed against the charms of a simpler, more primitive existence in harmony with an idealized Nature. The figure of the "noble savage" was increasingly invoked in these debates as a sort of discursive experiment, an effort to discover what Man would be in the absence of societal and cultural constraints. Cultural critics from Montaigne to Lahontan to Rousseau invoked the example of indigenous American peoples to condemn tyranny, religious persecution, social inequality, and artificial, alienating culture in Europe itself. While the Chinese mandarin had been the symbol most convenient for the advocates of enlightened despotism, the noble savage came to represent egalitarianism and a sort of romantic anarchy.

Native Americans would be invoked in a variety of philosophical debates throughout the course of the eighteenth century in France, and the figure of the "noble savage," though certainly the most popular and enduring such representation, was not the only lens through which they would be perceived and depicted. If secular cultural critics found an idealized "child of nature" well suited to their purposes, their clerical counterparts, particularly the Jesuit missionaries whose experiences with Native Americans were frequently more direct and sustained, sought to balance an image of an essentially good (if sometimes childlike) savage with the need to spread the Gospel and to affirm the essential unity of mankind. As the century progressed, a more negative vision of Native American peoples came to predominate, for reasons that we will consider below. Across these widely divergent representations, the Amerindian remained endlessly fascinating, a stock figure of philosophical discourse and a mirror through which Europeans could perceive and critique their own societies.

Perceived as a figure close to a hypothetical "state of nature," the American savage appeared to some Enlightenment observers as the key to unlocking the mysteries of man's innate character.

The Noble Savage and French Cultural Criticism

While the origins, character, and status of Native Americans were of obvious relevance to sixteenth-century Spaniards, who provided the first ethnographic and philosophical literature to come out of the New World, a number of early modern French writers and philosophers took interest in them as well, even before France began to carve out a vast but fragile empire in the far northern reaches of the continent. Amid the sixteenth-century wars of religion, Michel de Montaigne questioned the attribution of barbarism to Native Americans, observing that "everyone calls barbaric that which is not of his own custom."[1] In a formulation that would go on to have great influence on the Enlightenment, Montaigne described Native Americans as living a purely natural existence, declaring that "they are wild, just as we call wild those fruits which nature has produced of its own accord," observing that "they are still commanded by the laws of nature," living "without commerce, without knowledge of letters or numbers, without magistrates or political sovereignty, without servitude, without riches or poverty."[2] Montaigne acknowledged that the Amerindians practiced cannibalism, observing that they did so not for nourishment but as an act of "extreme vengeance," but argued that such acts were less culpable than the bloody acts of religious persecution committed in Europe, declaring that "there is more barbarism in eating a man alive, than in eating him once dead; in mutilating by hellish tortures a conscious being...than in roasting and eating him after he is deceased."[3] Montaigne went on to compare the stoicism and simplicity of Native Americans favorably with the customs of Renaissance Europe, and concluded on a note of cosmopolitan cultural relativism, denying that any culture had a privileged vantage point to judge another.

Montaigne's praise of the savage state would be echoed by numerous writers, philosophers, and learned travelers over the following centuries. The exploration and colonization of the Americas coincided with the consolidation of royal absolutism and Counter-Reformation orthodoxy, and those who were ambivalent or hostile to these changes within France looked across the Atlantic for an inverse image to juxtapose against the Bourbon kingdom. In the first years of the eighteenth century, a disaffected petty nobleman from southwestern France, the baron Louis-Armand de Lahontan, popularized the noble savage trope with a series of lively texts, notably a philosophical dialogue with a fictionalized Huron chief, Adario, who stressed the superiority of the natural simplicity and rational religion of the Native Americans to the artificial, alienating culture of Christian Europe.

Lahontan's most famous work, the *Dialogues de M. le baron de Lahontan et d'un sauvage*, was perhaps the most important work popularizing the figure of the "noble savage" in early eighteenth-century France. In this short text, published in 1704 as part of the third and final volume of the author's account of his travels and military service in Quebec from 1683 to 1693, two characters, the Huron Adario and the Frenchman "Lahontan" debate the merits of civilization and the state of nature (This device seems to have confused some readers, such as the German philosopher Leibniz, who assumed that Lahontan was a fictional character and asked one of his correspondents to discover the identity of the real author of the text).[4] Adario contrasts the primitive liberty and equality of the Hurons with the inequities produced among Europeans by private property and denounces the European obsession with the accumulation of wealth, declaring: "I say then that what you call money is the demon of demons, the tyrant of the French, the source of evil, the ruin of souls and the tomb of the living... This money is the father of luxury, of impropriety, of artifice, of intrigue, of lies, of betrayal, of bad faith, and generally of all the evils that are in the world."[5] Lahontan's ironic reply to this diatribe, which purportedly defends European institutions, reads against the grain rather as a celebration of anarchy:

> Do you not see, my friend, that the nations of Europe could not live without gold and silver, or some other precious thing? Already the gentlemen, the priests, and a thousand other sort of people who lack the force to till the soil would die of hunger. How would our kings be kings? What soldiers would they have? Who is he who would work for them, or for anyone? Who would risk taking to the sea? Who would forge arms for anyone other than himself? Believe me, we would be lost without recourse, it would be chaos and confusion in Europe, of the most frightful sort imaginable.[6]

I have argued elsewhere that Lahontan's invocation of the superior virtue of Native Americans was a rhetorical strategy in an ongoing intellectual confrontation between critics and defenders of royal absolutism and Counter-Reformation Catholicism in the France of Louis XIV.[7] A scion of the downwardly mobile provincial nobility, Lahontan rejected the expansion of state power and bureaucratization into French society, and celebrated the free, warlike peoples of Canada for the martial, aristocratic virtues that he believed were being lost in France itself. Similarly, he used the Hurons and other native peoples as a foil to critique the absurdities and hypocrisies of Western religion, projecting onto them a sort of enlightened Deism which, as Alain Beaulieu notes, has little to do with actual Amerindian religion.[8] Lahontan reported that the Hurons worshipped the Great Spirit or Manitou "in the most abstract way," and accused the Jesuit and Franciscan missionaries of New France of deliberately distorting the religious beliefs of Native Americans in order to mask their own failures to win new converts for Catholicism. The charge of deliberate distortion of the religious beliefs of the Hurons was turned back at Lahontan by his Jesuit critics in their reviews of his work. A review of Lahontan's works in the July 1703 issue of the *Mémoires de Trévoux* turned the author's claim of impartiality on its head, remarking, "not only is it difficult to guess if he is Catholic or Protestant; one finds it difficult to believe that he is a Christian." Far from being an impartial observer, the *Mémoires de Trévoux* suggested that Lahontan had an axe to grind, calling him "a man little touched by religion and who, by his own admission, is discontented with his country," who was not merely a bad writer, but a dangerous one, whose "Deist and Socininan" arguments were "capable of winning over weak minds."[9]

Lahontan responded to the charges made by the *Mémoires de Trévoux* in a letter that was published in the *Histoire des Ouvrages des Savans* in September 1705. In it, Lahontan affirmed (no doubt disingenuously) his Catholic faith, and turned the table on his adversaries, writing that "I doubt that *Messieurs les Journalistes* are as good Catholics as I; if they were, they would not seek to divide heaven between Confucius and Jesus Christ, nor to give communion to peoples who do not believe in the Incarnation," both references to the "Chinese rites controversy" that was discussed in the previous chapter.[10] Although Lahontan published no further work after the *Dialogues* and would die in exile in Hanover a decade later, his representations of Native American society continued to echo through French discourse on primitivism, natural religion, and human nature. Lahontan's charges against the missionary enterprise of conversion remained perhaps the most controversial aspect of his work, and continued to be the target for Jesuit responses over the following years.

Lahontan was a prominent figure in his own time; Jonathan Israel describes him as "the foremost champion in the era between Spinoza and Rousseau of 'natural man' as a tool of criticism of existing social and cultural realities."[11] If Lahontan is remembered today, however, it is primarily as a forerunner of Jean-Jacques Rousseau, the eighteenth-century writer most associated with the figure of the "noble savage" as a foil for "primitivist" cultural criticism. The son of a Swiss Calvinist watchmaker, Rousseau ran away from home as an adolescent and, after a stormy youth, gained notoriety for his contrarian *Discourse on the Sciences and Arts*, which won a prize offered by the Academy of Dijon on the topic of whether the advances in the arts and sciences had led to an improvement in morals. Rousseau's argument, further developed in his *Discourse on the Origins of Inequality* and subsequently in *The Social Contract*, was that the progress of civilization and refinement of the arts had not made man happier or freer, but had rather created social inequality, oppressive political and economic structures, and an artificial, corrupt culture that alienated man from his true nature.

Rousseau's discussion of "savage" peoples is abstract and universal in character, and he rarely focuses on a specific indigenous people to make his points. Most of the examples he considers, however, are taken from the Americas (with some others taken from Africa), and though he does not cite Lahontan's *Dialogues*, he echoes many of the same points once made by Adario regarding the superiority of primitive to civilized life, such as the greater health and vigor of the savage, his freedom from the concerns that make civilized man miserable, and the impossibility of subduing or enslaving a man who is truly independent, possesses nothing, and needs nothing from his fellow creatures. The savage state is thus defined in negative terms; Sankar Muthu has argued that it was precisely because Native Americans were perceived "as beings who inhabit a state of nature and who thus exhibit purely natural qualities," without the modifications produced by the institutions of church and state, that Rousseau and others considered them prime exemplars of what man would be in the absence of such distorting factors.[12]

Rousseau's arguments, however, are easily mischaracterized and misunderstood. He does not use the precise term "noble savage" that is often associated with him, and the "state of nature" that he evokes is, by his own admission, a hypothetical construct "which no longer exists, which perhaps never existed, which probably never will exist, and about which it is nevertheless necessary to have precise notions in order to judge our present state correctly."[13] In some ways, as both

Arthur Lovejoy and Ter Ellingson, approaching the topic from entirely different vantage points, have recognized, Rousseau's "primitivism" marks an end rather than a beginning, reflecting older Stoic and humanist perspectives subsequently displaced by evolutionary social thought.[14] The core of Rousseau's argument is that man is essentially good, that his central instincts of self-preservation and compassion incline him toward gentleness and altruism, and that society, beginning with the introduction of property rights, social distinctions, and institutions of government, corrupts that essentially good nature. Rousseau argues that it is necessary to imagine man in the state of nature in order to understand his original character, and though he acknowledges that none of the primitive peoples discovered in the Americas and elsewhere live in a state of pure nature, he nonetheless depicts them as happier and freer than civilized man, and cites as proof the inability of missionaries and colonizers to persuade the "savages" to abandon their carefree ways to adopt European norms and customs.[15] However, Rousseau's ideal is not the state of pure nature, but a simple, egalitarian society, governed by common consent and free of the inequalities, superfluous luxuries, and compulsions that make civilized man miserable. He describes such a society as "the happiest and most durable epoch...the best for man," and laments that "he must have come out of it only by some fatal accident, which for the common good ought never to have happened."[16]

The practical implications of Rousseau's primitivist theses are often misunderstood.[17] Voltaire referred to the *Discourse on the Origins of Inequality* as a "book against the human race" and declared that "never has so much intelligence been deployed in an effort to make us beasts,"[18] while a contemporary satirical play, Charles Palissot's *Les Philosophes,* mocked Rousseau with a character who entered the stage crawling on all fours and grazing on lettuce.[19] It was never Rousseau's intent, however, that civilized man should, as he put it, "destroy societies...and go back to live in forests with bears."[20] He invited those who were still able to reclaim their "ancient and first innocence" to "have no fear of debasing your species in renouncing its enlightenment in order to renounce its vices." However, he argued that this was not possible for "men like me, whose passions have forever destroyed their original simplicity, who can no longer nourish themselves on grass and nuts." For such men, the only choice remaining was to live virtuously and honestly within society, loving and serving their fellow men, and advising virtuous princes of "the greatness of their task and the rigor of their duty."[21] When Rousseau sketched out the principles of government in *The Social Contract,* he discussed the state of nature only briefly, in order to refute claims to legitimacy based upon birthright, property ownership, or the right of the strongest, and spent much of the remainder of the work extolling the virtues of small republics, civic spirit, and direct democracy, citing as models ancient Sparta, republican Rome, and the cantons of modern Switzerland.[22]

For French cultural critics from Montaigne to Rousseau, the primitives of the Americas were of interest primarily because of what they lacked. Symbols of a simpler life in harmony with nature, there was little that was culturally specific about them, since, as Sankar Muthu has observed, "the primary purpose of such accounts was not to produce an accurate ethnography...but to foster social criticism." Muthu further argues that in "noble savage" discourses Native Americans were "shorn of their distinctive cultural systems of meaning" to "become an amorphous, undifferentiated whole," which, he claims, "ultimately cast them as lacking the cultural agency that would have made them recognizably human."[23] With the notable exception of Lahontan, most of the writers in this vein had little if any direct contact with Native Americans.

The experience of the Jesuit missionary scholars of New France was entirely different. Many of them spent extended periods in residence in the colonies, learned native languages and observed indigenous customs directly, and were therefore in a position to be much more specific about the characteristics, not merely of "American savages," but of Iroquois, Hurons, Abenakis, Sioux, and so on. It would, however, be an error to see them as entirely empirical and objective observers of Native American society. Just as the secular cultural critics, whether humanists like Montaigne, libertines like Lahontan, or philosophes like Rousseau, the Jesuits embraced the figure of the Native American as a symbol in an ongoing discourse about human nature, human origins, and the universality of religious belief.

Native Americans and Jesuit Universalism

Exactly 20 years after Lahontan published his *Dialogues,* the Jesuit missionary-scholar Joseph-François Lafitau published a very different sort of book about the native peoples of New France. This text, the *Moeurs des sauvages amériquains, comparés aux moeurs des premiers temps,* presented Native Americans not as a discursively constructed Other with which to interrogate European customs and civilization, but rather as members of a universal human family, with customs and beliefs similar to the primitive peoples of Western antiquity, particularly the Scythians described by Herodotus and other classical historians. Lafitau specifically criticized Lahontan's representations of Native American religious beliefs as false, writing: "They do not in fact hold that Metaphysics which the Baron de Lahontan gives them in his *Dialogues*...All the arguments that he makes him give are of his own invention."[24] Instead, he argued, the religion of the Native Americans was a form of polytheism reminiscent of classical antiquity; a false religion, to be sure, but one that reflected vague, distant memories of divine revelation. "All the foundations of the ancient religion of the savages of America," Lafitau asserted, "is the same as that of the barbarians who first occupied Greece and later spread throughout Asia."[25] Lafitau further argued that all forms of paganism, both ancient and modern, were corruptions of the natural religion of the first patriarchs, spread by the sons of Noah to the ends of the world. This natural religion, Lafitau maintained, had originally been shared by all peoples, but had become corrupted into paganism and idolatry following the destruction of the Tower of Babel and the dispersion of peoples.

Lafitau arrived at this surprising conclusion for largely theological reasons.[26] Catholic orthodoxy had long maintained that the "universal consent" of peoples in the existence of a supreme being and in the immortality of the soul constituted positive proof of the truth of both propositions, whereas skeptics such as Pierre Bayle maintained that religion was not necessary for morality and that a society of atheists could exist and function effectively. While the seventeenth-century bishop and antiquarian scholar Pierre-Daniel Huet had argued a half-century earlier that all pagan religions were deformations of the teachings of Moses, Lafitau objected that if this were the case, "it would be true that before Moses, all of the Gentiles were without religion and without gods," invalidating the doctrine of universal consent.[27] Instead, Lafitau cited numerous passages from Genesis that indicated that patriarchs preceding Moses (notably Noah and Abraham) were in direct communication with the deity and honored him with sacrifices, and gave biblical examples of Gentile practitioners of the natural religion, such as King Melchizedek of Salem, Moses's father-in-law Jethro, and the long-suffering Job, to prove that divine revelation had not been limited to the ancestors of the Jews.

Although Lafitau's primary purpose was theological rather than anthropological, his extended residence in New France (from 1712 to 1717) allowed him to produce a more thorough and insightful description of Iroquois society than had previously been available for any of the native peoples of North America. His work, along with that of his fellow Jesuit Charlevoix, whom we will discuss below, contributed to a greater refinement of such knowledge, addressing not just an abstract, universalized "savage," as both Lahontan and Rousseau did, but a more culturally specific depiction and differentiation of various native peoples. [28] Following what Anthony Pagden has called the "principle of attachment...to assimilate the unknown to the known," Lafitau elaborated close parallels between the religions, customs, and practices of everyday life of Amerindians and those of the ancient peoples of the Old World.[29] Lafitau's hypothesis of direct connections between contemporary Native Americans and the peoples of early antiquity required him to record and analyze a wide variety of cultural practices, from religious rites to marriage customs, music and dance, hunting, and warfare. He was the first European observer to describe the matrilineal structure of Iroquois society, which he took as proof of a connection between the Iroquois and the matrilineal Lyciens of antiquity. Lafitau also found similarities between the snowshoes of the peoples of New France and similar footwear described by Strabo among the ancient peoples of the Caucasus, found the canoes used by native peoples along the St. Lawrence similar to the boats of antiquity, compared the scalping of enemies by Native Americans to the head-hunting of the ancient Scythians, and compared the caduceus of Mercury to the peace pipe of the Iroquois.[30]

The weakest link in Lafitau's argument, of course, is the assumption that cultural similarities between two peoples imply a direct connection between them. This belief led to errors of interpretation that Voltaire gleefully mocked in the *Essai sur les moeurs*, writing, "Lafitau has the Americans come from the ancient Greeks, and here are his reasons. The Greeks had fables, some Americans have them as well. The first Greeks went hunting, the Americans do so as well. The first Greeks had oracles, the Americans have sorcerers. The ancient Greeks danced at their festivals, the Americans dance too. One must admit that these reasons are convincing."[31] Interwoven with this rather elementary error, however, was a genuinely revolutionary insight that was to have a profound impact on eighteenth-century social and historical thought: the idea that the march of civilization consists of a series of developmental stages through which each people must pass, albeit at different times and at different rates of progress. This "stadial" approach to global history suggests that present-day "primitives" are functionally analogous to the remote ancestors of today's "civilized" peoples, because of similarities in their means of subsistence, level of technical proficiency, and knowledge of and mastery over the natural world. We shall see that many of the "philosophical historians" of the French Enlightenment would adopt this approach, although for purely secular rather than theological reasons.

By the time that Lafitau published his treatise, another French Jesuit, Pierre-François-Xavier Charlevoix, had embarked upon a tour of France's New World possessions. He compiled a journal of his travels in the 1720s, which was published both separately and as the third and final volume of his 1744 *Histoire de la Nouvelle France*. Charlevoix shared Lafitau's commitment to a single origin of mankind, and like his fellow Jesuit, he claimed to discern "feeble traces... of the ancient faith, and of the primitive religion" among Native American peoples.[32] However, while Lafitau had written a protoanthropological text for largely theological reasons, Charlevoix's discussion of Native Americans was embedded in a more strictly historical account of the foundation and development of France's New World colonies. While it would be incorrect to represent his work as entirely objective, as it was intended to further the twin causes of the colonization of America and the evangelization of its inhabitants, it was, on the whole, devoted more to "thick description" than to theoretical speculation. Charlevoix's writing on the Americas, produced over a period of a quarter century, from his initial departure from France in 1720 to the publication of his three-volume magnum opus in 1744, also marks a transition in French views of Native Americans and cultural primitivism. While some of his early writings echo Lahontan's romantic idealization of Amerindians, the final product of his labors takes a more critical and analytical stance, assessing native peoples according to their receptivity to the colonial project and assuming the superiority of European civilization to American primitivism.

Whereas Lafitau's treatise tended to elide the differences between different Native American societies, creating a single "Indian" identity that could be likened to the barbarians of classical antiquity, Charlevoix, particularly in his 1744 *Histoire de la Nouvelle France*, presented a more nuanced portrait, which drew distinctions between different groups, praising or blaming them according to their manners and their receptivity to Christian conversion. Charlevoix noted that the natives of Florida were "not so cruel toward their prisoners as the Canadians [Iroquois], and although they are cannibals like them, they do not push inhumanity so far as to take pleasure in seeing an unfortunate suffer, nor make an art of torturing him." In contrast, Charlevoix wrote of the Micmacs, allies of the French, that "not only have they never been cannibals, but one has always noted a great deal of mildness and docility among them." He described the Hurons, another people allied to the French, as "the most spirited people of Canada, but also the one with whom one must always be most on guard," given their capacity for dissimulation, "which one who has not seen it would find difficult to believe."[33] Charlevoix offered a mixed portrait of the Abenakis. He lamented their laziness, stating that "one has never been able to engage them to cultivate the earth, and they have even less concern for the future than other savages," but also affirmed that "their affection for their missionaries, the goodness of their character, their sincere attachment to the French, the essential services they have given to New France...and above all that their unshakable constancy in the faith, have greatly lightened the rigors of so difficult a mission."[34] Of the Illinois, a people only recently in contact with the French, Charlevoix wrote that before the arrival of the missionaries: "There were perhaps no savages in all of Canada who had fewer good qualities and more vices. They have always had mildness and docility, but they were cowardly, treacherous, flighty, dishonest, thieves, brutish, without honor, without faith, greedy, given to gluttony and to the most monstrous obscenity, almost unknown to the savages of Canada." Of the Choctaws, he quoted a missionary stationed in Louisiana that "one had never before seen anywhere in America...savages more insolent, more ferocious, more disgusting, more bothersome, and more insatiable."[35]

Charlevoix's most negative assessments, however, were for the Iroquois, longtime enemies of the French. He lamented their attacks on France's Huron allies, writing that "the most horrible deserts and the most impenetrable countries of the North were no longer safe refuges against the rage of these barbarians, and against the rabid thirst that they had for human blood."[36] By contrast, his highest praise was for those Huron converts who maintained their faith during captivity by the Iroquois, who "formed amid these infidels a church akin to that of the Hebrews during the Babylonian captivity," and speculated that "God had dispersed this nation among the other savages, like once the Jews in the kingdoms of Babylon and Persia, to make His name known and to prepare for new worshippers."[37]

Charlevoix's initial impressions of Native American converts to Christianity were favorable. In a 1720 entry in the journal of his voyage to the Americas, he gave a favorable account of his visit to Notre Dame de Lorette, a village of Huron converts, writing, "They are savages, but who have retained from their birth and origins only that which is estimable; that is, the simplicity and rectitude of the first age of the world, together with that which Grace has added, the faith of the patriarchs, a sincere piety, this correctness and docility of the heart that makes saints, an incredible innocence of manners, a pure Christianity, upon which the world has not yet blown the contagious air that corrupts it."[38] He contrasted the state of Eskimo slaves who had been converted to Christianity with their original, barbaric condition, writing that "servitude and distance from their country had softened the manners of these barbarians, as ferocious as the wolves and bears with which their horrid deserts are filled; without laws, without principles, without society, hardly different from those brutes, but for the human form, they soon became mild and reasonable, once they found themselves amid men who made use of their reason."[39]

Subsequently, however, Charlevoix became more doubtful of the possibility of winning and keeping lasting converts among the Native Americans. He described the experience of boarding schools for native girls established by the Ursuline order, observing that when the pupils returned from the convent to their villages, "their blood and nature soon won out, and soon all that was left of the good education that they had been given was an openness of spirit and new knowledge which soon became harmful through the abuse which they made of it." He concluded that efforts at full-scale acculturation were counterproductive, as "savages can be good Christians without taking on any of our refinements or our ways of living...serving God with piety and fervor, which makes them very suited to the most sublime operations of Grace."[40] Charlevoix argued that a century of efforts at conversion had demonstrated "that the worst system to govern these peoples well and to maintain them in our interests was to put them in contact with the French, whom they would have esteemed more, had they not seen them from so close," and went on to observe that Indians who had resided in Montreal had lost their piety and morals, while France's most faithful allies were the Abenakis, who had less contact with French colonists. [41]

On a related note, Charlevoix cited a 1685 letter of the marquis de Denonville, governor of Canada, on the failure of assimilation: "It has long been believed that it was necessary to bring the savages closer to us to Frenchify (*franciser*) them, but there is every reason to recognize that this was an error. Those who have approached us have not become French, and the Frenchmen who have frequented them have become savages. They affect to dress and to live like them."[42] Charlevoix noted that many French colonists who had been taken prisoner by the Iroquois during the wars of the 1690s did not want to return to Montreal after peace had been established, noting that "most of them, accustomed to the savage life, could not resolve to renounce it...The appeal of a liberty free of all sort of laws, and perhaps also a bit of libertinage, led these people to forget all that was hard in their condition, and all of the ease which they could find in their homeland."[43] Charlevoix again discussed the dangers of Europeans "going native" in the Americas when he described his encounter with survivors of La Salle's expedition who had found refuge with the Ceni people. Charlevoix wrote of one of these survivors that "he was naked as the savages, and hardly remembered how to speak French." When he encountered several other men in similar situations, he noted that "one would never have taken them for Europeans. Not only were they naked, but they had all of their bodies painted and pierced. They were married, and some had several wives...The libertine lives that they led had great attraction for them, and they retained almost no imprint of religion."[44] He made a similar point with regard to the pirate communities of the early Caribbean, writing that "if they had survived alone down to the third generation, their grandchildren would have been as little instructed in the principles of Christianity as the inhabitants of New Guinea."[45] Clearly, for Charlevoix, Native Americans were not the only "savages" in the New World.

If the noble savage of Lahontan and Rousseau is a proud child of nature, strong and free, who prefers his independent existence to the subservience and stratification of European society, the savages of the Jesuits Lafitau and Charlevoix resemble rather the promising but occasionally disobedient pupils of a strict Catholic boarding school, who must be disciplined and educated for their own good. Nevertheless, the Jesuit vision of the American primitives was a generous, ecumenical, and inclusive one, in which these peoples, however strange they might appear, formed part of a universal family of man. With the guidance of the Jesuit fathers, they could make up the distance between them, and claim their rightful place at the table of universal Christendom.

The Ignoble Savage: La Condamine in the Amazon

Defenders of the "noble savage," such as Lahontan and Rousseau, celebrated the virtues and independence of Native Americans as a means to critique social inequality, religious hypocrisy, and the artificiality of customs in contemporary Europe. Jesuit observers, such as Lafitau and Charlevoix, emphasized what Native Americans had in common with other peoples, and presented their religions and customs as degenerated versions of those of the early patriarchs, in order to support world-historical theories about the common origins of man and the universality of revealed religion. While both of these views played prominent roles in the intellectual debates of the eighteenth century, neither was universally accepted by enlightened readers, and in fact the tide was turning against both secular and clerical apologists for "natural man." In fact, the parallel that Lafitau suggested between the European past and the American present tended, in the hands of the "philosophical historians," to lead to a more negative assessment of the latter. For men of letters who adopted a progressive, evolutionary view of world history, "primitives" were not to be envied for the simplicity of their lives in harmony with nature, but rather were to be pitied or scorned, as remnants that recalled to civilized man the degraded condition that he had escaped. Ronald Meek has argued that the eighteenth-century pioneers of the social sciences drew heavily upon travelers' accounts of America and invoked what he calls the "ignoble savage" to support stadial theories of social evolution based upon changing means of subsistence.[46] Such approaches would lead to a new wave of much more negative portrayals of Native Americans, and other peoples considered "primitive," from the mid-eighteenth century onward.

That the French Enlightenment took an increasingly negative view of Native Americans as the eighteenth century progressed is due primarily to the influence of the learned traveler Charles-Marie de La Condamine, who presented his observations in the 1745 *Voyage à l'Amérique méridionale*. A onetime military engineer turned mathematician and man of science, La Condamine was the dominant figure in one leg of a two-part expedition sponsored by the Académie des Sciences in 1735 to determine whether the earth was indeed flattened at the poles, as Newton had hypothesized. La Condamine and his colleagues went to what is now Ecuador, while another expedition under Pierre Moreau de Maupertuis went to the Arctic Circle, and each measured an arc of latitude through a series of complex astronomical operations. After the purpose of the expedition was completed and Newton had been proven right, La Condamine decided to return to France via the Amazon, thereby becoming the first scientist to make the journey and to provide a detailed account of what remained largely *terra incognita*.[47]

La Condamine did not come to South America as an ethnographer, nor did his purposes require extensive interaction with Native

Americans, as did, for example, the work of missionaries, merchants, or military adventurers. Most of his ethnographic observations take the form of asides, inserted casually into his accounts of travel and descriptions of Amazonian flora and fauna. Because he did not linger for long in any of the stops along his route, he did not have the time to glean detailed, original information regarding the beliefs, practices, and forms of social organization of Native American peoples. However, La Condamine did not limit himself to a mere physical description, but also entered into discussions of the allegedly indolent, passive, and amoral character of these Amazonian peoples. He could have had but little occasion to observe these traits firsthand, and much of what La Condamine says is in fact derivative of the accounts of Spanish observers, particularly Jesuit missionaries who recorded the customs and cultures of native peoples even as they sought to convert them to the true faith. Neil Safier has recently demonstrated that La Condamine frequently plagiarized from the work of other observers, such as Jesuit missionaries and Spanish chroniclers, to produce descriptions of Native American peoples and their practices. One of these, the Swiss Jesuit Jean Magnin, met with La Condamine at the mission of San Francisco de Borja in 1743, and gave him a copy of his own manuscript accounts of the native peoples of the upper Amazon, from which the scientific explorer would borrow heavily and without attribution.[48]

La Condamine acknowledged that many differences were to be found among different Native American peoples, resulting from different environments and different degrees of contact and acculturation from Spanish and Portuguese conquerors and missionaries. Nevertheless, he reflected: "Just as all the nations of Europe, however different among themselves in language, manners, and customs, would nonetheless have something in common in the eyes of an Asiatic who examined them attentively, so all the American Indians of the different countries that I had occasion to see in the course of my voyage, seemed to me to have certain traits of resemblance with one another, and...I believe I recognized in all of them the same underlying character."[49] That character, which La Condamine went on to describe, was hardly flattering:

> Insensibility forms the base. I leave it to be determined whether it should be honored by the name apathy, or debased by that of stupidity. It doubtless arises from the small number of their ideas, which do not extend beyond their needs. Gluttons to the point of voracity, when they can satisfy their desires; sober when necessity

obliges, to the point of going without everything, without seem-
ing to desire anything; pusillanimous and cowardly to excess, if
drunkenness does not enliven them; enemies of work; indifferent
to all forms of glory, honor, or recognition; only preoccupied with
the present; incapable of foresight or reflection; given, when nothing disturbs them, to childish joy, which they express by leaps
and immoderate outbursts of laughter, without object or design;
they pass their lives without thinking, and they grow old without
leaving infancy, of which they conserve all the faults.[50]

Although La Condamine had little to say that was new regarding
Native Americans, his status as an eyewitness gave him authority
to his French audience. As a man of science who had been there,
and seen with his own eyes, his assessments, however hasty and
generalized, were taken as authoritative, and helped to shape the
Enlightenment image of Native Americans as static, indolent, and
resistant to civilization. The abbé Cornelius de Pauw, the age's most
polemical critic of the romantic idealization of the "noble savage,"
cited La Condamine's authority as an eyewitness in his dispute with
the abbé Pernety, writing, "why should one believe him [Pernety]
on his word, and refuse belief to a philosopher who spent ten years
among these Americans, whom he has depicted exactly as he saw
them?"[51] Among the few contemporary readers who doubted La
Condamine's negative appraisal of the Amazonian natives was the
Dutch Sephardic scholar Isaac de Pinto, who questioned whether
La Condamine had sufficient knowledge of indigenous cultures to
make such a sweeping assessment. Pinto later expressed these doubts
directly to the scientist/explorer, writing to La Condamine, "Since
you had no knowledge of their language, you were not able to divine
their thoughts."[52] De Pinto was, however, an isolated critic; the
Journal des Sçavans quoted La Condamine's ethnographic observations approvingly, noting that "while it was not the goal of M. de
La Condamine to instruct us on the manners and intellect of the
inhabitants, he has not neglected to report to us some aspects that
characterize the savages. If the ideas that he presents on this topic
are not extensive, they are exact."[53] La Condamine was recognized as
an authority on South America even by those, such as Rousseau, who
differed most strongly with him regarding the character of "natural
man," and dozens of entries regarding America and its inhabitants in
the *Encyclopédie* are in some way derivative of his writings.[54]

La Condamine's harsh assessment of Native American character
was echoed by the other members of the expedition. The Spanish

officers Jorge Juan and Antonio de Ulloa, who accompanied the
French scientists throughout their work and composed the official
Spanish chronicle of the expedition, described the natives as "populations possessed entirely by ignorance, full of rusticity, and only
slightly removed from an uncultured barbarity."[55] Pierre Bouger,
another member of the Académie who traveled with La Condamine
on the expedition to South America, described them as "stupid"
and of "extreme laziness," indifferent to riches, and responding to
requests for labor that they "were not hungry." He concluded that,
"were it not for their excessive love for a beer that they brew from
corn, they would form a great sect of Stoic philosophers, or rather
Cynics."[56] These apostles of progress and of the spread of civilization thus took primitivism as a starting point from which man was
destined to evolve and grow, rather than, as did Rousseau, a sort of
happy childhood of humanity to be evoked with fond nostalgia.

The materialist philosopher Claude-Adrien Helvétius, whose
treatise *De l'esprit* appeared in 1758, reflected the new evolutionary assumptions of social development, and presented the savagery
and anarchy of Native Americans as representing the childhood of
nations. In a footnote, he considered Rousseau's contention that
primitive man was happier than civilized man, and qualified this
sweeping generalization by pointing out that the question depended
entirely on a given individual's position within the hierarchy of a
complex and stratified society. While acknowledging the benefits
that the progress of civilization had brought to the upper classes,
Helvétius asked: "Who doubts that the state of the savage is preferable to that of the peasant?" Echoing Adario's praise of a simple life
free from the arbitrary authority of kings or priests, Helvétius wrote
that the Native American alone "enjoys the bounty of equality, and
especially the priceless good of freedom, so uselessly evoked by the
majority of nations."[57]

While Helvétius, like Rousseau (and Lahontan before him), contrasted the freedom and equality of the American "savages" to the
regimentation and social inequality of Europe, he did not roman-
ticize the condition of primitive peoples, perceiving it rather as a
purely negative and empty state, lacking the hardships and vexa-
tions of life in a civilized state, but also lacking all those things that
made life worth living. Citing the example of savages as depicted by
missionaries and travelers, Helvétius argued that man was naturally
lazy and indolent, but that these forces of inertia were countered by
his natural curiosity and desire for new sensations, characteristics to
which Helvétius attributed "the principle...of the perfectibility of

the human mind." Helvétius defended the positive role of the passions, writing that "the total absence of the passions, if it could exist, would produce in us perfect brutishness," and argued that the desire for possessions and material comforts jolted primitive man out of his initial lethargy and encouraged him to labor and invention.[58] Though just as opposed to oppression and inequality as Rousseau, Helvétius's vision of history is progressive and evolutionary, and he seeks the remedy for Europe's ills in the perfection of its civilization, rather in a retreat to a hypothetical prehistoric Eden.

The middle decades of the eighteenth century, the time in which Rousseau, La Condamine, and Helvétius debated the virtues and vices of Native American "savages," also marked the climax of the Anglo-French struggle for supremacy in North America, which reached a decisive conclusion with the British capture of Quebec and the collapse of French power in the region. These conflicts, and particularly the American theater of the Seven Years' War, provided the French military officers who served there with a closer view of Native Americans who fought against or alongside them, and eyewitness testimony from the frontier soon contradicted the Rousseauian image of man's natural goodness. Louis-Antoine de Bougainville, better known for his voyage to the South Pacific, which will be discussed in the next chapter, served as an aide-de-camp to the marquis de Montcalm in Canada, where he witnessed the capture of Fort William Henry in upper New York (an episode memorably depicted in *The Last of the Mohicans*). Bougainville was horrified by what he saw, writing that "the cruelties and the insolence of these barbarians cause horror and spread darkness in the soul. It is an abominable way to wage war; reprisals are terrifying, and the air that one breathes here makes one accustomed to insensibility."[59] Denis Diderot, who never visited America, nonetheless met with veterans who had served there, and recounted their tales of native treachery and cruelty in a letter to Sophie Volland, rhetorically asking: "Tell me then, where is the natural goodness? Who corrupted these Iroquois? Who inspired them to vengeance?"[60]

Diderot was once a close friend of Rousseau, who had encouraged the latter to present his *Discourse on the Sciences and Arts* to the Académie de Dijon in 1750, the success of which launched Rousseau to fame and notoriety.[61] Though he would at some points in his career embrace cultural primitivism as a means to critique contemporary French civilization (particularly in his "Supplement to the Voyage of Bougainville," which we will discuss in the next chapter), Diderot differed from Rousseau in rejecting the attribution of moral superiority to the savage and in celebrating the practical benefits of life in civilized society. In a letter written in 1755 to the abbé Le Monnier, Diderot wrote, "I do not care for acorns, caves, or the hollows of oak trees. I require a carriage, a comfortable apartment, fine linens, a perfumed lady, and I will gladly accommodate myself to the rest of the curses of our civilized state. I carry myself very well on my two hind legs, and whatever Rousseau says, I prefer that the hand that writes these letters be a hand to write that I love you dearly...rather than a lousy paw, dirty and clawed."[62] Similarly, Diderot wrote a decade later in a letter to Falconet, "I believe, my friend, that there are men, and even exceptional men in Russia; I even believe that they are to be found deep in the forests of the Abenakis or the huts of the Hottentots. But educated, enlightened, cultivated men, that is another matter. It is not trees that I propose to you, but gardeners. There are trees everywhere."[63]

As these examples suggest, the stance that individual French Enlightenment authors took with regard to Native American "savages" had more to do with their attitude toward European civilization, and specifically with the question of whether its refinements represented the cultivation of manners or rather their decadence and corruption, than it did with the specific vices and virtues of indigenous American societies. A constellation of factors, encompassing changing intellectual fashions, the experience and eyewitness testimony of travelers to the New World, and a growing emphasis on progress and the benefits of civilization, began to tip the balance away from the romantic depiction of the "noble savage," despite Rousseau's substantial influence over the culture and sensibility of the age. Both the positive and the negative images of "primitivism," however, formed part of the mainstream of Enlightenment discourse on America and the Americans, and would collide in the 1760s in one of the most notable polemical exchanges of the era.

The Dispute of the New World

This debate, which Antonello Gerbi has called "the dispute of the New World," marked a decisive shift away from the romantic primitivism of Rousseau and toward an evolutionary vision of history as a series of stages of development. The preconditions for the debate were set by Georges-Louis Leclerc, comte de Buffon, in his *Histoire naturelle*, which argued that America was a new continent, still covered by pestilential swamps, in which both human and animal life degenerated. Already in the third volume of the *Histoire naturelle*, published in 1749, Buffon had argued that racial difference among peoples was the result of climate, a theory that we will examine in greater detail in the fifth chapter. Noting the contrast between the racial diversity of the Old World and the relative homogeneity of Native American peoples across climate zones, Buffon had argued at that time that America was a newly settled continent, in which the forces of climate had not yet had sufficient time to operate changes in the nature of its inhabitants. Buffon developed this idea still further in subsequent volumes of the *Histoire naturelle*, which appeared over the 1750s and 1760s, which shifted in focus from humanity to the animal kingdom. Buffon claimed that there were no large quadrupeds that were native to the Americas, and that animals taken from the Old World to the New degenerated over the course of several generations. In the section entitled "Animals common to both continents," which appeared in 1761, Buffon wrote that in the New World "there are obstacles to the development and perhaps to the formation of large creatures; those which, by the gentle influences of another climate, have received their complete form and full extension, wither and shrink under this miserly sky and in this empty land."[64] Thomas Jefferson would later defend American wildlife against Buffon's charges in his *Notes on the State of Virginia*, going so far as to ship a stuffed moose across the Atlantic to prove the existence of large quadrupeds in the New World. Although Buffon's most complete elaboration of the theory of environmental degeneration of species in the Americas deals with animals, not human beings, both he and others sometimes cited environmental degeneration as a cause for the alleged inferiority of Native Americans to Europeans, and also for the supposed inferiority of white American-born Creoles to their European kin.

Buffon's scholarly musings turned into an acrimonious debate when his theories of environmental degeneracy in the Americas were picked up by more polemical popularizers and used to draw sweeping conclusions about the inferiority of the New World to the Old. Chief among these was the Dutch abbé Cornelius de Pauw, a member of Frederick the Great's Berlin Academy, who emphasized the brutishness and ignorance of Native Americans in his *Recherches philosophiques sur les Américains*. Gerbi describes the work as "a polemic against the reports of the missionaries and the admirers of the Noble Savage," which asserted that "nature in America is weak and corrupt."[65] While de Pauw's views were not entirely original, he stated them far more bluntly and categorically than his predecessors, reveling in examples of Native American brutishness to shock the sensibilities of his readers and to mock Rousseau and other exponents of cultural primitivism. He dismissed Rousseau's contention that primitive man was less vicious than civilized man, writing, "This outrageous judgment is that of a misanthrope or a madman who has sadly determined to search for reasons to hate the human race. If crimes are frequent among the most civilized nations, one should not condemn the sciences or the arts...but the cowardice of those who do not resist despotism."[66]

De Pauw also rejected the Christian universalism of the Jesuits, holding up for ridicule a passage in which Charlevoix had celebrated the Stoic virtues of Amerindians, declaring, "I read one of these bad chronicles, in which the compiler, to prove that these barbarians have a fine philosophy, cites the Iroquois that was brought to France in 1666. He did not admire Versailles, but he greatly admired a rotisseur's boutique in Paris, he fell upon the meats with incredible avidity, and it was impossible to pull him out of that boutique. The compiler concluded that this Iroquois was a philosopher; he esteemed, so it was said, useful things, and not useless things. To which I reply that a Canadian wolf would have done likewise."[67] What Charlevoix had celebrated as the Stoicism and utilitarian wisdom of the Iroquois appeared, half a century later and in a different cultural context, as a sign of the animalistic nature of the American "savages" to the eyes of de Pauw.

De Pauw shared with Buffon the idea that the alleged deficiencies of Native Americans resulted from the unhealthiness of their environment, though the two men differed in their assessment of the causes of that condition. While Buffon argued that the New World was indeed literally a new world, a continent recently emerged from the primordial waters, De Pauw asserted that the Americas had long been peopled, but had been decimated by a natural catastrophe, which had reduced its inhabitants to a state of "decrepitude and caducity."[68] He went on to elaborate, "If the savage life, if the absence of agriculture and alphabets were incontestable proof of the newness of a people, the Lapps and the Negroes would be the most modern of men. However, no professor of chronology disputes their antiquity."[69] Citing the experience of Spanish colonialism, de Pauw argued that Native Americans were "such stupid and degenerate men that one even abandoned hope of making them into slaves."[70] Although de Pauw's interpretation of human difference is ultimately based upon environmental rather than hereditary causes, he found the impact of environment to be so pervasive that its effects were, for all practical purposes, irreversible.

De Pauw's most persistent European critic was the abbé Antoine-Joseph Pernety. Pernety had accompanied the explorer Louis-Antoine de Bougainville on his first voyage to South America, which attempted to create a French colony on the Falkland Islands, which Bougainville was subsequently forced to surrender to Spanish authorities. Pernety, unlike de Pauw, had thus been to America, albeit briefly, and used his status as eyewitness observer to refute the criticisms of de Pauw, who had never left Europe. He observed in his preface that "M. de Pauw knows very little of America" while the categorical tone of his condemnations "could lead one to believe that he had traveled through all of the countries of this vast stretch of earth; that he had lived for a long time with each of the peoples who inhabit it."[71] He complained that "America is to the eyes of M. de Pauw a land that nature seems to have created in rage…over which she has generously poured all the evils, all the bitterness of Pandora's box, without allowing the slightest portion of the goodness which she possesses to escape."[72] He accused de Pauw of embracing "a hypothesis born of an imagination a bit too drunk with tenderness for our hemisphere and its inhabitants."[73]

Instead, Pernety romanticized the simple lives of Native Americans in terms that echoed Lahontan and Rousseau. After citing Lahontan's observations on the Hurons specifically, he wrote, "They live without chagrin, without worry, scorning gold and silver, like the Spartans. The prejudices of education make us regard them as men reduced to the last misery, but they are effectively happier than us."[74] Like Lahontan, he praised the absence of private property and monarchical rule among them, writing "these peoples whom we consider so stupid conserve such a feeling of freedom that they treat the Europeans as vile slaves for submitting blindly to the will of a single man, who disposes of them like a herd of sheep or as puppets which he can move at his will."[75] Pernety's view of indigenous society was certainly generous and well intentioned, but hardly more realistic than that of de Pauw, and owed more to Enlightenment philosophy and classical notions of the golden age of humanity than to any direct observation of American peoples. He had spent most of his single voyage to the Americas aboard a ship among French sailors and on the previously uninhabited Falkland Islands, and the only Native Americans he observed directly were not isolated "natural men," but members of the urban underclass of Montevideo, who offered the travelers animal skins in exchange for liquor.[76] He did, however, collect a good deal of secondhand information on Native American society from Spanish and Portuguese informants, which he would later draw upon in his polemical exchange with de Pauw.

De Pauw responded to Pernety's book with another volume of his own, called the *Défense des Recherches philosophiques sur les Américains*. In it, he defended himself against Pernety's charge that he had "condemned the Americans in order to humiliate the human race" by responding, "Either the peoples of Europe are not part of the human race, or it is not true that the author wished to humiliate the human race." Instead, he declared, "he wanted to demonstrate the infinite advantage of the social life over the savage life, the infinite advantage that the inhabitants of Europe have over the natives of the New World." He continued, "The nations that have produced such great men as Newton, Locke, Leibnitz, Descartes, Bayle, Montesquieu, s'Gravesende, are not only superior, but infinitely superior to the barbarians of America, who do not know how to read, write, or count beyond their fingers."[77]

The debate continued to rage on by proxy well after de Pauw and Pernety ceased to write, and was fundamentally incapable of reaching a resolution, as the two parties essentially talked past each other. Pernety, like Rousseau before him, was primarily concerned with equality, simplicity, and life in harmony with nature, whereas de Pauw, like Voltaire, though in a somewhat cruder and more categorical form, measured the progress of civilization by the refinement of the arts and sciences. De Pauw's work set off a storm of vitriolic exchange, as a phalanx of both European and American scholars sought to redeem the American continent and its inhabitants from de Pauw's admittedly polemical assertions. The doctor Rollin, who accompanied La Pérouse on a voyage around the world that included stops in Chile, California, and Alaska, as well as parts of Asia and Polynesia, took detailed measurements of the native peoples he encountered in accordance with his instructions from the Faculté de Médicine, and concluded: "The authors who have spoken of the Americans as a degenerated race have followed the tangents of their imagination, and have given nothing to truth."[78] Instead, Rollin argued, the various native peoples of the Americas were generally comparable to the French in size, form, strength, and general vitality.

What Civilization Can Learn from the Savage

Although the cultural primitivists Lahontan and Rousseau, the Jesuit universalists Lafitau and Charlevoix, and the Eurocentric scientist La Condamine differed in many respects, they shared a common vision of human diversity as defined by a discursive time-space continuum, in which modern-day "primitive" peoples were taken as analogues to the remote ancestors of today's civilized peoples. The English philosopher John Locke had already anticipated this linkage at the end of the seventeenth century, writing, "In the beginning, all the World was America," and that "America...is still a Pattern of the first Ages in Asia and Europe."[79] This association of contemporary America with Old World prehistory suggested that the present could be used to explain the past, and vice versa, so that classicists could look to the "savages" of the New World to fill in the lacunae of Old World prehistory, and explorers and travelers could consult the Greco-Roman classics in order to know what to expect from the "primitive" peoples whom they encountered. In its review of Lafitau's work, the *Mémoires de Trévoux* observed that Lafitau found the Native Americans to be "in the same relation of distance from us as the ancient Romans, Greeks, Gauls, [and] Persians."[80] The *Mémoires* then noted with enthusiasm the possible unexpected utility of the discovery of the New World, which it described as "a library...in which one discovers the entire history of the earliest times." "When America was discovered," the review continued, "who would have believed that it was antiquity that was reborn before our eyes? Could one have believed that in the depths of its barbarity it carefully conserved, perhaps without the slightest alteration, all the premises of the history of the human race?" [81]

The secular scholars of the later Enlightenment perceived the relationship between contemporary America and the ancient world in much the same way. Over 70 years after Lafitau's work was published, Joseph-Marie Degerando wrote: "The traveller-philosopher who sails to the farthest corners of the Globe, travels, in fact, along the road of time. He travels in the past. Every step he takes is a century passed. The islands he reaches are for him the cradle of human society."[82] By this point, the association of contemporary "primitives" and the remote past of Europe had become something of a commonplace, though the implications of this parallel remained the subject of considerable debate. For Lahontan and for Rousseau, the American savage was to be envied for the absolute freedom he was believed to enjoy, without kings, priests, or other masters above him, and without superfluous needs or desires to entice him into dependence upon others. Seen as living closer to nature, without the luxuries, social stratification, and religious and philosophical baggage of European society, these "noble savages" served to indict the artificial, alienating culture of contemporary Western civilization. For an observer such as La Condamine, by contrast, the savage state was one of wretched animality, sobering evidence that it was only through the civilizing process that man came to differ from the beasts of the forest.

What both sides agreed upon was that Native Americans were "good for thinking," and that their simple ways held the key to unlocking deeper truths of human nature. As Harry Liebersohn observes: "Exotic cultures held the promise of revealing truths about human nature; of showing what human beings were like at an earlier stage of their development."[83] The association of Native Americans with a state of pure nature allowed both primitivist and evolutionary social thinkers to use them, in Roger Mercier's words, as "a methodological instrument" for the study of man's essential character, unadulterated by the factors of religion, manners, or political institutions.[84] Denis Diderot, who as editor of the *Encyclopédie* was the great synthesizer of French Enlightenment thought, recognized this utility of the study of "primitive" cultures in a remarkable aside he inserted into the abbé Raynal's *Histoire des deux Indes*.

While some of Diderot's works, most famously his "Supplement to the Voyage of Bougainville," which will be discussed in the next chapter, reflect the cultural primitivism of his onetime friend Rousseau, he differed from Rousseau in conceptualizing history as an evolutionary process defined by the advance of civilization. The primary utility of primitive peoples, in Diderot's vision, is to inspire civilized peoples to return to nature's path by showing them the error of their ways and the falseness and artificiality of their institutions and customs. After discussing the beginnings of French colonialism in North America in the *Histoire des Deux Indes*, Diderot speculated on the coming extinction of Native American peoples in the wake of European expansion. Rather than focusing on the tragedy which this would represent for the native peoples themselves, however, Diderot laments the possible loss of a necessary corrective for the further growth of Western civilization:

> What then will posterity think of this sort of men who will exist only in the histories of travelers? The time of savage man will seem to them like what for us are the mythic ages of antiquity... Those of our writings that will have escaped the oblivion of time will seem like fictions akin to that which Plato has left us on ancient Atlantis... There will be systematic thinkers who will prove, through a variety of reasons taken from the dignity of the human race... that man has never been naked, errant, without society or laws, reduced to the animal condition...
>
> Doubtless it is important for future generations never to lose sight of the spectacle of the lives and manners of savages. It is perhaps due to this knowledge that we owe all the progress that

moral philosophy has made among us...Since it has been shown
that social institutions do not derive from the demands of nature
or the dogmas of religion, as countless peoples live independently,
without religion or property, we have discovered the vices of morals and legislation at the beginnings of societies...This discovery has spread great enlightenment, the seed of the benefits that
reform brings. It is therefore, so to speak, from the ignorance of
savages that the civilized peoples have become enlightened.[85]

Whatever the destruction of traditional native society might have
meant to the natives themselves, Diderot's primary concern in this
passage is for the fate of man in civilization. Arguing that philosophers and theologians have constructed a false representation of
human nature and human origins in order to ensnare and deceive
their followers, Diderot celebrates the savage state as a precious reser-
voir of truth, with which these lies and deceptions can be unmasked,
and worries that it is on the verge of running dry. Even as the
advances of European colonialism were displacing and destroying
the remnants of native society in the Americas, however, European
explorers and travelers were uncovering other new worlds for commerce, colonization, and philosophic contemplation. It is to those
newest "new worlds" that we will turn in the next chapter.

Conclusions

Once the terms of the "dispute of the New World" were set, the
debate came to have relatively little to do with what one thought
of Native Americans themselves, but rather with attitudes toward
Europe-specific debates regarding the progress and decadence of
civilization. In fact, as Sankar Muthu laments, "the presentation of
New World peoples that served as the anthropological basis of unor-
thodox, or even radical, moral and political claims ultimately came
at the price of presenting them as largely hard-wired automatons,
rather than as creative agents who were embedded within and who
shaped and altered cultural systems of meaning and value."[86] This
framing of the issue, though useful for abstract social theorizing,
stripped native peoples of their own culturally specific traits in order
to use them as stand-ins for the Scythians, Gauls, or other barbarians of antiquity. Cultural primitivists like Rousseau, influenced by
the classical notion of a pastoral "golden age" of humanity and by a
neo-Stoic condemnation of luxury as a corrupting influence on morals, invoked the example of the American primitives to recall their

countrymen back to the virtuous path from which they had strayed. Advocates of science and progress, such as La Condamine, dismissed the same Amerindian peoples as remnants and reminders of a barbaric past that Europeans had thankfully left behind, and trumpeted Europe's superiority over the natives of America as evidence of the benefits of the scientific progress they so enthusiastically embraced. Even the careful and nuanced protoethnographies of the Jesuit missionary-scholars, which were of all of the texts we have considered the most sensitive to cultural difference, were framed by the intellectual need to defend the universality of humankind and the practical need to justify and encourage evangelization. In this sense, the "dispute of the New World" was really a dispute about Europe itself. The same would also be true with regard to European discussions of Africa and Oceania, as we shall see in the following chapter.

4
The Last Frontiers

French Enlightenment interest in the non-European world was not confined to Asia and the Americas. As Enlightenment thinkers sought to elaborate a new universal science of man, they supported their competing theories with a wide range of examples, drawing not only upon Greco-Roman antiquity and contemporary Europe, but also upon travel narratives from distant lands. They recognized, however, that much of the available information regarding the peoples of these remote regions was unreliable. The medieval belief that distant countries were populated by monstrous races such as cyclopses and dog-headed men had not completely dissipated, and even in the eighteenth century, serious scholars debated whether there existed giants in Patagonia or men with tails in the Philippines. In a footnote to the 1755 *Discourse on the Origins of Inequality*, Rousseau wrote:

> We know nothing of the peoples of the East Indies, who have been frequented solely by Europeans more desirous to fill their purses than their heads. All of Africa and its numerous inhabitants, as distinctive in character as in color, are still to be examined; the whole earth is covered by nations of which we know only the names—yet we dabble in judging the human race! Let us suppose a Montesquieu, Buffon, Diderot, Duclos, d'Alembert, Condillac, or men of that stamp traveling in order to inform their compatriots, observing and describing, as they know how, Turkey, Egypt, Barbary, the empire of Morocco, Guinea, the land of the Bantus, the interior of Africa and its eastern coasts, the Malabars, Mogul, the banks of the Ganges, the kingdoms of Siam, Pegu, and Ava, China, Tartary, and especially Japan; then, in the other hemisphere, Mexico, Peru, Chile, the straits of Magellan, not forgetting the Patagonias true or false, Tucuman, Paraguay if possible, Brazil, finally the Caribbean islands, Florida, and all the savage countries: the most important voyage of all and the one that must be undertaken with the greatest care. Let us suppose that these new

Hercules, back from these memorable expeditions, then at leisure wrote the natural, moral, and political history of what they would have seen; we ourselves would see a new world come from their pens, and we would thus learn to know our own.[1]

The possibilities for such accumulation of ethnographic knowledge were greater in Rousseau's time than at any previous moment in history. The eighteenth century was an age of rapidly expanding networks of commerce, colonization, and exploration, which by the eve of the Revolution had encompassed nearly the entire world. The academicians Pierre Moreau de Maupertuis and Charles de Brosses recommended French exploration and colonization of the uncharted Pacific Ocean, and a number of intrepid explorers, notably Louis-Antoine de Bougainville and Jean-François de La Pérouse, followed their suggestion, failing to discover the long-anticipated southern continent, but expanding French influence into Oceania and reigniting the Enlightenment fascination with "natural man." At the same time, though with less fanfare, a number of French travelers were expanding contacts with West Africa, previously known only as a source of slaves for the tropical colonies. These encounters further stimulated French curiosity regarding human diversity, giving new life to ongoing debates regarding race, environment, and the comparative merits of civilization and the state of nature. They also contributed to a gradual shift away from the primitivism of Lahontan and Rousseau toward the stadial, evolutionary theories that were more typical of the later Enlightenment. Paradoxically, as we shall see, this shift gave rise to an increasingly patronizing view of non-European populations, but also led to the recognition of these "savages" as autonomous cultural agents in their own right.

Science, Philosophy, and Colonial Expansion

Pierre Moreau de Maupertuis, who made his reputation in 1735 by leading the Arctic leg of the Académie des Sciences's two-pronged expedition to test Newton's hypothesis that the earth was flattened at the poles, was a man of many interests. The son of a successful Saint-Malo corsair, whose experience on the high seas had taught him the value of mathematics and astronomy for navigation, Maupertuis retained something of the swashbuckling ways of his ancestors, and developed a keen interest in voyages of exploration and colonial expansion.[2] Maupertuis recognized, however, that the days of the solitary genius and the lone explorer were past, and that the state had a prominent role to play in promoting the advancement of knowledge. His 1752 *Lettre sur le progrès des sciences* made the case that certain branches of scientific inquiry could only be promoted through the engagement of the resources of the monarchy. "There are certain sciences," he wrote, "that need the power of sovereigns to make progress; these are the ones that demand greater expenditures than can be made by private citizens, or experiences that are not practicable in the normal order of things."[3]

Chief among such areas of inquiry, Maupertuis argued, was the search to discover the *terres australes,* the long-suspected southern continent. He wrote, "Everyone knows that in the southern hemisphere there is an unknown space where there could be located a new part of the world larger than any of the four others, and no prince has had the curiosity to investigate if it is land or sea which fills this space, in a century in which navigation has been taken to so high a degree of perfection."[4] Maupertuis suggested that the unexplored southern zone of the Indian Ocean was the most promising location in which to search for a new continent, and argued that its discovery would not only be of great commercial utility, but would also substantially advance knowledge about man and the natural world. He observed that the three continents of the Old World were joined together, and formed in fact "but a single continent," to which even America might be connected, and which shared the same forms of plant, animal, and human life. The undiscovered *terres australes,* cut off from all contact with the rest of the world for innumerable centuries, were another matter entirely. Maupertuis wrote, "It is certain that they are absolutely isolated, that they form, so to speak, a new world apart, in which one cannot predict what will be found. The discovery of these lands could thus offer great utility to commerce, and marvelous spectacles for science."[5]

In addition to the southern continent, Maupertuis advocated the systematic exploration of the islands of the Pacific, writing, "It is in the islands of this sea that travelers assure us of having seen wild men, hairy men, bearing tails, an intermediate species between the apes and ourselves. I would rather have an hour of conversation with them than with the greatest minds of Europe."[6] He suggested new voyages of exploration to Africa, writing that "all of this vast continent is almost as unknown to us as the *terres australes.*" Noting the riches that ancient civilizations once drew from Africa and the continued trade in gold along its western coast, he suggested that "the discoveries that would be made in Africa would not be useless to commerce." [7] He also suggested a new voyage of exploration to Tierra del Fuego to verify the alleged existence of Patagonian giants, writing, "So many credible accounts speak to us of these giants, that one cannot reasonably doubt that there are in this region men whose size is quite different from our own."[8] "In examining the matter philosophically," he wrote further, "one may be surprised that there is not to be found among all the men of which we know the same variety of size that we observe in many other species... From a little sapajou to a great ape there is more difference than separates the smallest Lapp from the greatest of these giants of which the travelers speak."[9] In any case, he concluded that "these men are undoubtedly worthy of being known; the great size of their bodies would be perhaps the least matter to observe; their ideas, their knowledge, their histories would be worthy of greater curiosity."[10]

Just a few years before Rousseau would propose the dispatch of a network of the greatest scientific minds of Europe to the far corners of the globe in order to gather reliable information about exotic people and places, Maupertuis proposed the converse, suggesting the creation of a "college des sciences étrangères" in Paris, writing, "When we consider the long sequence of centuries in which the Chinese, the Indians, the Egyptians have cultivated the sciences, and the objects of art that come from their countries, we cannot help but regret that there is not more communication between them and us." [11] In this way, he suggested, European scholars would be better able to study the languages, cultures, and knowledge of the most distant peoples.

Maupertuis's appeals for further voyages of exploration to the far reaches of the southern hemisphere were soon taken up by other scholars and supporters of French colonial expansion. Chief among them was Charles de Brosses, president of the Parlement of Dijon and member of the Académie des Inscriptions, who in 1756 published a compilation of travel narratives, *Histoire des navigations aux terres australes*, preceded by an introduction that appealed to Louis XV and his subjects to carve out a new French empire in the southern hemisphere. De Brosses was inspired by Maupertuis's *Lettre sur le progrès des sciences*, which was discussed in detail at the provincial academy of Dijon, in which de Brosses played an active role, and, encouraged by his close friend and fellow Burgundian, the Comte de Buffon, he decided to pursue his own project.[12] Echoing Maupertuis, de Brosses argued that the far south was the last unexplored frontier of the globe, and wrote, "All of the southern part of our globe is still unknown. It is not likely that so vast a space should be filled only by the seas. Capes and coasts have been discovered, certain signs of a continent."[13] He stated a geophysical theory, incorrect but widely shared at the time, that a massive southern continent must exist, "capable of holding the globe in equilibrium in its rotation, and to serve as a counterweight to the mass of northern Asia," without which, he declared, the earth would rotate along the poles rather than the equator.[14]

De Brosses went on to describe the great discoveries and riches that Portugal and Spain had drawn from overseas exploration and conquest, and lamented that France, despite several noteworthy early voyages, had been left so far behind, commenting, "If there is a nation which should ardently seek to repeat such attempts, it is undoubtedly the French nation, which should show itself jealous of its honor, and mark its regret to have allowed foreigners to reap all the glory of such discoveries."[15] He argued that the discovery and settlement of a new colony would benefit France greatly, writing, "How can one doubt that such a vast extent of land would furnish, after the discovery, objects of curiosity and opportunities for profit, perhaps as much as America offered in its newness? How many peoples, differing among themselves and surely very unlike us, by their appearance, their manners, their customs, ideas, and religions?"[16] De Brosses further argued that the benefit to France, though great, would pale in comparison to the benefit to the yet-to-be-discovered *Australiens* themselves, who would gain access to the science, technology, and knowledge of modern Europe. He even held out the prospect of discovering "some civilized nation from whom we ourselves might learn an infinite number of things," though he added, "I admit that one should not expect to do so." In any case, he observed, if the French were to find advanced civilizations in the southern continent, they would not destroy them, as the Spaniards had destroyed the Aztec and Inca empires.[17]

While de Brosses promised humane treatment for any indigenous *Australiens* who might be discovered in these voyages of exploration, he nonetheless envisioned the yet-to-be-discovered lands of the south as potential settlement colonies. "Colonies," he wrote, "offer inexhaustible resources to produce, occupy, and nourish an abundant population."[18] Much as Britain would soon do with the real Australia, de Brosses argued that the *terres australes* could serve as a vast open-air reformatory in which the misfits and outcasts of society could be regenerated and turned into productive citizens. After discussing the pros and cons of galley ships, banishment, prisons, and other forms of punishment, he suggested that criminals could be disposed of most advantageously to the state by employing them as forced labor in the colonies, writing, "No one should find it strange that I propose to renew the servitude of free-born citizens; the loss of their liberty is the fair price to have made use of it against society. During this interval, they can render good services in a colony, rather than remaining useless, imprisoned for a term or forever in a *maison de force*."[19]

De Brosses's clarion call did not immediately stir the French monarchy into action. From 1756 to 1763, the French state was engaged in one of the most far-flung, costly, and ultimately disastrous wars of its history. Not only did France lose Canada to the British, but the enemy also blockaded its Caribbean colonies, occupied the smaller islands of Martinique and Guadeloupe, and destroyed much of the French fleet in the process. Once the peace was established, however, patriotic French statesmen and explorers would look for new avenues to make good the losses that the kingdom had suffered, and de Brosses's call for voyages of exploration to the south would be taken up. One of the most diligent and determined of these new explorers, Louis-Antoine de Bougainville, was directly inspired by de Brosses's appeal, and the accounts of his travels would stir the imagination of the enlightened public of readers and writers.

The Newest New World: Bougainville in Tahiti

In April 1768, two French vessels, the frigate *La Boudeuse* and its supply ship *L'Etoile,* approached an unknown island in the South Pacific. Their crews were exhausted, having made a harrowing journey through the Straits of Magellan before sailing across the vast and uncharted open sea, part of their quest to become the first French expedition to circumnavigate the globe. What happened next would become one of the most celebrated cultural encounters of the eighteenth century. The young captain Louis-Antoine de Bougainville, leader of the expedition, remarked with astonishment: "The boats were full of women, whose faces conceded nothing in beauty to the majority of European women, and whose bodies could rival them all. Most of these nymphs were nude...I ask, how could one keep at work, amid such a spectacle, four hundred young French sailors, who had not seen a woman in six months?" After a young beauty boarded his ship and "appeared before the eyes of all as Venus appeared to the Phrygian shepherd," Bougainville and his men subsequently landed on the island, Tahiti, and spent nine days of rest and relaxation there before continuing their voyage westward. [20] Their accounts contributed to the lasting European image of the South Pacific as an idyllic paradise, free from the artificial moral constraints of Christian

Europe. The French reading public, which Rousseau's writings had already prepared to celebrate the simple charms of life in harmony with nature, eagerly embraced Bougainville's seductive portrait of the island, which he named "New Cythera" after the Greek island of love. As Matt Matsuda has shown, Tahiti and the rest of Polynesia would remain associated in the French imagination with natural beauty and unbridled sexuality from the age of Bougainville to that of Paul Gauguin and Pierre Loti, and even beyond.[21]

One may easily establish a direct line between the theoretical speculations and patriotic exhortations of Maupertuis and de Brosses and the voyage of Bougainville, the most famous French explorer of the late eighteenth century. As a young man coming of age in the 1750s, Louis-Antoine de Bougainville was inspired by both of these texts, and had personal connections to both of their authors: Bougainville's elder brother, Jean-Pierre de Bougainville, was a classicist and pupil of the érudit Nicolas Fréret, and succeeded his mentor as secretary of the Académie des Inscriptions, of which de Brosses was also a member, while Louis-Antoine himself was trained in mathematics by d'Alembert, who was Maupertuis's colleague in the Académie des Sciences. Louis-Antoine de Bougainville shared these men's commitment to reviving France's flagging colonial power, and when war broke out again between France and Britain, he sought and received a commission in Montcalm's army in Canada. Described by Harry Liebersohn as both a "strategic thinker" with ambitious plans for French imperial renewal and a "master courtier" who was able to capitalize on his connections at court and among learned society, Bougainville offered his services to the duc de Choiseul even before the final peace treaties were signed.[22] He was subsequently sent on two missions, first to establish a (short-lived) French colony in the Falkland Islands, and later to embark on a voyage of exploration through the Straits of Magellan and beyond into the uncharted South Pacific.

Like the contemporaneous travels of his English counterpart, Captain James Cook, Bougainville's voyage was a scientific expedition, and the explorer was accompanied by the botanist Philibert Commerson and the astronomer Pierre-Antoine Veron, who took samples and made detailed observations all along their two and a half year journey. An enlightened and humane traveler, Bougainville took particular pride in the fact that, despite the many hardships encountered along the route, he only lost nine men in the entire journey. He returned to France in 1769 amid general acclaim. Although Bougainville's visit to Tahiti lasted only nine days, and takes up only four chapters out of an extensive two-volume travel narrative, it was this section of the work that most enchanted his contemporaries, for the idyllic portrait of Tahitian society that Bougainville and others depicted touched the romantic sensibilities of the somewhat jaded readers of the late Old Regime. Most interesting to Parisian society was his human subject, the Tahitian Aotourou, who was a sensation in the salons and academies of Paris during his 11-month stay in France.

Bougainville's depiction drew both on the biblical paradise and on the classical legends of a primeval golden age of humanity. Bougainville described the beauty of the tropical landscape, remarking, "I believed myself transported to the Garden of Eden...A numerous people there enjoys the treasures that Nature pours out openhanded upon it."[23] Most of his comparative references, however, were classical rather than biblical, notably his decision to name the island New Cythera, after the Greek island of love. Bougainville bid a romantic farewell upon leaving Tahiti, writing, "I cannot depart from this fortunate isle without renewing the praises that I have already made. To describe fully what we have seen, it would take the pen of Fenelon, to depict it, the charming brush of Albano or Boucher. Farewell happy and wise people! I will never recall without delight the few instants I spent among you and, as long as I live, I will celebrate the happy isle of Cythera. It is the true Utopia."[24] Philibert Commerson, the naturalist who accompanied Bougainville on his voyage, offered an even more enthusiastic praise of Tahiti in a 1769 letter to the *Mercure de France*, calling it "the only corner of the world where men live without vices, without prejudices, without needs, without conflicts," and considered the island as proof that "in the state of nature man is born essentially good, exempt of all prejudices and following without defiance or regret the sweet impulses of an instinct which is always sure, as it has not yet degenerated into reason."[25] The superiority of savage to civilized life, celebrated by Rousseau from the early 1750s, received a decisive boost from these travelers' tales. Glyndwr Williams has observed the ethnographic potential of the Enlightenment-era voyages to the South Pacific, noting that "for students of primitive peoples the Pacific held advantages over North America and West Africa, ravaged and contaminated as they were by centuries of European exploitation...Here in unspoilt surroundings would surely be found evidence to prove or disprove the presumptions of the 'noble savagery' school of thought, and indicate more reliably the relationship between western and primitive man."[26]

Despite the seductive legend his own work helped to launch, which contributed to wide public interest in the South Pacific back in France, Bougainville the romantic traveler coexisted with Bougainville the man of reason and budding social scientist. There is a fairly marked contrast between chapters one, two, and four of the second part of Bougainville's travel narrative, which were written as a journal at the time the events occurred, and chapter three, which was composed after the fact as a more dispassionate, analytical examination of Tahitian society. In this chapter, Bougainville discusses the racial composition, social structure, and religious beliefs of the Tahitian people, and offers a more sober and realistic, if not necessarily negative, portrait of "new Cythera." He observed that he had been incorrect in first assuming that Tahitian social structure was egalitarian, remarking that instead its chiefs held the power of life and death over their slaves, and perhaps also over the commoners under their jurisdiction. He presented the Tahitians as essentially childlike, observing, "Everything strikes them, nothing occupies them; amid the new objects that we presented to them, we were never able to fix their attention on any of them for more than two minutes. It seems that the slightest reflection is for them an unbearable toil, and that they flee the fatigues of the mind even more than those of the body." He also described them as credulous and superstitious, noting that "priests have the most fearsome authority among them."[27]

The product of a classical education and the younger brother of the secretary of the Académie des Inscriptions, Bougainville rather naturally fell into the paradigm, perhaps most explicitly developed by Lafitau with regard to Native Americans, of drawing parallels between contemporary "primitives" and the peoples of remote antiquity. In a letter to his brother Jean-Pierre during his Canadian campaign, Louis-Antoine confessed that he found solace from the boredom and brutality of military life in rereading the classical authors Horace, Virgil, and Tacitus. This odd juxtaposition of activities suggested to Bougainville's fertile mind many surprising conclusions regarding primitivism, civilization, and the relationship of the Old World to the New. "One finds in the manners of the savages traces of the ancient customs of the Greeks," he wrote. "Principally I believe I find in their warlike manners and customs those of the heroes of the Iliad and the Odyssey."[28] He wrote of the Plains Indians that "they form, like the Tartars, errant hordes, they follow the beasts from whose hunting they live, their abodes are tents of skins."[29] Bougainville compared the ritual dances of the Indians to the Greek bacchanalia, likened the prominent role of women in Iroquois councils to the authority of the matrons of the ancient Gauls, and compared a ceremony for departing warriors to a similar ritual of ancient Persia.[30] He likened the oratory of the Iroquois leaders to the "figurative style of the Orientals."[31] A decade later, during his Pacific voyage, he drew a similar parallel in discussing the Tahitian custom of tattooing the hips and thighs, comparing it to the body painting of the ancient Picts: "It is noteworthy that in all times this painting has been in fashion among peoples still close to the state of nature. When Caesar made his first descent in England, he found this custom of self-painting established there."[32]

Bougainville did not share the cultural primitivism made fashionable by Jean-Jacques Rousseau, and specifically condemned Rousseau's abstract theorization of human nature and his dismissal of eyewitness accounts that he considered unreliable. He wrote in the preface to his travel account that he wrote not to establish or combat any hypothesis, and rejected "this spirit of system, so common today, and yet so little compatible with true philosophy." He went on to state, somewhat ironically, that he had little hope that his account would be believed in learned circles, writing, "I am a traveler and a sailor, that is to say, a liar and an imbecile in the eyes of that class of superb and lazy authors who, in the shadows of their cabinets, philosophize themselves blind over the world and its inhabitants, and imperiously submit nature to their imaginations." Bougainville further complained that "these people who, having observed nothing for themselves, only write and dogmatize based on observations borrowed from those same travelers to whom they refuse the faculties of seeing and thinking."[33]

Bougainville's anthropological reflections, I would argue, were more typical of French Enlightenment thought regarding human diversity and the course of history than were the somewhat iconoclastic and polemical treatises of Rousseau. Like such illustrious predecessors and contemporaries as Montesquieu, Buffon, Raynal, and Diderot, Bougainville took a more optimistic view of progress than did Rousseau, and credited Europe with a central role in its forward march. Like these other Enlightenment figures, Bougainville attributed the development of culture to a combination of the influence of climate and diet and the legacy of lawgivers or legislators who brought civilization to formerly barbarous peoples. If the Tahitians, a half-civilized people living in tranquility under a gentle and abundant climate, were to be envied, more savage peoples, abandoned to the harsh elements of extreme environments, were far less fortunate. Bougainville's description of a Patagonian people he calls the Pécherais contrasts sharply with his idyllic depiction of the Tahitians:

> Of all the savages I have seen in my life, the Pécherais are the most lacking of everything: they exist in exactly what one could call the state of nature, and if in truth one should pity the fate of a free man, master of himself, without duties or affairs, content with his lot because he knows nothing better, then I would pity these men who, with the privation of that which makes life comfortable, must suffer the harshness of the most awful climate of the universe.[34]

At the same time, however, Bougainville denied that even these most primitive of men truly lived in the solitary fashion that Rousseau described as the state of nature. Instead, he reflected, man was a naturally social creature, and social inequality and interpersonal conflicts exist even in the simplest societies:

> These Pécherais form the least numerous society of men that I have encountered in any part of the world; however...one finds charlatans among them. The fact is, once there is assembled more than one family...interests become complicated, and individuals want to dominate by force or by imposture. The name of family changes to that of society, and were it established in the middle of the woods, were it formed only by cousins, (one) will soon discover the seed of all the vices to which men assembled in nations, becoming civilized, have given names, vices that cause the greatest empires to rise, evolve, and fall. It follows from the same principle that in those societies called civilized, there arise virtues of which men still close to the state of nature are not susceptible.[35]

Harry Liebersohn has argued that European voyages to the Pacific contributed to the emergence of a more nuanced and complex understanding of indigenous societies, writing, "It was one thing for European philosophers to speculate on natural man; the Pacific presented an extraordinary diversity of political societies within the clearly defined boundaries of isolated island societies."[36] Bougainville's own career attests to the truth of this assertion. While he romanticized the simple, happy existence of the Tahitians, Bougainville ultimately gave preference to civilization, and suggested that certain essential characteristics were shared by all peoples. By declaring that Iroquois warriors exhibited the same courage, vigor, and cruelty as the heroes of Homer's epics, or that tattooed Tahitians shared the aesthetic values of the Picts that Caesar encountered in ancient Britain, he suggested that all of these peoples could be situated along an evolutionary scale. Iroquois, Tahitians, and even the benighted Pécherais were not ontologically different from modern Europeans, but rather stood at a greater or lesser distance below them on a universal ladder of progress. This framework implied that contemporary primitives could offer new insights into how Europeans' own ancestors had once lived and, conversely, that the Western classical canon could contribute to an understanding of newly discovered exotic peoples. We will return to this means of representing the unity and diversity of humankind, which I have dubbed "progressive universalism," in the final chapter.

Diderot and the "Supplement to the Voyage of Bougainville"

Today, Bougainville's own travel journals and memoirs are less often read than is the "Supplement to the Voyage of Bougainville," a short, somewhat whimsical piece written by Denis Diderot, which uses the simplicity and sexual freedom of the Tahitians as a device to decry the hypocrisy and absurdity of European morals. Given that Diderot's "Supplement" is far better known than the text by Bougainville that it purportedly complemented, it should be noted that Diderot took substantial creative license with Bougainville's account. For example, in the second part of the "Supplement," "The Old Man's Farewell," Diderot makes use of an island elder, who appears but does not speak in Bougainville's account, to decry the evils of European civilization and of colonialism, much as Lahontan had done with Adario nearly a century earlier. Imploring Bougainville to leave the Tahitians in peace, Diderot's old man declares, "We are innocent, we are content, and you can only spoil that happiness. We follow the pure instincts of nature, and you have tried to erase its impression from our hearts. Here, everything belongs to everyone, and you have preached I can't tell what distinction between 'yours' and 'mine.'" Referring to the symbolic act of appropriation by which Bougainville claimed the island for France, the old man declares:

> So this land is yours? Why? Because you set foot on it! If a Tahitian should one day land on your shores and engrave on one of your stones or on the bark of one of your trees, "This land belongs to the people of Tahiti," what would you think then?... When one

of the miserable trinkets with which your ship is filled was taken away, what an uproar you made, what revenge you exacted! At that very moment, in the depths of your heart, you were plotting the theft of an entire country!...This inhabitant of Tahiti, whom you wish to ensnare like an animal, is your brother. You are both children of Nature. What right do you have over him that he does not have over you?[37]

Diderot further contrasted the naïve sexual freedom of the Tahitians with the hypocrisy, repression, and perversion of European society. This contrast is most evident in the third part of the "Supplement," "The conversation between the chaplain and Orou," in which an obliging Tahitian host pressures a French priest into having sexual relations with each of his daughters. While the chaplain is a character invented by Diderot for anticlerical comic effect, Bougainville's account did describe how his hosts offered young women as sexual partners to the visiting sailors and expressed amazement at the public, even ritualistic, celebration of sexuality in Tahitian society. Diderot's discussion of sex and reproduction is frankly utilitarian, as Orou seeks above all to multiply his posterity, without regard for the niceties of Christian morality, and the priest, despite his misgivings and protests regarding his "holy orders," surrenders to the call of nature with each new temptation.

Larry Wolff has stressed the significance of the fact that Diderot's "Supplement" begins and ends as a dialogue, which allows the author to contrast opposing points of view regarding nature, civilization, and morality without committing himself unambiguously to either. Wolff writes that "the relative counterpoint of differing customs rendered all morality problematically uncertain...the multiplicity of perspectives...encouraged the emergence of an anthropological discourse based on the principle of cultural relativism."[38] Diderot does not make a simple, categorical choice between primitivism and civilization, but acknowledges the virtues and vices of both conditions, using the contrast between them to highlight the situational and relative nature of laws and customs, which he expressed in the comment, "Let's follow the good chaplain's example and be monks in France and savages in Tahiti."[39] Claudia Moscovici interprets this ambivalent advice as an argument for an ethical theory balanced between universalism and relativism, in which "only individuals who can question the ethical norms of not only different cultures but also of their own gain a truly ethical consciousness that benefits from cultural exchange."[40] Through this discursive play of multiple perspectives and contrasting

points of view, which Moscovici calls a "doubled dialectical process,"
Diderot questions and challenges both European and exotic customs,
in an approach that is sufficiently relativist to acknowledge profound
cultural difference, yet sufficiently universalist as to make cross-cultural comparison and communication possible.

In the fourth and final section of the "Supplement," also written
in dialogic form, Diderot draws the moral lessons from Bougainville's
encounter with the Tahitians. He offers a proto-Freudian interpretation of the reasons why, in his view, the primitive man is happier
than the civilized man:

> Would you like a historical sketch of almost all our misery? Here
> it is. Once upon a time there was a natural man; inside him was
> introduced an artificial man, and within his breast there then
> broke out a continual war, lasting the whole of his life. Sometimes
> the natural man is stronger, sometimes he is laid low by artificial,
> moral man; in either case the miserable monster is racked, torn,
> tortured, stretched on the wheel, constantly groaning, ceaselessly
> wretched, whether moved to delirium by a false striving for glory
> or bowed down and battered by misbegotten shame.[41]

Evoking the evolutionary assumptions of cultural development that
we have already encountered, Diderot wrote, "The Tahitian is close
to the origins of the world and the European near its old age. The
gulf between us is greater than that separating the new-born child
from the decrepit dotard. The Tahitian either fails entirely to understand our customs and laws, or he sees them as nothing but fetters
disguised in a hundred different ways, which can only inspire indig-
nation and scorn in those for whom the love of liberty is the deepest
of all feelings."[42] He lamented the loss of primitive man's innocent
happiness, writing that "as soon as physical factors, such as the need
to overcome the infertility of the soil, have brought man's ingenu-
ity into play, the momentum drives him well beyond his immediate
objective; so that when his need has elapsed he comes to be swept
into the great ocean of fantasy from which he cannot pull out. May
the happy Tahitian stop where he is!" He further wrote that the
Tahitians, "who have kept strictly to the law of nature, are nearer to
having good laws than any civilized people" because "it's easier to
abandon one's excessively primitive ways than to retrace one's steps
and reform one's abuses."[43]

Diderot had thus arrived at the same impasse which Rousseau
had reached in the *Discourse on the Origins of Inequality*, arguing that

primitive man was freer and happier than civilized man, but recognizing that time moves inexorably forward, rendering impossible the dream of a *retour en arrière*. Tzvetan Todorov writes that "the vision of the world and of history that Rousseau proposes is much more tragic than that of his primitivist contemporaries; society corrupts man, but man is truly man only because he has entered into society; there is no way out of this paradox."[44] Though Diderot's tone is witty and urbane where Rousseau's is grave and tragic, the two men reach more or less the same conclusion: that the best that civilized man can hope for is to take lessons from the study of primitive man, which he can then apply to the reform of his own society. Liebersohn writes that, for the Enlightenment, "Pacific islands were laboratories for social observation, places for comparing European hierarchies with diverse alternatives."[45] While Rousseau and Diderot (and Bougainville, for that matter) agreed that civilized man could learn valuable lessons from a sojourn in a primeval forest or on a tropical island, neither intended for him to stay permanently there. One contemporary reader who recognized this purpose was Immanuel Kant, who remarked that "Rousseau did not really want man to *go* back to the state of nature, but rather to *look* back at it from the step where he now stands."[46] By looking backward at the path he had traced from savagery to civilization, Enlightenment thinkers hoped, civilized man could build a new, better society upon the ruins of the old.

The Eclipse of the Noble Savage: La Pérouse as Ethnographer

Although both Bougainville and Diderot depicted Tahitian society in terms that recalled the simplicity and happiness of the Garden of Eden or the classical golden age, they balanced the romantic celebration of the "noble savage" with a historical vision that was largely progressive and evolutionary. As Europeans became more confident regarding the future and the accomplishments of modern civilization, celebrations of the noble savage gradually receded into the past, like a favorite childhood toy that is fondly remembered but no longer needed. Real encounters with actual indigenous people in the Pacific and beyond, and infamous incidents like the death of Captain James Cook, the most famous of Enlightenment explorers, at the hands of hostile Hawaiian islanders, also contributed to this shift. Even Rousseau, shocked by reports of violence and cannibalism among the Maori of New Zealand, is said to have exclaimed, "Is it possible that the good children of nature can really be so wicked?"[47] Once the savages lost their nobility, they became less useful for philosophic arguments regarding the natural goodness of man.

This change in perspective is particularly notable in the journals of the Pacific explorer Jean-François de La Pérouse, whose final journey took him from Brest to Chile, Hawaii, Alaska, China, and Australia, before he and his entire crew perished in a shipwreck in the South Pacific. La Pérouse was well aware of the fate that had befallen Captain Cook, whom he greatly admired, and on several occasions lamented that the gentle and indulgent policies that his orders required him to adopt with regard to the native peoples he encountered only encouraged the latter to become more insolent and demanding, and thereby precipitated rather than avoided conflict. Following the massacre of a landing party by the natives of the Solomon Islands in December 1787, La Pérouse recounted how the beauty and tranquility of their lush tropical surroundings and the apparently warm welcome of the islanders had lulled his men into a false sense of security. "What imagination would not paint a scene of happiness in such a delightful setting?" he remarked. Even in this bucolic tropical idyll, however, things were not as they seemed. "We were fooled," La Pérouse went on, "this beautiful scene was not one of innocence...Man, almost savage and in anarchy, is a being more cruel than the most ferocious animals."[48]

In one of his final letters, sent on February 7, 1788, from Botany Bay in Australia to his friend Pierre Claret de Fléurieu just before his disappearance into the South Pacific, La Pérouse reflected bitterly on the contrast between Rousseau's celebration of "natural man" and his own experiences, writing, "I am nevertheless a thousand times more angry with the *philosophes* who exalt savages, than with the savages themselves. Poor Lamanon, who they massacred, was telling me on the eve of his death, that these men were better than us...I have always dealt with the natives with the greatest moderation; but I confess that if I had to undertake a new voyage of this kind, I would ask for other orders."[49] He further wrote, "A navigator leaving Europe should consider the savages as enemies, very weak ones, in truth, whom it would be ungenerous to attack without motive and whom it would be barbaric to destroy, but against whom one has the right to take precautions when one is authorized by justified suspicions."[50]

Even before this misfortune, La Pérouse argued that Rousseau's celebration of the natural goodness of man was misguided, and that man only became truly human and virtuous in society. He told Fléurieu in the letter cited above that "my opinion on uncivilized peoples was fixed long ago; my voyage has only confirmed it."[51] In his travel journals, La Pérouse described the native Alaskans as being "as vulgar and barbarous as their soil is rocky and barren," and declared, "I will admit, if one wishes, that it is impossible that a society may exist without some virtues, but I am obliged to recognize that I did not have the insight to perceive any (among the Alaskans)."[52] Drawing upon his authority as eyewitness, La Pérouse wrote, "The *philosophes* will protest in vain against this tableau. They write their books by the fireside, and I have traveled for thirty years; I am witness to the injustices and trickery of those peoples which are depicted as so good, because they are very close to nature." Drawing upon an analogy with the natural world, La Pérouse went on to argue that Nature could only achieve its potential through cultivation, writing, "It is impossible to penetrate in the woods that the hand of civilized men has not pruned, to cross plains filled with stones, rocks, and flooded by impassable swamps, or finally to enter into society with the man of nature, because he is barbaric, wicked, and deceitful."[53] Human nature, La Pérouse thereby argued, is a rough stone, which must be hewn and polished through education and the civilizing process in order to become the precious gem that exists beneath the savage exterior.

At the same time, however, La Pérouse recognized that the peoples he encountered were not pure "natural men," but rather social creatures embedded within a specific cultural context, whose societies were not frozen in time, but rather progressed and evolved in the same ways as those of Europe, albeit at their own pace and along their own path. For example, during a brief visit to Concepción, situated on the margins between the Spanish colony of Chile and the unconquered Mapuche people to its south, La Pérouse noted that contact with Europeans, and particularly the introduction of horses, had transformed the native culture, giving the Mapuches "a more marked resemblance to the Tartars or the inhabitants of the shores of the Red Sea [i.e., the Arabs] than to their ancestors who lived two centuries ago."[54] Similarly, when visiting Easter Island, La Pérouse observed that the native islanders did not live in a state of nature, but rather, as he ironically observed, "they have on the contrary made great progress in civilization, and I consider them as corrupt as they could be relative to the circumstances in which they find themselves."[55] After noting the islanders' skills at farming and handicrafts, La Pérouse noted that they carefully observed the structure of his ships, remarking, "They did not view our arts as stupid beings."[56] In the course of his journey along the coast of Siberia, approaching the Bering Strait, La Pérouse remarked upon the similarities between the peoples he encountered and the natives of North America. Although his own journey bore witness to the proximity between Siberia and Alaska, La Pérouse attributed these similarities not to a common origin, but rather to a common human nature and a common adaptation to similar environments at a comparable stage of social development, concluding that "men, at the same degree of civilization, under the same latitudes, will adopt almost the same practices, and, if they were in exactly the same circumstances, they would perhaps not differ more between one another than the wolves of Canada differ from those of Europe."[57]

As these comments suggest, La Pérouse had adopted, consciously or not, a conceptualization of the progress of civilization in terms of the successive advance through a series of stages of socioeconomic development, similar to that elaborated by his countrymen Turgot and Condorcet and by the Scottish "conjectural historians" Ferguson and Kames. These "stadial" theories of history, which we will discuss in greater detail in the final chapter, assumed that hunter-gatherer societies were more "primitive" than those that drew their livelihood from agriculture. Accordingly, La Pérouse expressed surprise at the polite manners and level of knowledge he encountered among the natives of the Bay of Langle, writing, "It was very contrary to our ideas to find among a hunting and fishing people, who do not cultivate any production of the earth and who have no flocks, manners generally milder, more solemn, and perhaps an intelligence more expansive than among any nation of Europe."[58]

La Pérouse's observations also reflect the skeptical empiricism of the late eighteenth century, which (as was often the case) he framed in explicit opposition to the "system-builders" and metaphysicians of the seventeenth. He remarked upon the similarities and differences in skin color, body size and shape, cultural practices, and languages he observed among the peoples he encountered, and frequently offered conjectures on whether two or more of these peoples shared a common origin. At the same time, however, he acknowledged that "it is very difficult to excavate and to know how to read the archives of the world, in order to discover the origins of peoples, and travelers should leave the systems to those who will read their relations."[59]

Though often painted in unflattering colors, the natives who appear in La Pérouse's journals are not stock philosophical characters, but real people of flesh and blood, capable of doing good or evil, and displaying a wide range of cultural practices and skillful adaptations to the environments in which they live. In this sense, La Pérouse deserves recognition as one of the greatest ethnographers of the late Enlightenment, and were it not for his tragic death, he would likely have gone on to play a formative role in the emergence of the *sciences humaines* in the early nineteenth century. His observations reflect both a growing sophistication in late Enlightenment perceptions of "primitive" peoples, and also the increasing self-confidence and adoption of evolutionary, stadial models of development that enabled European learned travelers to assert their superiority over the indigenous peoples they encountered on their voyages.

Enlightenment Encounters in West Africa

Africa remained something of an enigma to eighteenth-century Europeans, at once broadly familiar and largely unknown, as Maupertuis recognized in the *Lettre sur le progrès des sciences*. Africa had been known to the West since antiquity, and its western coasts were the sites of intensive European commercial activity, focused primarily, though not exclusively, on the trans-Atlantic slave trade. If the coast of Africa was well known, its interior remained largely uncharted, a state of affairs due largely, as Daniel Headrick has observed, to the lack of navigable rivers and to the presence of tropical diseases that decimated all European expeditions prior to the mid-nineteenth century's advances in prophylactic medicine.[60] The slave traders, merchants, soldiers, and sailors who plied its coasts left few memoirs of their activities. Africa also suffered, in the European estimation, from its association with slavery and from racial prejudices that will be discussed in more detail in the next chapter. Nevertheless, in the middle decades of the century, a scientist and a cleric, Michel Adanson and the abbé Demanet, would both produce works that presented a generally favorable portrait of Africans, echoing the image of the "noble savage," which had been constructed with regard to the natives of the Americas. Few of their contemporaries embraced this representation, however, and Africa remained far more associated with savagery than with nobility in the eyes of most Europeans.

Michel Adanson, an aspiring scientist whose "universal curiosity" and "real sympathy" for West African society have been praised by the editors of his unpublished works,[61] was just 21-years old when he departed for Africa. A newcomer and a protégé of Bernard de Jussieu who sought to win recognition, and perhaps academy membership, through his work, Adanson's self-imposed task was the open-ended project of surveying the fauna and flora of Senegal, a region where French and other slave traders had been active for over a century, but which had not yet been examined in detail by European naturalists. Unable to obtain financial backing from the Académie des Sciences, he enrolled as a low-level clerk in the Compagnie des Indes, which arranged for his passage and residence in West Africa. Though stationed on Gorée Island, Adanson was able to spend several months in remote locations, away from other Europeans and in regular contact with Africans. He also claimed to have learned enough of the Wolof language to be able to communicate without an interpreter.

Adanson's descriptions of Africans drew upon existing discourses and stereotypes, as might perhaps be expected. At one point, he compared playful African children to "little monkeys," and he declared that Africans' own sense of inferiority with regard to Europeans was a useful prejudice that should be encouraged, remarking, "One should as much as possible, maintain them in this sort of submission."[62] On the other hand, given his extended sojourn in West Africa, Adanson encountered Africans in a variety of different settings, and he presented a nuanced portrait that reflected their essential humanity. He described the Wolof of Senegal as physically attractive, finding them "the handsomest people of black Africa," describing the men as "taller than average, well-built and without defect," and the women equally "well-built," with fine and soft skin, "well-proportioned" facial features, and concluded, "there are many of perfect beauty. They have great liveliness, and above all an air of casual freedom that pleases."[63] Adanson in fact seems quite taken by the beauty of Senegalese women, for after noting that they went about with their breasts uncovered, he remarked, "As they are usually well-built, they always have a very good appearance in this undressed state, especially once one is accustomed to their color. Those who are not accustomed to it should content themselves with looking at their figures, which is what is most beautiful about them."[64] As we shall see in this and the following chapter, Adanson was far from alone among European travelers and theorists in allowing aesthetic criteria and the attractions of desire to influence his appraisals of exotic peoples.

Adanson described a charming scene that occurred while he was busy with botanical research in a remote African village, in which the ethnographic gaze was suddenly reversed, and the French explorer's own body (specifically, his long, red hair) became the object of curiosity for a group of African children:

> I was soon surrounded by a troop of children of both sexes attracted by curiosity...Most of them having never seen a white person so close up, some touched my clothing, others took hold

of my hat and my hair...But what was their surprise, when...my hair fell down to my waist!...The singular scene that I had just experienced, unexpectedly, led me to several reflections upon leaving. It occurred to me that the color white, so opposed to the blackness of Africans, was the first thing that had struck these children; these poor creatures were in the same state as our children, when they see a Negro for the first time.[65]

Adanson also wrote against the grain of stereotypes of African ignorance in his discussion of evenings spent in tree houses with native peoples, where he listened to traditional folktales and observed their knowledge of the stars. "They distinguished even the twinkling of the stars that were just becoming visible," he wrote. "For a people whose knowledge is very limited, it is striking that they reason so pertinently about the stars, and there is no doubt that with the proper tools and will, they would become excellent astronomers, inhabiting a climate where the air is extremely calm nearly all the year, and where, living outside, they have all possible occasions to examine at each instant that which happens in the sky."[66] Here Adanson clearly sides with the Enlightenment advocates of the perfectibility of man against those of their contemporaries who argued for the innate inferiority of nonwhite peoples. Reynaud and Schmidt, editors of a recent edition of Adanson's travel narrative, observe that this assertion, given the contemporary consensus regarding the ignorance of Africans, "has a militant, almost polemical character."[67] The *Mémoires de Trévoux*, however, in reviewing Adanson's chronicle, downplayed the potential of this observation to refute prevailing prejudices, and instead integrated it into a seemingly unrelated European debate regarding historical chronology and the astronomical knowledge of the ancients, writing, "This observation may perhaps make probable Newton's system of chronology. Could not Chiron the Argonaut, who is the keystone of this hypothesis, know as much about the globe as these good Africans, born in barbarity and lacking all assistance for their education?"[68] In other words, the ethnographic fact that Africans carefully studied the sky is interpreted by the reviewer not as a mitigating factor in the assumption of African barbarity, but rather as evidence that even barbarians may have an elemental knowledge of astronomy, a conclusion that is quickly applied to an ancient European context.

Adanson's depiction of West Africans, though certainly not without condescension and a sense of European superiority, affirms the essential humanity of the subjects in question, and alludes to an evolutionary understanding of the history of society, in which Africans are not intrinsically inferior to Europeans, but rather stand below them on a common ladder of civilization. He presents a pleasant tableau of bucolic scenes, in which a friendly, appealing, if somewhat childlike people lives happily in harmony with nature:

> In every direction I looked during this happy sojourn, everything I saw there traced for me the most perfect image of pure nature, an agreeable solitude that was bounded on all sides only by the view of a charming landscape, the pastoral position of cottages amid the trees, the idleness and softness of Negroes lying in the shadow of their leaves, the simplicity of their dress and their manners, all of that recalled to me the idea of the first men; it seemed to me that I saw the world at its creation.[69]

Describing the Wolof in primitivist terms reminiscent of Rousseau or Lahontan, Adanson, who appears to have received friendly welcomes almost everywhere he went, noted that "there was much to refute in what I had read everywhere, and what I had heard said of the savage character of Africans."[70] Later in the same account, he stressed his own eyewitness credentials, having "stayed a long time with them, alone and distant from contact with those of my own nation," which gave him "occasion to know in depth their character, their manners, their way of life, and their customs," and asserted that the Wolof "are in general very humane and hospitable."[71] The *Mémoires de Trévoux* once again discounted the progressive and egalitarian thrust of Adanson's description, writing that Africans "appear to be born for slavery, they have all of the inclinations of good and bad servants," but concluded reassuringly that Adanson "has been so well received as to encourage those who travel to Senegal not to fear commerce with these barbarians."[72]

Adanson's travel narrative was published in 1757 in the first tome of what he hoped would be a nine-volume series on the natural history of Senegal. Unfortunately, the first volume was a commercial failure, and no publisher was willing to assume the risk of underwriting Adanson's magnum opus. Sadly, Adanson never reaped the rewards he anticipated for his scientific expedition to Senegal. He was repeatedly passed over for positions in the Jardin du Roi, and was accused of plagiarizing the work of his mentor by the latter's nephew, Antoine-Laurent de Jussieu. Though he secured royal support for a time, as Louis XV allowed him to move into the basement of the

Trianon Palace and to cultivate a botanical garden on its premises, he was subsequently evicted from the premises by Marie-Antoinette, who converted the building into her private retreat. Adanson thereafter withdrew from public life and spent his final decades alone and in poverty, working tirelessly on his own unfinished encyclopedia, intended to remedy the flaws that he observed in the work edited by Diderot and d'Alembert. He was almost entirely forgotten at the time of his death in 1806, and it was not until many years later that his signature achievement—the system of natural classification of species—was credited to him.[73]

Adanson's prospectus for his intended series on the natural history of Senegal, though the work was never completed, offers a sense of what he had in mind. While the majority of the volumes, as would be expected, focused on the plant and animal life of the region, he also proposed a volume dealing with the "civil history" of Senegal, which he said would "destroy many errors or fundamental faults that have slipped into it, whether by ignorance, or by carelessness in earlier relations."[74] He further declared that the Wolof, far from being "savages or the most primitive peoples, is the first of Africa, and one of the most spiritual and most polished of the globe, albeit one of the simplest in its manners and customs" and argued that their language "has been developed to the point to rival the perfection of the most civilized and learned peoples of Europe."[75]

Paradoxically from a twenty-first-century standpoint (though quite logically from an eighteenth-century one), Adanson combined genuine admiration and fondness for the Wolof people of Senegal with an equally strong desire to spread French civilization and extend French control into the region. He visited Africa during the brief interlude between two of the principal wars of the eighteenth century, the War of the Austrian Succession and the Seven Years' War. In both of these conflicts, most of France's overseas possessions fell to the mercy of the English, who dominated the seas. Out of patriotism, Adanson declined to sell his research notes and maps of Senegal to the enemy, and after the Seven Years' War, he wrote a brief to the Duc de Choiseul, who was determined to reestablish France's presence abroad, to stress the resources of Senegal and the contributions that it could make to French commerce. Most of his recommendations, suitably enough for a botanist, regarded plants and possible agricultural exports, such as rubber trees. Accordingly, his biographer Auguste Chevalier, writing at the high point of French imperialism in West Africa, described Adanson not only as a great scientist, but also as "a very great colonialist," who sought to expand

French commerce and influence in tropical Africa a century prior to Marchand and Brazza.[76]

Where the early twentieth-century French historian Chevalier praised Adanson for being a "great colonialist," more recent African scholars have criticized him for the same reason. David Diop has recently written that Adanson's generally favorable, yet patronizing portrait of the Wolof reflects his colonialist agenda. After noting his description of the village of Sor as a tropical Garden of Eden, Diop notes, "the botanist does not lend this mythic age of humanity the same meaning as does Rousseau." Rather, it "serves to reinforce the colonialist ideology in its certainty of the incapacity of Africans to exploit on their own, without the assistance of the French, the riches of nature which surround them."[77] Diop argues that Adanson adopts an evolutionary model of history and anticipates the "mission to civilize" of the French republican colonizers of West Africa. For this reason, Diop argues, Adanson presents Africans as vigorous and intelligent, and therefore capable of reaching the highest degree of civilization, but lacking initiative and remaining still in the earliest stages of social development, and thus needing French tutelage in order to achieve their innate potential. While Diop is largely correct in this assessment, I would argue that one should not simply dismiss Adanson as a lackey of imperialism without noting his sincere conviction that such a colonial arrangement would benefit the Wolof by integrating them into global networks of commerce and improving their standards of living through modern agriculture and the construction of roads, harbors, and markets.

Another French learned traveler to West Africa, the abbé Demanet, who served as *aumônier du roi* in the region during the same period, offered a similar report on Africans as promising candidates for French civilizing outreach. He condemned African rulers as cruel despots, and blamed many of Africa's problems on false religion and oppressive rule. His assessment of the common people of Africa is remarkably equivocal. On the one hand, he praised the simple virtues of the African people in a romantic tone that echoes depictions of the "noble savage," while on the other, he lamented that their "laziness and indolence" prevented the exploitation of the potential riches of the continent. "These people," he wrote, "who desire no riches…only work to the extent that is necessary to ensure their subsistence; these people, I say, leave the land uncultivated, ignore its riches or disdain them; they do not know the other commodities of life." Demanet noted their indifference to the mineral wealth that surrounded them, remarking that "they would even cast the gold underfoot, were the European not avid enough to cross the seas, expatriate himself, and expose himself to a thousand dangers, to give it a value in this nation." [78] Given this admirable disdain for money and precious metals, which Demanet called "the idols of Europeans," he noted that "if they were instructed in the principles of the Christian religion, one would see among them the purest morals, luxury and ambition would be but chimerical names, and simplicity would be their character."[79]

After praising the Stoic simplicity of the West Africans, however, Demanet proposed, "If this people had the industriousness of Europeans, either to cultivate the earth or to exploit its gold mines, and to bring into value many other rich products of the land, Africa would have enough revenue to enrich the other parts of the universe." Demanet blamed Africa's degeneration from past glory on the pernicious impact of false religions, writing that "error and falsehood have established their rule there, and the unfortunate inhabitants of a great region have engaged themselves as followers of a false and impious prophet."[80] He went on to argue that it would be in France's national interest to promote the evangelization of Africa, stating that "in little time, one would see this part of the idolatrous world become a precious asset to religion. It would also be so for the state, for the number of Christians and good French subjects would be as one, for there is no nation more attached to its prince than the African. They would be subjects on whom one could rely, both to enable and facilitate commerce and to defend the nation's territories, and soon they would form with us, in the spiritual, civil, and political order, a single body, a single spirit, whose only goal would be the public good."[81]

Adanson and Demanet both reflected attitudes toward Africa that were at once humanitarian and colonialist. Genuinely sympathetic to the people of the region and concerned for their well-being, they remained convinced that Africans would be better off as Christian French subjects than as pagans and savages, and both took an interest in the region's potential for economic development. Their nuanced and generally favorable portraits of West Africa had little impact, however, on the broader French perspective on the continent, as most of their contemporaries considered it primarily as a source of captives for the trans-Atlantic slave trade. It is primarily as a source of slaves that the African coast appears in the 11th book of the *Histoire des deux Indes*. Although, as we will see in the sixth chapter, the authors of the *Histoire*, particularly Diderot, bitterly condemned the institution of slavery, their depiction of Africa and its inhabitants reflected prevailing stereotypes of primitive savagery.

Most eighteenth-century French observers concurred in perceiving West Africans as "primitives" living close to a state of nature. Africans thus exemplified an earlier stage of human social development, in much the same way as did the Native American "savages" we considered in the previous chapter. As living vestiges of a distant epoch that had long vanished from Europe itself, they could therefore also serve as a key to unlock the mysteries of the past. For this reason, Charles de Brosses, who never traveled farther south than Italy, took West African "fetishism" (taken from the Portuguese *fetisso*, meaning a talisman or magical object) as his point of departure for analysis of the polytheism of the ancient Egyptians. De Brosses argued that the Egyptians, Greeks, and Romans had developed a religion similar to the "fetishism" of West Africa, centered on the veneration of totems such as sacred animals, locations, and objects, during an early, barbaric stage of their development, and had maintained that religion long after they became civilized. De Brosses stated that "what is today the religion of black Africans and other barbarians, was once that of ancient peoples."[82] De Brosses advanced an evolutionary theory of history, which asserted that all civilized peoples, including the ancient Greeks and Egyptians, as well as the Gauls from whom contemporary Frenchmen were descended, had their beginnings in a state of barbarism of which contemporary Africans and Native Americans offered living examples. "Just as one passes through childhood before becoming a grown man, [peoples] have had their centuries of childhood before their centuries of reason. Almost everywhere that we can go back to the first traditions of a civilized people, we find them savage or barbarian." [83] De Brosses's assessment did have the virtue of embracing West Africans as worthy objects of scholarly study, but it also had the vice of situating them at the lowest rung on the ladder of progress, where they would remain in Western anthropological discourse for the next two centuries.

Conclusions

The voyages of exploration and discovery of the latter half of the eighteenth century offered new information regarding distant parts of the world, as such diverse proponents as Maupertuis, de Brosses, and Rousseau had hoped that they would. They raised as many new questions as they answered, giving new life to the discursive figure of the "noble savage" and to the debate over whether primitive or civilized man was happier. The voyages of exploration also gave new impetus to the scientific description and analysis of human diversity, and to new taxonomies and debates regarding racial difference. The presence of groups with very different physical appearances, such as the Melanesians and Polynesians, in the same environment complicated the traditional association of skin color with climate, and subjective aesthetic criteria influenced European assessments of the merits of these peoples in often unacknowledged ways, as David Bindman has noted.[84] This is certainly the case with Bougainville, who repeatedly praised the beauty of the Tahitians, observing, "I have never encountered better built or proportioned men," and situated them on the margins of whiteness, writing that "if they were clothed, if they lived less exposed to the air and the sun, they would be as white as we are."[85] By contrast, Bougainville described the natives of Melanesia as "small, ugly, badly built, and mostly ravaged by leprosy," noting that the few women he saw were "no less disgusting than the men," and later reflected that "we have observed over the course of this voyage that in general black men are much more wicked than those whose color approaches that of the whites."[86]

Bougainville, it need hardly be said, was not an isolated figure, and many of his contemporaries were also quick to make evaluative judgments regarding the merits of peoples based upon superficial observation and aesthetic tastes. Nowhere was the Enlightenment's blindness regarding its own subjective biases and its tendency toward broad generalization based upon scanty evidence more damaging than with regard to the construction of race. There was not, however, a single Enlightenment view of racial difference, and egalitarian and exclusionary discourses competed with one another over the course of the century. In the next chapter, we will examine the roots, development, and course of racial thought in Enlightenment France.

5

The Varieties of Man: Racial Theory between Climate and Heredity

Numerous historians of racism in Western culture have argued that the eighteenth century marked a critical milestone in the construction of race, with George Mosse going so far as to declare that "eighteenth-century Europe was the cradle of modern racism."[1] The race concept was not an invention of the Enlightenment; recent studies have highlighted precedents such as ancient Greek representations of Persians and other "barbarians," the growing preoccupation with "purity of blood" in late medieval Spain, which led to the racialization of religious identities, and the sixteenth-century debates over whether indigenous American peoples were "natural slaves" in the Aristotelian sense.[2] Nevertheless, the taxonomic impulse of eighteenth-century thought led to a growing tendency to classify human beings into a precise number of biologically defined and allegedly invariable racial categories, while the secularization of European thought during the Enlightenment made possible new narratives of human origins that broke with the framework of the Book of Genesis to argue that different "races" of humankind did not share a common origin. For these reasons, it is often argued, as Emmanuel Eze has written, that "Enlightenment philosophy was instrumental in codifying and institutionalizing both the scientific and popular European perceptions on the human race," thereby generating the strain of scientific racism that became predominant in the nineteenth and early twentieth centuries.[3]

It is not my contention that this allegation is false, but rather that it is incomplete, and that a teleological reading of the development of racial theory that leads directly from the Enlightenment to Auschwitz or apartheid fails to do justice to the complexity, diversity, and ambiguities of eighteenth-century thought. The concept of race was much more fluid than it would later become, and lacked clearly defined boundaries between the contributing factors of heredity, environment, and culture. While, as Colin Kidd has noted, postrevolutionary France proved more receptive to polygenist theories of human origins than did Victorian Britain, such views were far from dominant in the prerevolutionary period, when only a few rare iconoclasts (such as Isaac La Peyrère in the seventeenth century and Voltaire in the eighteenth) explicitly argued that different "races" of man stemmed from separate origins.[4] We shall see that, as in the Anglo-American case, which Kidd has studied, religion continued to shape ideas of race in France well into the eighteenth century. While it is possible, and not entirely false, to represent the Enlightenment as the crucible of scientific racism, I would argue that it is more accurate to envision it as marking the last stand of a much older paradigm, which attributed physical and alleged mental or spiritual differences between human groups to the influence of climate. Climate determinism, with a pedigree dating back to Aristotle and Hippocrates, was endorsed by two of the most prominent thinkers of the period, the comte de Buffon and the baron de Montesquieu, and was accepted by many (though not all) of the others. Ultimately, as we shall see, the weaknesses and contradictions within climate determinism would cause it to give way to theories emphasizing heredity, and the fluidity of Enlightenment theories of man would harden into the rigid racial hierarchies of the nineteenth century.

The Beginnings of Racial Classification

As was noted above, the Enlightenment did not "invent" the race concept, or the tendency to ascribe distinctive characteristics to particular groups of human beings. However, the Enlightenment arguably did invent systems of racial taxonomy, classifying all humanity into a series of allegedly fixed and invariable categories. Prior to this time, as Pierre Boulle has noted, the term "race" was generally used to refer to noble lineages or to different breeds of dogs, horses, and so forth, rather than to categorize human beings into clearly defined groups according to skin color.[5] The first sign of a new usage for the term appeared in the *Journal des Sçavans* in 1684, in a short article entitled "A New Division of the Earth," published anonymously, but written by François Bernier, who, as we saw in the first chapter, spent eight years in India as a physician at the Mughal court and was a principal source for the theory of Oriental despotism.

Bernier began his essay by noting that, while geographers generally divided the world according to political boundaries or geographical features, "that which I have seen of men in my long and frequent voyages has given me the idea of dividing it differently." He went on to assert that "men are almost all different from one another according to the different parts of the earth in which they live...I have remarked that there are in particular four or five sorts or races of men among whom the difference is so notable, that it may serve as the just foundation of a new division of the earth."[6] Bernier's first and principal race was what later racial theorists would describe as "Caucasian," including all Europeans as well as the inhabitants of North Africa, Asia Minor, and the Indian subcontinent. Bernier's second race was made up of sub-Saharan Africans, which he justified considering as a different "variety" because of the shape of their noses and lips, their black color, which he presented as an essential characteristic, their relative lack of facial hair, and their hair "which is not properly hair, but rather a sort of wool." Bernier's third race was made up of the peoples of central and east Asia, whom he described as "truly white," but with different features, such as wide shoulders, flat faces and noses, and "little pig eyes, long and dark." Bernier described the Lapps of Scandinavia as a fourth and distinct race, which he situated on the outer margins of humanity, describing their faces as "quite horrid, and resembling those of bears," and calling them "vile animals." Bernier justified including Arabs and Indians among his first "variety" by arguing that their skin color was the result of "accidental" environmental causes, and he denied that Native Americans constituted a different variety of men, writing that "they are in fact mostly olive-colored, and have their faces shaped in a different manner than ourselves, but I do not find enough difference to make them a particular and distinct *espèce* than our own." By contrast, he argued that the blackness of Africans was inherent and hereditary, observing, "if one transports a black man and woman from Africa to a cold country, their children will not cease to be black, as all their descendants will be until they marry with white women." He seemed unsure whether to distinguish between different groups of Africans, observing that "the blacks of the Cape of Good Hope seem to be a different sort than those of the rest of Africa." While Bernier was willing to question the very humanity of the Lapps, he acknowledged that "I only ever saw two of them, at Danzig" and admitted that his assertions were based on "the portraits which I have seen and the reports made by people who have been in their country."[7]

As this brief summary indicates, Bernier's theories of race were unsystematic and highly personalized, based primarily on his own aesthetic preferences. The second half of Bernier's short essay is a sort of voyeuristic *tour du monde*, which recounts which countries have, in his opinion, the most beautiful women. In this sense, Bernier's tastes appear varied and eclectic, for he reported seeing on his travels beauties of Egypt, "who reminded me of the lovely and famous Cleopatra," and encountered women of African origin who, lacking the wide noses and full lips that he found distasteful, had such "surprising beauty, that they surpassed in my opinion the Venus of the Farnese Palace of Rome." He reported that "I have seen some in Moka, fully nude, who were for sale, and I can declare that there is nothing more beautiful to be seen in the world," but lamented that "they were very expensive, for they were priced three times more than the others."[8] Pierre Boulle notes that "Bernier's insistence that the transmission of characteristics by inheritance predominates over environmental or cultural determinants...constitutes a startling departure from contemporary beliefs." He further observes, however, that Bernier's influence was limited in his own time, perhaps a result of the arbitrary and personalized nature of his categories, and that his essay was rarely cited in eighteenth-century discussions of racial difference. Nevertheless, Boulle argues, Bernier's taxonomy is indicative of a shift in European scientific culture at the end of the seventeenth century "from a system of evidence based on analogies to one supported by fixed laws of nature, and...from a view of forms as well-nigh accidental, or at least molded by all sorts of external forces, to a belief in the permanence of species."[9]

The taxonomic exercises begun by Bernier at the end of the seventeenth century would be taken up by subsequent European scholars, most notably the Swede Carl von Linné (or Linnaeus), whose *System of Nature* (1735) identified four human races, and the German Johann Blumenbach, whose *On the Natural Varieties of Mankind* (1775, 3rd ed. 1795) identified five. This lack of agreement was not unusual; Benjamin Isaac has observed, "If no other form of proof [that race does not exist] were at hand, then it would still suffice to observe that no two scholars who wrote about race agree on the number of human races: they range from two or three or four, five, six to ten, eleven, thirteen, fifteen, sixteen, twenty-two, thirty-two, thirty-four up to sixty-three."[10] Colin Kidd concurs with this assessment, and adds: "All theories of race...are examples of cultural construction superimposed upon arbitrarily selected features of human variation."[11] In addition to differing on the number of races, eighteenth-century

European writers who discussed the physical differences among different groups of peoples were inconsistent in their use of terminology. David Bindman has observed that "'race' in the eighteenth century was but one category of 'human variety,' but confusingly 'varieties' and 'nations'...were often used where 'race' appears to have been meant, and 'race' was sometimes used when it clearly was not."[12] While the classification systems of Linnaeus and Buffon developed the modern concept of "species," French authors frequently used the word *espèce* interchangeably with the term *variété*, rather than in the strict scientific sense of the term, which Buffon defined as the ability of male and female exemplars to mate and to produce fertile offspring. While even Enlightenment polygenists did not go so far as to assert that whites and nonwhites belonged to different species, they and other eighteenth-century authors disagreed sharply regarding the causes and significance of differences in pigmentation and other physical features.

Race and Religion: The Curse of Ham and the Mark of Cain

One of the reasons why Bernier's essay on racial classification stands out in the context of the late seventeenth century is its purely secular approach. Bernier made no reference to sacred texts and did not pronounce on the question of whether all human beings share a common origin. Colin Kidd has convincingly demonstrated that, for much of the early modern era and even into the nineteenth century, debates regarding race had a strong religious component, leading him to conclude that "the spectre of Genesis haunted the birth of ethnology."[13] Religious skeptics, such as Lahontan and Voltaire, cited racial difference as prima facie evidence against the biblical account of humanity's common descent from Adam and Eve, while more devout authors, assuming the truth of Genesis, debated the family trees of distant and diverse peoples. Despite what twenty-first-century readers might assume, early modern scholars engaged in the debate between monogenesis and polygenesis (that is, whether or not all human beings shared a common origin) lined up not according to how "racist" they were, but rather according to their assessment of the credibility of the biblical account of the creation of humanity and the dispersal of peoples. While, as we shall see in the following chapter, political and economic relations of power would later become decisive in the classification and valuation of different groups of human beings, particularly in the Caribbean colonies, for philosophers and theologians in the French metropole in the seventeenth and early eighteenth centuries, racial difference was first and foremost a religious question.

For at least two centuries following Columbus's voyage, the origin of Native American peoples was among the most contentious debates engaging Western Christendom. Giuliano Gliozzi notes that "there was no respectable travel narrative which did not devote one of its first chapters to the problem of the 'origins of the Americans,' and there was hardly a jurist, theologian, or philosopher who did not, in his reflections on the New World, attempt to respond in some fashion to this problem."[14] Most Spanish commentators derived the Native Americans from Old Testament peoples, such as the Canaanites expelled from the Promised Land or the ten tribes of Israel lost during the Babylonian captivity, but a few preferred classical sources, such as Francisco López de Gómara, official historian of the conquest of Mexico by Hernán Cortés, who cited Plato's *Timaeus* and *Critias* to argue that Native Americans were the survivors of the lost continent of Atlantis.[15] A purportedly medieval chronicle published in sixteenth-century England, the *History of Cambria*, traced the origin of Native Americans from the Welsh prince Madoc, who sailed to the west in the twelfth century, never to return.[16] The learned Dutch jurist Hugo Grotius developed a particularly convoluted theory, in which natives of North America derived from Norwegians, the Maya of the Yucatán from Ethiopians, the peoples of the Amazon from the Malays, and the Incas from the Chinese. Although already in the late sixteenth century the Spanish Jesuit José de Acosta had advanced the correct hypothesis that the earliest Americans had crossed a land bridge from Asia in the far north, this topic continued to inspire speculation and debate well into the eighteenth century.

One possible, and in some ways logical, response to the overwhelming diversity of mankind was to assert that the different "races" or "varieties" of humanity were the product of separate acts of creation. Even before the discovery of America, the "pre-Adamite" heresy was advanced by those, such as the fourteenth-century Spanish monk Tomás Scotus, who believed in an eternal, uncreated world.[17] This view was expressed by a number of different writers in the sixteenth century, such as Giordano Bruno and Paracelsus, the latter of whom wrote that "some hidden countries have not been populated by Adam's children but through another creature, created like man outside of Adam's creation."[18] The Catholic Church stridently condemned polygenism, with the Spanish Jesuit Martín del Río writing in 1606 that "nothing can be more mad, more blasphemous, and more distant from the true faith," noting that, if Adam were not the father of all men, then the sacrifice of Christ, the "second Adam," would not have universal significance for man's salvation.[19] Despite such condemnations, polygenism developed as a clandestine intellectual current, and from the mid-seventeenth century into the modern era was most commonly associated with one notorious figure, the erudite libertine Isaac La Peyrère.

La Peyrère argued that Adam was not the first or only man created by God at the beginning of the world, but merely the first of his race, from whence the Jewish people were descended. Rather than a single moment of creation, La Peyrère thus imagined multiple creations of different groups of human beings in different regions of the globe. He offered his own exegesis of a New Testament passage, Romans 5:12–14, which declares that "sin was in the world before it was imputed," arguing that this suggested that human society was in existence prior to the "original sin" of Adam and Eve in the Garden of Eden. La Peyrère also drew upon the noncanonical, but widely shared belief in a "natural religion" of the patriarchs, which, he argued, was imparted directly by God to Adam, and served to govern the conduct of Adam's descendants until the next revelation of the divine law to Moses atop Mt. Sinai, and argued that St. Paul's assertion that "sin was not imputed before the Law" referred to this first law of Adam, rather than (as was generally accepted) to the law of Moses.[20]

Born in Bordeaux in 1596 to a Huguenot family of Portuguese Jewish origin, La Peyrère approached theological and historical issues with the purpose of bringing about the conversion of the Jews and the reconciliation of Catholics and Protestants, a prospect that he had already advocated in *Le Rappel des Juifs* (1643). Richard Popkin notes that La Peyrère insisted on the essential sameness of humanity, despite its diverse origins, and hoped that all the races would eventually become united in the body of Christ.[21] Similarly, David Livingstone describes La Peyrère's "pre-Adamite" theory as "fundamentally a theological project, universalistic in impulse and messianic in character," but also notes that it allowed the author "to reconcile the shortness of biblical chronology with the latest findings of geography, anthropology, and archeology."[22] In my view, La Peyrère's own work demonstrates that his "pre-Adamite" hypothesis derives less from his reading of what is, in fact, not really that ambiguous a biblical passage, than from his efforts to reconcile belief in the Genesis narrative of prehistory with the documented antiquity of other ancient peoples. La Peyrère observed that "the most ancient records of the Egyptians, Ethiopians, and Scythians" extended to ages prior to the Biblical Deluge, and that "those unknown countries, to which the Hollanders have sailed of late," do not appear in biblical accounts of the dispersal of peoples. He argued that Moses, in writing the Pentateuch, did not compose the history of all humanity, but the history of his own people, "as is usual amongst all Historiographers." As additional proof, he cited a favorite argument of skeptics of biblical literalism, the origins of Cain's wife, reasoning that "because Adam had as yet begotten no daughter, he must marry a wife of the daughters of the Gentiles, who was sprung from the men of the first creation." Similarly, La Peyrère argued that the Biblical Deluge had been only a local disaster affecting Palestine and Mesopotamia and asked how, if only eight people survived the Deluge (Noah, his sons Shem, Ham, and Japheth, and their wives), "could it be possible that in five generations...that they could inhabit China, America, the Southland, and Greenland, and whatsoever land lies betwixt them?"[23]

Despite the explosive potential of his theories, La Peyrère did not consider himself a heretic, and in fact argued that Jews and Gentiles, though biologically unrelated, could be united by "mystical adoption" and become brothers in Christ.[24] He later protested that he had written not to attack religion, but to strengthen it, and that he had hoped that his theories would contribute to the conversion of the Jews to Christianity. Nevertheless, La Peyrère's book, initially published anonymously in Holland, was almost immediately condemned by the Catholic Church, and La Peyrère was soon identified as its author. In February 1656, while he was traveling through the Austrian Netherlands in the retinue of his master, the prince de Condé, ecclesiastical officials ordered La Peyrère's arrest on charges of heresy. He was subsequently questioned by the grand vicar of the archbishop of Malines and by several other priests. The emperor Leopold, the secular ruler of the territory, declared that he had no authority over ecclesiastical courts, while La Peyrère's master, the prince de Condé, found himself torn between his obligation to protect his vassal and his duty to obey the dictates of the Church. Finally, with no other hope of rescue, La Peyrère decided to throw himself upon the mercy of the pope, renouncing his pre-Adamite theories and converting to Catholicism.[25] He thereafter published the *Lettre de la Peyrère a Philotime*, a recantation of his pre-Adamite theory and an account of his experience of arrest and imprisonment.

La Peyrère's frightening experience served as a cautionary tale to subsequent writers who might dare to question the literal truth of the Book of Genesis, forcing those who would advance polygenist arguments to do so very carefully. For example, when the baron de Lahontan, whom we have encountered as a creator of the "noble savage" trope, cited the apparent fact of racial difference as a means of discrediting the Genesis account of creation, he prudently distanced himself from the polygenist argument he presented, attributing it instead to "a Portuguese doctor, who had made several voyages to Angola, Brazil, and Goa." The doctor claims that the peoples of Asia, Africa, and the Americas must be descended from three different fathers, and goes on to cite their physical differences as proof. Americans, the doctor declares, "have neither body hair nor beards, their facial features, their color, and their customs are different," whereas Africans were "black and pug-nosed, with monstrous lips, flat faces, wooly heads, and with nature, customs, and temperament different from the Americans." Lahontan goes on to relate that the doctor "found it impossible that these two sorts of people could draw their origin from Adam, whom the doctor gave more or less the features of a Turk or a Persian."[26] Lahontan replies by invoking a climate-based theory of racial differentiation, and the exchange then turns into a debate over whether blacks and whites could change color by living in different environments. Responding to Lahontan's claims that the descendants of Africans taken to Europe "would produce children who in four or five generations would infallibly be as white as the oldest Europeans," the doctor responds that the rays of the sun in Europe, "more oblique and less burning" than in Africa, might cause Africans to lose their "luster," but would not change their skin color. The doctor then cites cases of Africans resident in Lisbon, and Portuguese on the Angolan coast who had maintained their original skin color over many generations. After this remarkable exchange, Lahontan concludes, in a very carefully worded denial, that "his principle is very false and very absurd, for it is not permitted to doubt, without a lack of faith, good sense and judgment, that Adam is the lone father of all men."[27] Not surprisingly, the *Mémoires de Trévoux* was not convinced by this half-hearted disavowal, and condemned the section in its entirety, declaring that "the declarations of his Portuguese doctor are...suited to weaken the belief that we should have in the books of the Old Testament."[28]

As Lahontan's example suggests, by the eighteenth century, the debates regarding Native Americans were increasingly superseded by the debate regarding the blackness of Africans, a reflection both of the growing centrality of plantation slavery to the Atlantic world economy and of the importance of neoclassical aesthetic criteria that associated blackness with ugliness and deformity. African identity was racialized to a much greater degree than was that of other exotic peoples; there was no analogous debate regarding the causes of the skin color of Asians or Native Americans. Within the Christian tradition, a long-held belief, which was perpetuated into the eighteenth century and beyond, held that the blackness of Africans was the visible manifestation of the curse of Ham, one of Noah's three sons, who had mocked his father's nudity. George Fredrickson observes that the curse of Ham "operated more on the level of popular belief and mythology rather than as formal ideology," noting that the biblical text places the curse upon Ham's son Canaan rather than on his brother Cush, who was generally considered the ancestor of black Africans.[29] The Book of Genesis contains multiple curses, however, and a variety of individuals and peoples who pass mysteriously in and out of the sacred narrative. The Jesuit journal *Mémoires de Trévoux* published a quite extraordinary exchange on this topic in 1733 and 1734, with an anonymously published "Mémoire sur l'origine des Nègres et des Américains" drawing a sharp rebuke from the journal's editor, Father René-Joseph Tournemine.[30]

The first essay, whose author has been identified as the French Jesuit Auguste Malfert, was written in an effort to refute the pre-Adamite thesis of Isaac La Peyrère, and to account for racial difference within the sacred narrative. Malfert claimed that black Africans were the descendants not of Ham but of Cain, and that black skin was the "mark" by which God had identified Cain "in order to distinguish him from others, to obligate him to flee, to wander toward other regions, and to establish a new people of another color than that of Adam."[31] Arguing that "all of the Negroes are descended from Cain," the author declared that "all of the children of Noah were white," and that "it is not the climate that has caused their blackness; if it were so, all of the peoples of America, from Mexico to Peru, would be as black as those of Africa." To account for the peoples of America, he identified another obscure Old Testament curse, that of Lamech, and wrote, "because his sin was greater than that of Cain, God demanded a greater satisfaction, not only punishing him with a third color and obligating him to flee...but he also deprived all of his race until the fifteenth century of the manifestation of our Savior, in the plenitude of time, to all the men of Asia, Europe, and Africa."[32]

After a brief digression on the topic of the crossing of races in the New World, Malfert then went on to argue that miscegenation was the unpardonable sin that had provoked God to unleash the Deluge. "God had punished the Negroes and the Americans by...different colors, so that they should not mix with one another," Malfert wrote. "But the sons of Seth transgressed this law; they abused the daughters of Cain and perhaps also those of Lamech...and they soiled the purity of their blood in uniting with them." Malfert went on to argue that this interpretation explained the enigmatic sixth chapter of Genesis, which speaks of prohibited unions between the "children of God" and the "daughters of men," and declared that "God was enraged by these monstrous marriages, by the mixing of different blood, which had no principle and object but lust, and to end this order, he decided upon the destruction of the guilty."[33] After the Deluge, Malfert suggested, the different races of man were separated, and their intermixing came to an end, at least until the modern era. The editor of the *Mémoires de Trévoux*, Father René-Joseph Tournemine, objected to this theory of racial difference, not because of its striking racism, but because it flirted with heresy by suggesting that Noah's family were not the only survivors of the Flood, and instead asserted the orthodox position that Africans were descended from Ham.[34]

While theologians continued to debate the curses of Cain, Ham, and Lamech into the eighteenth century, such arguments held little weight among the secular thinkers of the Enlightenment, who ridiculed such claims if they deigned to notice them at all. The abbé Prévost, editor of the multivolume *Histoire générale des voyages*, in 1747 dismissed the attribution of racial difference to the curse of Ham or Cain as a "chimera" without further explanation.[35] Nevertheless, religion and race remained intertwined for erudite libertines and anticlerical philosophes, who frequently cited the apparent "fact" of racial difference as evidence against the religious dogma of the unity of humankind and its common descent from Adam and Eve.

In the middle decades of the eighteenth century, the most prominent critic of the Genesis account of human origins was Voltaire. Although race was not the central analytical theme of any of Voltaire's works, he frequently invoked racial difference as evidence against the biblical narrative of creation, notably in a *Traité de métaphysique*, written in 1734 for Emilie du Châtelet but not published during his lifetime. In this treatise, Voltaire imagines himself as an extraterrestrial investigator who descends to earth "from Mars or Jupiter." Seeking to learn about humankind, Voltaire's alien observes men in Africa and Asia, and encounters "a man in a long black robe" who offers to instruct him. "'All of these men that you see,' he tells me, 'are born from the same father.'" The alien listens to the priest's teaching, but rejects his contention that all of the peoples of the earth are descended from Adam and Eve. Voltaire's imagined alien asks the priest "if a Negro and a Negress, with black wool and flattened noses, ever produce white children, with fair hair, pointed noses and blue eyes." Upon receiving a negative response, he concludes "that men are like trees, that pear trees, evergreens, oaks, and apricot trees do not come from the same tree, and that bearded whites, wooly Negroes, black-haired yellow men, and men without beards, do not come from the same man."[36] Voltaire returned to the same argument at various stages over the course of his career. Decades later, he began his *Philosophie de l'histoire* with a taxonomy of race, declaring, "Only a blind man can doubt that the whites, the Negroes, the albinos, the Hottentots, the Lapps, the Chinese, the Americans, are entirely different races."[37] Similarly, in the *Essai sur les moeurs*, he wrote, "The whites, blacks, red men, Lapps, Samoyeds, and Albinos clearly do not come from the same soil. The difference between all these species is as marked as that between a greyhound and a spaniel. It is therefore only a poorly instructed and stubborn Brahman who would pretend that all men descend from the Indian Adimo and his wife."[38] All of these passages, written over the course of 30 years, share the common theme of invoking racial difference in order to attack religious orthodoxy, in the final example going so far as to suggest that the Genesis narrative of creation was a simple copy of an older Indian myth.

The Climate Theory of Racial Difference

Religious and philosophical controversies played a determinant role in the ways in which opposing positions regarding racial difference were defined and defended in the seventeenth and early eighteenth centuries. Freethinkers, libertines, and religious nonconformists often cited racial difference as tangible evidence that disproved the historical veracity of Genesis, an argument that required the corollary contention that racial identity was fixed and invariable. By contrast, devout Christians, whether Catholic or Protestant, were obliged to defend the common descent of all humanity from Adam and Eve, and therefore were forced to argue that skin color and other physical characteristics, such as the texture of hair and the shape of facial features, were subject to change. The most commonly cited cause for such change in the early Enlightenment was the climate in which different peoples lived. Benjamin Isaac notes that this position had the added prestige of classical authority, for the idea that climate determined physical and moral character was first advanced in the treatise *Airs, Waters, Places*, composed in the fifth century BC and attributed to Hippocrates, and was subsequently endorsed in Aristotle's *Politics* and in Galen's medical commentaries. Isaac further argues that Montesquieu, the Enlightenment author most associated with climate theory, "elaborated and expanded, but did not really add anything to the ancient environmental theories."[39] Eighteenth-century thinkers who sought to reconcile science and religion found climate theory particularly useful, as Margaret Hodgen observes that the climate theory of racial difference "helped to keep the Negro and other darker-skinned peoples theoretically in the family of Adam, thus upholding their dignity as human beings."[40] Similarly, David Bindman has noted that "climatic theory was compatible with the Creation story, for it assumed that there was once an original unitary people that was forced by some kind of fall into a diaspora, spreading to the far corners of the earth." [41]

As of the late seventeenth century, there were very few nonwhites living in northern Europe, and many contemporaries still considered it an open question whether family lines could change skin color over multiple generations. The abbé Jean-Baptiste du Bos responded in the affirmative in his *Réflexions critiques sur la peinture et la poésie*, arguing that, although "the difference...is prodigious between a Negro and a Muscovite...this difference can only come from the difference in the air in the countries where the ancestors of the Negroes and Muscovites of today, all of whom descend from Adam, went to inhabit." Du Bos suggested that the forces of climate could have brought about the racial differentiation of humanity within the short timeline of biblical chronology, arguing that "ten centuries would have sufficed to make the descendants of the same father and mother as different as today are the Negro and the Swede." As proof of this proposition, du Bos cited the descendants of Portuguese colonists living on the west coast of Africa, who "no longer resemble the Portuguese born in the kingdom of Portugal," and suggested that "a colony of Negroes established in England would finally lose its natural color."[42]

The missionary-scholars of the Jesuit order were particularly prominent among the defenders of the unity of mankind and, consequently, of the climate-based theory of racial differentiation. For example, Charlevoix denied that Native Americans constituted a different race of men, writing that their "dirty and dark red color...is not natural to them," but rather resulted from "the frequent ointments they use" and from their exposure "to smoke in the winter, to the great heat of the sun in summer, and in all seasons to all the harshness of the air."[43] Charlevoix perceived skin color as a relatively minor factor, and attributed its variation to environmental causes, particularly the heat of the sun and the exposure of the skin to the elements. Consequently, he attributed the blackness of Africans to the heat of the Torrid Zone, and expressed doubts of travelers' reports of seeing black men in Greenland, writing, "One must admit that it would be a strange thing for black men to live so close to the Pole, and under a climate in which even the bears are white." Instead, he suggested that "the pygmies of the north of America seem to me to be the same race as the Lapps and the Samoyeds, and prove fairly well, I think, an easy passage from Europe to America by Greenland."[44]

David Bindman has observed that the climate theory of racial differentiation could be invoked both to assert the unity of all mankind and to affirm the superiority of white Europeans, born under a climate uniquely favorable to human development. According to this interpretation, he notes, those peoples "at the antipodes of north and south, Lapps and Africans, took on the most extreme characteristics; the former became nomadic hunters stunted by deprivation in extreme cold, the latter, scorched by the sun, were made lazy by the heat and the fecundity of nature." By contrast, the mild climate of Europe enabled "a balanced way of life that encouraged activity and allowed reflection, and therefore civilization."[45] For example, du Bos wrote that "men born in Europe, and along the coasts bordering Europe, have always been superior to other peoples in the arts, the sciences, and in civil government. Everywhere that Europeans have carried their arms, they have subjected the natives of the country." As evidence of this proposition, du Bos cited past conquests of Alexander and Caesar as well as the more recent Spanish conquest of the Americas, which, he claimed, "prove the superiority of the genius of our Europe."[46] This interpretation, which gave apparent scientific status both to the religious belief in a common origin of humanity and to the contemporary conceit of European superiority, was not new to the eighteenth century. On the contrary, Isaac notes that both the Greeks and Romans perceived themselves as inhabiting an "ideal land in the middle" between the vigorous but dimwitted barbarians of the north and the clever but weak peoples of the south and east.[47]

In the French Enlightenment, the climate theory of racial difference was most clearly articulated by Georges-Louis Leclerc, comte de Buffon, the dominant figure in the biological sciences in France for nearly half a century. A prosperous landowner who rose from the upper bourgeoisie to the nobility and a gifted writer with a talent for popularizing the new science to a general audience, he was also an accomplished naturalist and prolific scholar, whose *Histoire naturelle* ran to dozens of volumes and remained unfinished at the time of his death. His position as director of the Jardin du Roi and as a prominent member of the Académie des Sciences placed him at the center of academic life, and his theories were broadly influential in a wide variety of areas.

Bruce Baum writes that Buffon "was perhaps the first naturalist to use the 'race' concept in a systemic way in relation to the concept of 'species.' His species consisted of 'the constant succession and uninterrupted renewal' of the individuals that comprise it. That is, he defined a species in terms of biological reproduction that results in the succession of similar and fertile individuals across time. From here, he theorized racial variation within the human species."[48] In his essay "De l'Âne"(Of the Donkey) in the *Histoire naturelle,* Buffon distinguished cross-breeding between different species, such as the production of mules from the mating of a horse and a donkey, from the intermixing of varieties within the same species, writing, "If the black and the white could not reproduce together, if the product of their union remained infertile, if the mulatto were a true mule, there would be two distinct species . . . but this very supposition is disproven by facts, and since all humans can interact and breed together, they all come from the same origin and belong to the same family."[49] Because human beings of different skin colors are able to mate with one another and thereby to produce fertile offspring, Buffon concluded that all of humanity formed a single species, which therefore, he deduced, must share a common origin.

Buffon's essay, "Des variétés de l'homme," was a synthesis of several centuries of travel writing and missionary accounts. The essay takes readers on a rather rambling journey through the different parts of the world, beginning with the far north, then traveling southward through Asia, west to Africa and Europe, and on to the Americas, commenting on the appearance, customs, and oddities of an enormous variety of peoples. Buffon drew upon a wide range of sources; Michèle Duchet writes that he "is undoubtedly the man of his century who best knew and explored travel literature, for this knowledge was the very foundation of his work." She also notes the drawbacks of this approach, however, for as Buffon himself remained in France and crystallized his treatise out of secondhand observations, "the validity of his work is at the mercy of testimonies which he could neither neglect nor verify."[50] Buffon included some suspect information, such as the assertion, from a missionary chronicle of

1719, that on the Philippine island of Mindano, there was "a race of men...who have tails four or five inches long,"[51] though he did note that the various accounts of men with tails contradicted one another and could not be confirmed. Belief in such monstrous figures on the margins of humanity died hard. The Jesuit scholar Charlevoix was reluctant to dismiss accounts of monstrous races of headless men in the Americas, remarking, "Who can be sure of knowing all the caprices and all the mysteries of Nature?"[52] As late as 1785, when the Société de Médicine crafted a series of questions for the scientists accompanying La Pérouse on his voyage around the world to investigate, it included requests for more information regarding reports of hermaphrodites and breastfeeding men in the Americas.[53] The physician Rollin, who accompanied La Pérouse on his voyage, subsequently reported back that such peoples did not exist.[54]

Buffon's discussion of human variety is heavily inflected by classical Western aesthetics and notions of beauty. Buffon argued that peoples born under the same latitudes, at least within the Old World, shared similar characteristics. Those living between the twentieth and thirty-fifth parallel, from the East Indies through Arabia to North Africa, he described as "brown and bronzed, but handsome and well built." He noted that nearly all the Old World peoples who lived between the eighteenth parallel north and the eighteenth parallel south were black, remarking, "It appears that this portion of the globe was reserved by Nature to this race of men." By contrast, Buffon declared that those "who inhabit a more temperate climate...are the most beautiful, the whitest, and the best shaped in the world."[55] In this group, he included all of the peoples of Europe, those of the Caucasus (which he notes was famous for the beauty of its women), and the northern parts of India. He also commented on differences in stature and coloring between northern and southern Europe, and concluded that "color depends greatly on the climate, though one cannot, however, say that it depends entirely upon it." Arguing that diet, clothing, and shelter from the elements also affected the physical constitution of peoples, Buffon hypothesized, "If we suppose these two different peoples under the same climate, one can believe that the men of the savage nation will be more bronzed, uglier, smaller, and more wrinkled than those of the civilized nation." Buffon then concluded, "I recognize three causes which act together to produce the varieties that we observe in the different peoples of the earth. The first is the influence of climate; the second, which owes much to the first, is diet; the third, which perhaps depends even more on the first and the second, are customs."[56]

Despite these aesthetically inspired preferences for white Europeans over all others, Buffon's vision of humanity was not a system of rigidly fixed categories, but a spectrum whose nuances shaded imperceptibly into one another. He described the Hottentots of South Africa as "not true Negroes, but men who in the black race begin to approach the white, as the Moors of the white race begin to approach the black."[57] Buffon argued that "there are as many varieties in the black race as in that of whites," and distinguished between the "true" Negroes of the equatorial zone and the "Caffres" of the southern tip of the continent. He further remarked that in exploring Africa, "we will find all the nuances from brown to black, as we found among the white races all the nuances from brown to white," contrasting, as Adanson would also do, the Moors of the Sahara region to the "Negroes" from Senegal to the south.[58] Buffon took the existence of Caffres or Hottentots in South Africa as proof of his theory that "color depends principally on the climate," observing that while they "could only derive their origin from the black nations, they are nonetheless the whitest of the peoples of Africa, because they live in the coldest climate of this part of the world."[59]

As these examples suggest, the empirically minded Buffon remained skeptical of far-reaching systems of classification. Indeed, the root of his long-standing debate with the other great biologist of the century, the Swede Carl von Linné or Linnaeus, was his rejection of the Linnaean taxonomy as an artificial imposition upon the diversity of nature.[60] For this reason, although he described the multiple "varieties" of mankind, he did not classify them systematically into groups. Claude Blanckaert has noted that the nineteenth-century French physical anthropologists who lionized Buffon as the founder of their discipline could not agree on the number of "races" Buffon was believed to have identified.[61] On the contrary, Buffon insisted on the unity of the human race despite its phenotypical diversity, and recognized that, as one moved across the globe, the various nuances of color and characteristics faded imperceptibly one into another.

Buffon acknowledged that the peoples of America, who shared a similar skin color despite living in very different climates, might seem to contradict this theory, suggesting that one would expect to find blacks in the tropics and brown or white peoples in the colder regions. However, he argued, "If one pays attention to the migration of different peoples on the one hand, and on the other to the time it may take to blacken or to whiten a race, one will see that all this may be reconciled with the sentiments of the ancients."[62] Buffon argued that the New World was, literally, a new world, created and populated much later than the continents of the Old World, writing that "if one pays attention to the small numbers of men who have been found in the vast expanses of the lands of North America, and that none of these men were yet civilized, one cannot refuse to believe that all of these savage nations are but new tribes produced by a few individuals who have escaped from a more numerous people."[63] Buffon wrote that, with the exception of the Eskimos, who resembled the Lapps of the Old World, "All the rest of this vast part of the world contains men among whom there is almost no diversity, while in the old continent we have found a prodigious variety among different peoples." Arguing that Native American peoples either remained in the state of savagery or, in the case of the Aztecs and Incas, were only "newly civilized," Buffon concludes that "they have preserved the characteristics of their race without great variation, because they have all remained savages, they all live more or less the same way, their climate is not as varied in heat and cold as that of the old continent, and being newly established in their country, the causes that produce varieties have not acted for long enough to create notable effects."[64]

Buffon rejected the notion that the Native Americans were a different variety of men from those of the Old World, or that they were the product of a separate creation. He wrote, "With regard to their first origin, I do not doubt that, independent of theological reasons, it is the same as ours; the resemblance of the natives of North America to the Oriental Tartars leads one to suspect that they derive originally from these peoples." He noted that the Russians had recently discovered islands and lands beyond Kamchatka, and suspected that Asia and North America were close enough in the far north to make possible migration from the one to the other. "I am led to believe," Buffon concluded, "that the first men who came to America arrived on the lands to the northwest of California, that the excessive cold of this climate then obliged them to go to the more southern parts of their new home, where they first established themselves in Mexico and Peru, from which they subsequently dispersed to all the regions of North and South America."[65]

Buffon concluded his tour du monde with the argument, which we have already seen in the writings of du Bos and in his classical antecedents, that extremes of both hot and cold stunted human development, and that man could reach his greatest potential in the temperate zone. He wrote that "the most temperate climate is from the fortieth to the fiftieth degree; it is also in this zone that one finds the most beautiful and best-built men; it is in this climate that one should form an idea of the true natural color of man, it is there that one should take the model of the unity to which all the other nuances of color and beauty should be brought; the two extremes are equally distanced from the true and the beautiful."[66] Though he maintained that the peoples of the temperate zone represented the highest development of humanity, Buffon nonetheless affirmed the essential unity of mankind.

He concluded from his researches into the subject that "the human race is not composed of essentially different species, but rather that there was originally but a single species of man, which in multiplying and spreading across the surface of the earth, has experienced different changes from the influence of climate, different diets, different ways of life, through diseases, and also through mixture, varying to an infinite degree of more or less similar individuals."[67] These variations, transmitted from generation to generation, eventually created such great differences that some of his contemporaries could falsely claim that the different races were entirely different species of men. Nor had this process necessarily come to a halt in the present. On the contrary, Buffon argued, as civilization spread to the savage peoples of the world, "it is quite probable that [these differences] will disappear little by little, or even that they may become different from what they are today."[68]

Toward a Theory of Genetics

The scientist and mathematician Pierre Moreau de Maupertuis, whom we have already encountered in the previous chapter, was drawn to the topic of racial differentiation by the visit to Paris of an African albino child. This so-called *nègre blanc* (white Negro) became a momentary sensation, and was displayed before the members of the Académie des Sciences on January 8, 1744, where his appearance inspired debate as to the original color of man and the causes of racial difference. Maupertuis addressed this issue in his 1745 work, *La Vénus physique,* in which he described the "nègre blanc" as "a child of four or five, with all the traits of a Negro, and whose very white and blemished skin only increased his ugliness. His large and badly formed hands resembled more the paws of an animal."[69] What the child thought of Maupertuis is unknown.

It is worth recalling that, not only did the science of genetics not yet exist at the time that Maupertuis wrote, but even the basic principles of reproduction were still being debated among "spermists," "ovists," and "preformationists."[70] Despite this uncertainty, Maupertuis's discussion of reproduction came relatively close to discovering its principles, though his discussion expresses genuine insights with awkward terminology and mixes them with bizarre flights of fancy. He began by considering both sperm and egg theory in isolation, and arguing that each had some validity, but were insufficient to explain the variation of human traits. He further noted that while children generally resembled their parents, certain traits could skip generations, and concluded, "Nature contains the seed of all of these varieties, but chance or artistry places them in motion."[71] He followed this up with an insight that comes close to anticipating evolution through random variation, suggesting that new organisms were formed from an assemblage of a great number of "parts" contributed by their parents, and argued, "The parts analogous to the father and mother being the most numerous, and those with the greatest affinity, are those that unite ordinarily, and produce animals similar to those from which they are produced. Chance, or the lack of family traits sometimes produce other assemblages, and one can see black parents produce a white child, or maybe even a black child from white parents, though this last phenomenon must be much rarer than the other."[72] He also cited the random production of "monsters" or deformed organisms by the same process of variation, though noting that these were usually incapable of reproducing and soon disappeared.

After describing the racial extremes of Scandinavia and Africa, where he found "too much uniformity" of color, he declared that French women were the most beautiful in the world, stating that "it is on the banks of the Seine that one finds this happy variety."[73] In a flight of male fantasy that appears rather discordant in this scientific text, Maupertuis reflected, "Why do these blasé sultans, in their harems that enclose women of all known types, not devote themselves to the production of new varieties? If I were, like them, reduced to the single pleasure that could produce such forms and traits, I would soon have recourse to these varieties."[74] Fortunately, Maupertuis did not have the opportunity to pursue this Orientalist fantasy, though his biographer Mary Terrall notes that he was an avid pet breeder who meticulously recorded the outcomes of his experiments, including the transmission and reappearance of recessive traits.[75]

Even as his researches laid the groundwork for the subsequent development of genetics,[76] Maupertuis still attributed a significant role to environmental causality, remarking upon the fact that the Torrid Zone "is only inhabited by black or swarthy peoples," while the colder zones of northern Europe were inhabited by whites.[77] This observation, increasingly a commonplace in the eighteenth century, led him to hedge his bets somewhat, and to qualify his essentially hereditary argument with the possibility of environmental modification. "Furthermore," he wrote, "although I assume here that the foundation of all of these varieties is found in the seminal liquids themselves, I do not exclude the influence that climate and diet may have. It seems that the heat of the Torrid Zone is more apt to foment the parts that turn the skin black than those that turn it white. And I do not know to what point this influence of climate or diet can reach over the long course of centuries."[78] Philip Sloan has observed that Maupertuis's approach blends genetic and environmental causes by assuming the heritability of acquired traits, a theory that would subsequently become associated with Jean-Baptiste Lamarck, and notes Maupertuis's conclusion that "the gradual but cumulative influence of the environment, operating on the hereditary material transmitted from one generation to another, is a possible explanation of the origin of the races from a common historical root."[79]

Maupertuis endorsed theories of the mutability of species at least in part to defend the biblical doctrine of the common origin of mankind against polygenists like La Peyrère and Voltaire, writing, "This difficulty regarding the origin of the blacks, so contested, and which some people wish to place against the history of Genesis, which teaches us that all the peoples of the earth are descended from a single father and a single mother, is lifted if one accepts a system which is at least as probable as that which has been imagined up to now to explain reproduction."[80] Nevertheless, Maupertuis, like Buffon, took white Europeans as the norm from which other races had degenerated. The example of the *nègre blanc* led him to reflect, "From the sudden appearance of white children among black peoples, we may conclude that white is the original color of man, and that blackness is but a variety which has become hereditary over many centuries, but which has not entirely erased the white color which always tends to resurface."[81] Leaving aside the fact that albino Africans look nothing like white Europeans, as Maupertuis himself noted in describing the young "nègre blanc," the evidence Maupertuis cited could with at least as much plausibility be used to argue the (no doubt to him) distasteful theory that whiteness was a sort of mutation or degeneration from the original blackness of humanity. To his credit, however, Maupertuis did suggest that differences in skin color, however aesthetically unappealing he may have found them, were ultimately of trivial importance, writing, "It is quite probable that the difference between black and white, so apparent to our eyes, is of very little importance to Nature."[82]

Similarly, Buffon denied that the "nègre blanc" described by Maupertuis or the albinos observed by travelers in the East Indies and in Panama represented distinct races, noting that they were born of dark-skinned parents, and concluded instead "that these white men who are found at such great distance from one another are individuals who have degenerated from their race by some accidental cause." Buffon concurred with Maupertuis that the appearance of albinos among black or brown peoples was proof that white was "the original color of nature, which climate, diet, and custom can alter and change, even to yellow, brown, or black, and which reappears under certain circumstances, but with such alteration, that it no longer resembles the original white, but has been denatured by the causes which we have indicated."[83] The ethnocentric preconceptions of Buffon and Maupertuis thus led them to draw false conclusions that made white Europeans the normative standard for humanity, rather than but one of a great number of randomly produced variations on a common theme.

Enlightenment Debates over Racial Difference

The theory of climate determinism, despite the many factors that recommended it, not the least of which was its ability to reconcile science and religion, would ultimately collapse under the weight of its own internal contradictions. Although Buffon and the other scientific exponents of climate causality argued that racial changes would occur only very slowly, over the course of many centuries, the observable fact that white Europeans transported to the colonial tropics, or black Africans taken as slaves or free servants to Europe, did not change color over the course of several generations (absent intermixing across racial lines) served to discredit the climate explanation in the eyes of many contemporaries. Indeed, as we shall see in the following chapter, the colonial experience of hybridization inspired the creation of extensive taxonomies of intermediate racial types and the emergence of debates regarding the proper role and status of mixed-race individuals in the colonial French Caribbean. The excesses of some advocates for climate determinism also contributed to discrediting the theory, as they advanced arguments that were demonstrably false.

The abbé Demanet, who served in Senegal as a royal chaplain in the years following the Seven Years' War, devoted much of his *Nouvelle histoire de l'Afrique française* to elaborating an extreme environmentalist perspective on the source of the blackness of Africans, claiming that his eyewitness experience in the region gave him insights into "the origin and the true cause of a phenomenon that has long confounded scientists."[84] He began by noting that the equatorial Torrid Zone was, across all continents and oceans, inhabited by dark-skinned peoples, "some of which are absolutely black, others brown, others red, relative to the climates in which they live, which vary the color of peoples, proportionally to the reverberations of the sun, more vivid and ardent in one region than another." By contrast, he observed that "the farther one travels from the equator, the more the color of peoples lightens by degrees...it is in the extremities of this zone that one finds the whitest peoples, for the sun, the climate and the humidity make the least impressions on the skins of these peoples." This racial differentiation had led some observers to the heretical conclusion of polygenesis, for "the blond Dane astonishes the traveler by his whiteness, who cannot comprehend that the figure that he sees in the frozen lands of Denmark, and the African he has just seen in the Torrid Zone, are both men, and if he examines with exactitude the physical causes of these phenomena, he will soon say that this variety is the result of different influences, powerful for blackness in Africa, and powerful for whiteness in Denmark."[85]

Demanet then went on to reconcile this environmentalist account, which borrowed heavily from Buffon and Maupertuis (for example, he echoed the latter's conclusion that the appearance of albinos in Africa proved that white was the primeval color of humanity), with theological arguments drawn from the Book of Genesis. Demanet insisted that "it is certain that Adam and Eve, as well as their descendants, were white, and that all of the latter perished in the universal flood, except Noah, his three sons, and their respective wives, who were saved in the Ark. From Adam to the Deluge, no black people appeared on the face of the earth; the fact seems fairly certain, as otherwise the phenomenon would have been remarked upon by sacred and profane historians."[86] Demanet followed these assertions, for which he offered no supporting evidence, with several examples from ancient and modern history. The first, taken from sacred history, was the dispersion of peoples following the destruction of the Tower of Babel, after which the descendants of Ham, still white, settled in Africa, whereupon "the air, the climate, the reverberations of the rays of the sun turned them first bronze, then half-black, and after several generations, they were all more or less black." Demanet also claimed, as du Bos had done a half-century earlier, that the reverse transformation was also possible, asserting that "it is beyond doubt that the descendants of Negroes and Negresses in

Europe would recover their natural color, and become white. The fact is proven by experience."[87]

Demanet did not elaborate on which experiences proved his final point, but continued to discuss the more modern examples of Arabs and Portuguese settling in Africa in the seventh and fourteenth centuries, respectively. He claimed that the original Arab conquerors of the Maghreb had been white, but that "after several generations, they changed color, and became as black as the ancient inhabitants of Africa, and none of them conserved their original color under the Torrid Zone. Their language, their religion, their laws, and their customs transformed Africa, just as Africa transformed their color." He also, as Maupertuis had done before him, cited the Portuguese of Cape Verde as examples of Europeans who changed color in Africa, claiming that "after several generations, they saw themselves transformed, and as black as the natives of the country." He then joined to this account the authority of eyewitness testimony, declaring that he had in 1764 baptized the black, African-born children of Portuguese colonists, "so transformed that I could hardly distinguish them from Negroes."[88] Demanet did not discuss the biological process of reproduction, nor, apparently, did he consult the mothers of these "transformed" Portuguese children, which would perhaps have convinced him of the far more probable cause of their multigenerational transformation into black Africans. Like Maupertuis, however, he affirmed that skin color was of relatively little importance, declaring that "the nature of man has not changed, it is everywhere the same, and it will never change."[89]

Race figures prominently in the "dispute of the New World," which we briefly examined in chapter 3, but not in the ways in which a twenty-first-century reader might expect. Whereas we, conditioned by the development of scientific racism in the nineteenth century and beyond, would tend to associate racial prejudice with hereditarian arguments emphasizing the immutability of race, in this particular eighteenth-century debate, it was the archracist Cornelius de Pauw who endorsed environmental determinism, while the abbé Pernety, who sought to defend Native American peoples against de Pauw's vitriol, insisted that skin color was a matter of inheritance rather than climate-based acquisition. De Pauw cited Demanet's environmental determinist arguments approvingly in his *Recherches philosophiques sur les Américains*, and interrupted his diatribe against the alleged vices of Native Americans to discuss what he saw as the environmental causes of blackness. "There exist no Negroes," he wrote, "other than in the most excessively hot countries of the world."[90] He compared Demanet's observations regarding the "blackening" of the Portuguese in Africa over several generations to observations made by Arab and Jewish writers, particularly the twelfth-century Benjamin of Tudela on changes in color among the Sephardic communities of the Diaspora. Drawing conclusions that were at once antiblack and anti-Semitic, de Pauw declared, "If one takes notice that these bandits, unsociable because of fanaticism, never cross their debased race, and that they regard the mixture of foreign blood with their own as an abomination and a sacrilege, one cannot deny that the climate has blackened these expatriate Hebrews."[91]

Just as Buffon had done in the *Histoire naturelle*, de Pauw concluded that humanity would reach its full potential only in the temperate zone, which he called "the seat of [man's] power, of his greatness and of his glory." By contrast, de Pauw argued that, "beyond the polar circle...[man] becomes a stunted brute," while "under the equator, his skin is burned and darkened...the fires of the climate shorten the term of his days, and in augmenting the heat of his passions, they restrict the sphere of his soul; he loses the ability to govern himself and does not mature beyond childhood." De Pauw, however, drew much harsher conclusions from these observations than Buffon himself had done, declaring that "if one excludes the inhabitants of Europe, if one excludes four or five peoples of Asia, and a few small cantons of Africa, the remainder of the human race is only composed of individuals who resemble less men than savage beasts." He elaborated that "the Negroes burned in the Torrid Zone, and the Lapps frozen under the polar circle, have never written treatises of philosophy, and will never write them...one has never found in all the extent of the New World, despite the great diversity of climates, a man of ability superior to another."[92]

In his response to de Pauw, Pernety rejected environmental determination of race, and argued that skin color was instead a matter of heredity. Denying that the color of Native Americans was the result of the heat of the tropics, he cited the example of the peoples of frigid Patagonia, writing that "their natural color is bronzed, leaning toward a copper red...It is not an effect of the quality of the air that one breathes, but a particular affectation of the blood, for the descendants of the Spaniards who were established there and married with Europeans and conserved without mixture with the [indigenous] Chileans, are of a whiteness and a blood more beautiful and fresh than those of Europe, however born in Chile, nourished in more or less the same way, and commonly nursed by the natives of the country." Noting that this "bronzed" skin color was "common to all the inhabitants of the two extremes of the New World, and to those who live between the two tropics," Pernety concluded that "cold and heat therefore contribute nothing to it."[93]

As we have already had occasion to note, Voltaire insisted upon the separate origins of different "races" of humanity for primarily theological reasons, seeing racial difference as a powerful argument against the Genesis account of creation. Consequently, in an age in which his scientifically minded contemporaries, such as Buffon and Maupertuis, were becoming increasingly aware of the mutability of species, insights that would culminate in the Darwinian synthesis of the next century, Voltaire remained stubbornly attached to an older vision of a universe in which all species were fixed and invariable. Where Buffon, as we have seen, argued that all human beings were essentially similar, and were separated from the nonhuman primates by an ontological chasm, Voltaire suggested that the difference between whites and blacks was as great as that between the latter and the great apes, as the extraterrestrial narrator of his *Traité de métaphysique* declares, "I see men who appear superior to these Negroes, as these Negroes are to the apes, and as the apes are to oysters and to other animals of this sort."[94] Similarly, in the *Essai sur les moeurs*, Voltaire wrote of the African albinos described by Maupertuis that "nature has perhaps placed them below the Negroes and the Hottentots, and above the monkeys, as one of the degrees descending from man to the animals. Perhaps there have also been inferior intermediate species whose weakness has caused them to perish."[95]

Voltaire cited racial difference and alleged the inherent superiority of white Europeans to explain why the latter had successfully conquered the Americas and enslaved African peoples in the plantation colonies they created there. Voltaire argued that "the race of Negroes is a breed of men different from our own...They are native to that part of Africa, like the elephants and the monkeys...and believe themselves born in Guinea to be sold to whites and to serve them." He further argued that the differences in mental and moral character of different human varieties was as pronounced as their physical differences, declaring, "Nature has subordinated to this principle the different degrees of genius and the characters of nations which one rarely sees change. This is why the Negroes are the slaves of other men. They are purchased on the coasts of Africa like beasts, and the multitudes of these blacks, transported to our American colonies, serve a small number of Europeans. Experience has further taught what superiority these Europeans hold over the Americans who, easily defeated everywhere, have never dared to attempt a revolution, even when they were more than a thousand to one."[96] For Voltaire, racial differences were fixed and invariable, and the superiority of white Europeans over the darker inhabitants of Africa and the Americas was an unshakable law of history.

Some of Voltaire's contemporaries, however, took a contrary view. If Voltaire's emphasis on racial difference as fixed and hereditary may be said to constitute one pole of the spectrum of Enlightenment views on the topic, the other pole was occupied by those writers who argued that differences between nations and peoples were entirely the result of custom, and therefore eminently malleable. While such writers did not generally challenge the contention of the present superiority of Europe over non-European peoples, they differed from Voltaire in seeing these differences as entirely contingent, and subject to change.

Claude-Adrien Helvétius rejected the determinism of climate in favor of an evolutionary model of history, in which all peoples, regardless of where they live, must pass through a series of stages from barbarism to civilization, and rise and fall according to factors of culture, education, and good governance. Helvétius rejected the notion, shared by du Bos, Montesquieu, and Buffon, that the temperate climate of Europe made its inhabitants superior to those raised in extreme environments, writing, "The climate which would generate such a [superior] people is yet unknown. History does not show in any of them a constant superiority of spirit over the others; it proves on the contrary that from Delhi to Petersburg, all peoples have been successively stupid and enlightened."[97] An avowed materialist, Helvétius ignored the theologically inspired arguments that divided his compatriots between polygenesis and monogenesis. Accepting physical differences as a given without interrogating their origins, he nonetheless rejected the contention that these external differences between peoples implied differences in intellectual capacity, writing, "It would, however, be easy to perceive that the exterior difference that one notes, for example, in the physiognomy of a Chinese and a Swede can have no influence on their minds and that, if all of our ideas, as M. Locke has demonstrated, come to us through our senses, the northern peoples do not have a greater number of senses than the Orientals, so each of them consequently have, from their physical formation, equal dispositions of mind."[98] With a playful irony, Helvétius invoked one of the most stigmatized peoples of the globe to turn the tables on his fellow countrymen, writing, "The Hottentots do not wish to reason or think. 'Thinking,' they say, 'is the scourge of life.' How many Hottentots there are among us!"[99]

The philosopher and statesman Anne-Robert-Jacques Turgot rejected environmental determinism, writing that "I know that the opinion of the influence of climate on the spirit of man is very widespread. Nothing is more common than to hear the lively, volatile imagination of the Orientals juxtaposed to the weightiness of the peoples of the North. The abbé Dubos, who was given to building systems upon common prejudices and extending them to the strangest paradoxes, has adopted this idea without reserve." Turgot, however, rejected this interpretation, declaring, "The inhabitants of barbarous countries do not have less spirit than others for common affairs... There is between souls a real inequality, but it will be forever unknown to us, and can never be the object of our reasoning. All the rest is the result of education."[100] Turgot further elaborated that climate theory was "disproved by experience, for peoples are different under the same climate, and under climates very unlike one another, one often finds the same character and the same spirit."[101] Turgot's protégé, the marquis de Condorcet, would make this case even more stridently in the prerevolutionary debates regarding slavery in the colonial Caribbean, as we shall see in the following chapter.

Conclusions

There was not a single Enlightenment position on race, but rather a spectrum of opinion, with substantial disagreement over whether perceived racial differences were the result of climate-based causes, secondary factors such as customs, diet, dress, and exposure to the elements, or rather were inherent, inalterable characteristics passed down across the generations. Though most Enlightenment thinkers could be classified as racist by today's standards, there were significant disagreements among them, and Voltaire's gratuitously harsh assessments of Africans and other nonwhite peoples appear far more culpable than the environmentalist arguments of Buffon and his imitators. Marvin Harris has observed that "scientific racism remained a minority point of view until after the French Revolution. With a radical form of environmentalism as the guiding doctrine of the *philosophes*, permanent hereditary disabilities could not very well be conceived as the key to the understanding of history." Furthermore, Harris concludes, "the racism of the eighteenth century... remained a modest doctrine, circumscribed by environmentalism and plagued with doubts about the respective merits of the noble savages and their vice-ridden civilized conquerors."[102] While some Enlightenment theorists, such as Voltaire, argued that racial hierarchies were fixed and invariable, others, such as Helvétius, argued that they were entirely contingent, and that even the most degraded "races" could, through education, become the equals of white Europeans. Full-fledged scientific racism, though undoubtedly drawing upon Enlightenment ideas, debates, and texts, was a product of the nineteenth century.

If Paris-based philosophes encountered race as an abstract, purely intellectual issue, such was not the case for their counterparts across the Atlantic. Questions of race, hybridity, slavery, and assimilation took on much greater salience in the Caribbean colonies, particularly as these became ever more central to French economic prosperity and military strategy following the loss of Canada. The colonial sphere formed a crucible for the forging of new identities, new theories, and new political and social conflicts, and forced issues onto the metropolitan agenda. The following chapter will examine the expansion of slavery and colonialism in the eighteenth-century French Atlantic world, and the responses of writers, officials, and intellectuals on both sides of the Atlantic to the contradictions between enlightened philosophy and plantation slavery.

6

"An Indelible Stain": Slavery and the Colonial Enlightenment

Writing of the need to preserve strict legal segregation and white supremacy in the colonial Caribbean, the jurist Michel-René Hilliard d'Auberteuil declared that "self-interest and security demand that we burden the black race with such great scorn that whoever descends from it, down to the sixth generation, be covered by an indelible stain."[1] To the eyes of some contemporary critics, however, it is the French Enlightenment's own alleged indifference to the moral outrage of slavery that casts an "indelible stain" on its legacy. Louis Sala-Molins has declared that "the crucial test for the Enlightenment is the slave trade and slavery,"[2] while Michèle Duchet has denounced the "myth of the anti-colonialism of the philosophes," arguing that their halfhearted reformism merely "contributed to the maintenance of the established order."[3] On the other hand, Jean Ehrard has sought to defend the philosophes against charges of complicity in slavery, arguing instead that, while they did not have the power to free the slaves, their works made possible the rise of an antislavery movement in the final years of the Old Regime.[4]

This chapter will argue, by contrast, that neither sweeping condemnation nor an unqualified exoneration is appropriate, as there was no single Enlightenment response to the ethical dilemmas raised by plantation slavery. A fundamental divide separated the proslavery colonial Enlightenment from the majority of metropolitan *philosophes*. While there was a nearly universal consensus among the latter that slavery was a brutal institution that violated natural law by stripping man of his personal freedom, defenders of the colonial plantation complex, both in the Caribbean and in France itself, argued that slavery was a necessary evil, justified by economic utility and the demands of the harsh tropical climate. Contemporaries on both sides of the Atlantic worried that racial hybridization in the colonies threatened the biological and cultural integrity of the

French nation. They also debated whether the moral evil of slavery might be mitigated by the benefits it brought through the increase of national wealth and prosperity, the pleasant commodities that it provided to European consumers, and even the opportunity it offered to the slaves themselves to become civilized through contact with a more advanced culture. Finally, even the sharpest critics of slavery harbored doubts as to whether its immediate abolition was desirable or even possible, without provoking a conflagration that virtually all French observers hoped to avoid.

The French Atlantic World

French colonial involvement in the New World was marked by numerous false starts and reverses. The French monarchy took an early interest in the Americas; François I famously asked, regarding the papal Treaty of Tordesillas dividing the non-European world between Spain and Portugal, where in Adam's will the pope had been granted such authority. French efforts at establishing colonies in Brazil and Florida in the sixteenth century were thwarted by the Portuguese and Spanish, respectively, and while Jacques Cartier had explored the far northeastern coast of North America in the 1530s, no permanent French settlement was established there, although fishermen from France's Atlantic provinces traveled repeatedly to the cod fisheries of the Great Banks in the following decades. Samuel de Champlain finally established a permanent French colony at Quebec in 1608, but this languished for many years and was even abandoned from 1629 to 1632 following a devastating attack by the native population on the French interlopers. In the middle decades of the seventeenth century, the development of "New France" along the shores of the St. Lawrence River proceeded steadily, though the colony remained vulnerable to attacks from the Iroquois and their Dutch and English allies throughout the period of French rule.

In comparison with New France, the French colonial presence in the Caribbean developed more slowly and initially attracted less attention. The first Frenchmen and Englishmen to settle in the region were pirates attracted by the Spanish treasure fleets that sailed laden with gold and silver from the American mainland back to Europe. French corsairs and merchants established footholds on the "lesser Antilles" of Martinique, Guadeloupe, and several smaller islands, as well as the depopulated western shore of Hispaniola, which was to become the French colony of Saint-Domingue. The island colonies experienced a similar transformation from largely unregulated "frontier" societies of adventurers into more settled and stratified plantation societies producing tropical commodities such as tobacco, coffee, indigo, and above all sugar, with the smaller islands undergoing the shift after about 1660, and larger Saint-Domingue experiencing the same transformation in the first decades of the eighteenth century.

In the early years of the plantation colonies, the labor force consisted largely of white *engagés* or indentured servants. However, from the beginning, African slaves, already utilized as a labor force in the Spanish and Portuguese colonies, were also brought to cultivate the island plantations. The relative lack of white indentured labor (far fewer Frenchmen than Englishmen, Spaniards, or Portuguese emigrated to the Americas), and the drawbacks presented by its utilization soon led to a shift toward the use of African slave labor, which was authorized by Louis XIII in 1638. Thereafter, the black population of the French Caribbean colonies increased exponentially whereas their white population grew much more slowly, and the ratio of slaves to free colonists, roughly one to one in the seventeenth century, expanded to more than ten to one by the middle of the eighteenth.[5]

Important institutional changes took place during the same period. Under Louis XIV's reforming minister Jean-Baptiste Colbert, the formerly autonomous or proprietary colonies of the Caribbean were brought under the authority of a centrally chartered Compagnie des Indes Occidentales, and governors-general and intendants were named from Versailles to administer them. A special legal code, the Code Noir, was introduced in 1685 to regulate the status of African slaves in the colonies, and despite its harshness on many points, it included numerous clauses intended to protect the slaves from abusive treatment (which were generally ignored by the planters and unenforced by colonial authorities). Over the following decades, Philip Boucher observes, a "mature plantation system" took root, in which the immigration of white women redressed the previous gender imbalance of the colonies and allowed the reproduction of a Creole planter elite, massive importations of African slaves provided a readily exploitable and seemingly limitless supply of labor, and "poor white inhabitants, free blacks, and people of color, as well as the few island Caribs were slowly but inexorably pushed to the margins of society."[6]

As the plantation system matured over the early eighteenth century, the Caribbean colonies gained in economic importance within the French empire, and the triangle trade in tropical commodities, French-made goods required or desired by the colonists, and African slaves needed as plantation labor made the fortunes of Atlantic port cities such as Nantes, La Rochelle, and Bordeaux. When disaster struck, with the British defeat of French forces in Quebec and on the Atlantic in the Seven Years' War, France's long-standing presence in North America was irretrievably lost, and the Caribbean islands became not only the most lucrative, but virtually the only remaining overseas possessions of the French state (the exceptions, a series of small islands in the Atlantic and Indian Oceans and a few trading posts in India, could hardly compare with the splendor and wealth of the Antilles). While the smaller islands, particularly Martinique and Guadeloupe, remained important to France, it was Saint-Domingue, the "pearl of the Antilles," that received the lion's share of attention from the metropole, absorbed the greatest number of slaves and free immigrants, and made the greatest contribution to the national wealth.

John Garrigus has noted that the planter elite of Saint-Domingue remained largely beyond the control of the French state, and ignored the provisions of the Code Noir and the mercantilist restrictions prohibiting trade with the British, Dutch, and Spanish empires, writing, "Notorious for their independence and materialism, the colony's ex-freebooters would not accept Versailles' guidance as to how to drive and discipline their slaves...It was more profitable for many estates to export the maximum amount of sugar and import new Africans than it was to reduce working hours and provide good food so slaves would live longer."[7] Philip Boucher describes this period as an "era in which French would-be millionaires strove at any cost for quick riches," particularly through a plantation system characterized by the "massive, brutal, and wasteful importation of Africans."[8] Doris Garraway observes the consequences of this system, writing, "Nowhere in the colonial world were people so swiftly driven to death...It was a genocidal state of affairs maintained by an astounding rate of slave consumption."[9] As the plantation complex became more oppressive, however, it also grew more lucrative, and Caribbean planters and colonial merchants became increasingly influential in French affairs.

While the anomalous development of the Caribbean colonies troubled few Frenchmen in the early eighteenth century, the difference and distinctiveness of the tropical colonies became a topic of lively political and philosophical discourse at home and abroad in the period following the Seven Years' War, as the islands took on a greater role in French strategic calculations, a new wave of *petit-blanc* colonists arrived there to seek their fortunes, and the economic importance of the plantation colonies to French commerce increased.

Colonial governors and intendants sought to strengthen centralized rule and to build up military infrastructure in preparation for a coming war of revenge against Britain, and rejected the planters' claims to autonomy and immunity within their domains. The "patriot party" of white colonists sought to defend and expand the scope of local governing institutions, to resist the imposition of compulsory militia service and the excise taxes that financed island defense, and to assert the superiority and independence of white colonists as masters in their own house, resisting both the political ambitions of the upwardly mobile free people of color and the governmental efforts to intervene in plantation discipline and to come between the masters and their slaves. [10] Finally, a growing number of influential figures in metropolitan French society, ranging from jurists and civil administrators to philosophers and pamphleteers, took interest in colonial matters, and increasingly condemned the existence of plantation slavery as incompatible with a free civil society.

Enlightenment Condemnations of Slavery

Jean Ehrard credits Montesquieu with being the first French theorist to make a substantive argument against the institution of slavery, concluding that as a result of his work, "The struggle of ideas on behalf of the slaves could finally be engaged."[11] An extensive section of the *Esprit des Lois* is dedicated to the question of slavery. Montesquieu discusses the different forms of slavery (civil, domestic, and so forth) that have existed in the ancient and modern worlds, and also discusses the relation of the institution to climate and culture. In Book 15, Chapter 5, Montesquieu purports to list the arguments in favor of African slavery in the American colonies:

> If I had to defend the right we had of making Negroes slaves, here is what I would say:
> The peoples of Europe, having exterminated those of America, had to make slaves of those of Africa in order to use them to clear so much land.
> Sugar would be too expensive if the plant producing it were not cultivated by slaves.
> Those concerned are black from head to toe, and they have such flat noses that it is almost impossible to feel sorry for them.
> One cannot get into one's mind that God, who is a very wise being, should have put a soul, above all a good soul, in a body that was entirely black...

A proof that Negroes do not have common sense is that they make more of a glass necklace than of one of gold, which is of such great consequence among nations having a police. It is impossible for us to assume that these people are men because if we assumed that they were men one would begin to believe that we ourselves were not Christians.[12]

In just a few lines, Montesquieu summarizes and skewers many of the received ideas of the age, such as the links between culturally specific aesthetic qualities and the worth of individual human beings, the notion that economic utility could excuse immoral actions, and the intrinsic value of functionally useless luxury commodities such as gold. While Montesquieu's intent is clear to readers familiar with the use of irony and satire in Enlightenment discourse, this passage has, remarkably, been misread as a straightforward defense of racism and slavery, first by British colonists in colonial Jamaica and more recently by the Parisian daily *Le Monde*.[13]

Montesquieu was not the only philosopher of the age to condemn slavery as immoral. In a famous footnote to his extensive treatise *De l'esprit* (1758), Helvétius considered the amount of human misery required to produce one tropical commodity, sugar, and wrote:

Humanity, which demands the love of all men, wishes that, in the slave trade, I weigh equally the suffering and death of my compatriots and those of so many Africans, resulting from combat in the hope of taking prisoners and the desire to exchange them for our merchandise. If one estimates the number of men who perish in these wars, and also in the crossing from Africa to America, if one adds to these the number of Negroes who, arriving at their destination, become the victims of the caprice, greed, and arbitrary power of a master; if one joins to them the number of citizens who perish in fire, shipwreck, or scurvy; if finally one adds that of the sailors who die during their stay at Saint-Domingue, or from diseases resulting from the temperature of this climate, or as a result of a libertinage that is so dangerous in this country, one must conclude that not a single cube of sugar arrives in Europe which is not stained with human blood. What man, in the sight of the misery that results from the cultivation and export of this commodity, would refuse to go without it, and would not renounce a pleasure purchased with the tears and the death of so many unfortunates? Let us turn our gaze away from this tragic spectacle, which brings so much shame and horror to humanity.[14]

Michèle Duchet has criticized Helvétius, rather unfairly in my opinion, for drawing an equivalency between the suffering of African slaves and that of French sailors and workers implicated in the slave and sugar trades, and for his final sentence, which "displays a feeling of impotence before a system which demands so great a consumption of men."[15] It is not entirely clear, however, what she would have had him do; certainly neither Helvétius nor any of the other Enlightenment authors with whom we are concerned had the power to put an end to the horrors of slavery, and given the absence of other avenues through which to pursue political change under an absolute monarchy, Helvétius's suggestion of a boycott of sugar seems an appropriate first step. One may further note that drawing an equivalency between black and white deaths caused directly or indirectly by the production of sugar, however disproportionate such a comparison may seem to our eyes, was a radically egalitarian position to take in the context of the eighteenth century. Certainly Helvétius's declaration, which was, after all, merely a footnote in an extensive work devoted to an unrelated topic, had the effect of raising awareness of the relationship between the rise of consumer society in eighteenth-century Europe and the development of the plantation complex. Voltaire's *Candide*, published the following year, drew the same connection between the abuse of slaves and the consumption of sugar, as the mutilated slave whom Candide encounters in Surinam tells him, "This is the price paid for the sugar you eat in Europe."[16] The theme also surfaces in Louis-Sebastien Mercier's utopian novel *L'an 2440*, which will be discussed shortly.

Helvétius returned to the theme of the slave trade later in the same work, drawing a connection between the injustice of the slave trade and the absence of a recognized standard of justice between nations and peoples, writing that "the nations are, in relation to one another, precisely in the condition of the first men before they came together in society, when they knew no other rights but force and dexterity."[17] Helvétius's contemplation of the injustice of the slave trade led him to propose the expansion and collective enforcement of international law to guarantee the peace and autonomy of all peoples, a sweeping proposal, which in the context of the eighteenth century can only be considered utopian (and whose record in our own times is checkered at best). As this example demonstrates, slavery was so much a part of the early modern international system that its abolition would require fundamental changes to the political and economic order. We will confront this dilemma again later in the chapter with regard to the debate over abolition on the eve of the Revolution.

Jean-Jacques Rousseau was also a consistent and categorical oppo-
nent of slavery. His most famous work of political theory, *The Social
Contract*, begins with the famous line, "Man is born free, and everywhere he is in chains," and the first chapters of the work are dedicated to refuting justifications of slavery and subordination based
upon the right of conquest or the right of the strongest. He argued
that "to renounce one's liberty is to renounce one's quality as a
man," and that "it is a vain and contradictory convention to stipu-
late on one side an absolute authority, and on the other an unlimited
obedience." He further observed that, even if a man could somehow
renounce his own freedom, he would have no right to alienate the
natural liberty of his children and descendants. Rousseau concluded
that "the right of enslavement is null, not only because it is illegiti-
mate, but because it is absurd and meaningless. These words, *slave*
and *right*, are contradictory, they exclude one another."[18] Although
it is true, as Sue Peabody has argued, that Rousseau moves quickly
from civil to political slavery, and uses the institution primarily as
a symbol to critique despotic authority, his rejection of all forms of
involuntary servitude and his sweeping refutation of conventional
justifications for the enslavement of captives are no less significant,
and it would be impossible to take him for an apologist for slavery.[19]

Other Enlightenment figures, however, took a less categorical
stance. Voltaire's position on the issue is particularly difficult to pin-
point. As we have just observed, it is Candide's encounter with a
wretched slave who has been beaten and mutilated by his master
that finally leads him to renounce his tutor Pangloss's maxim that
"everything is for the best in the best of all possible worlds."[20] In the
Essai sur les moeurs, by contrast, Voltaire rationalized the institution
of slavery, writing, "We only purchase domestic slaves from among
the Negroes. We are reproached for this commerce, but a people that
traffics in its children is still more blameworthy than the purchaser.
This commerce demonstrates our superiority; he who gives himself
a master was born to have one."[21] This harsh assessment is qualified
in a footnote to the Kehl edition of Voltaire's complete works, probably inserted by Condorcet, which reads, "Certainly the petty Negro
king who sells his subjects, he who wages war to have prisoners to
sell, the father who sells his children, commit a horrible crime, but
these crimes are the work of Europeans, who inspired in the blacks
the desire to commit them. The Negroes are but the accomplices and
instruments of Europeans, the latter are the truly guilty."[22]

Perhaps the most famous Enlightenment denunciation of slavery
appears in Louis-Sebastien Mercier's utopian novel *L'an 2440,* which

will be discussed in greater detail in the next chapter. Mercier's narrator, an eighteenth-century Frenchman transported in a dream 700 years into the future, encounters a remarkable monument in the Paris of the future, declaring, "I saw upon a magnificent pedestal a [statue of a] Negro, his head bare, his arm raised, his eye proud, his attitude noble and imposing. Around him was the debris of twenty scepters. At his feet were the words, 'To the avenger of the New World!'"[23] His guide then recounts the story of these momentous events with a sort of bloodthirsty glee:

> Nature finally created this astonishing man, this immortal man, who was to deliver the world from the most atrocious, long, and insulting tyranny. His genius, his courage, his patience, his firmness, his righteous vengeance were rewarded: he broke the chains of his compatriots. So many slaves oppressed under the most hateful slavery seemed only to await his signal to become so many heroes. The torrent that breaks through its dikes, the lightning that strikes, has a less sudden and violent effect. In the same instant they shed the blood of their tyrants. Frenchmen, Spaniards, Englishmen, Dutchmen, Portuguese, all were the prey of iron, poison, and flame. The land of America avidly drank this blood which it had long awaited, and the bones of its ancestors, cowardly slaughtered, seemed to rise up and to skip for joy.[24]

Mercier went on to describe the "avenger" as "the exterminating angel to whom the God of justice had given his sword."[25] Diderot inserted an allusion to Mercier's "avenger of the New World" in the 1774 second edition of the *Histoire des deux Indes.* "Where is this great man," Diderot asked, "whom nature perhaps owes to the honor of the human race? Where is this new Spartacus, who will find no Crassus?" By the 1780 third edition, the direct classical reference to Spartacus had been dropped, but the prediction of a black avenger was more emphatic, as the question cited above was followed by the affirmation, "He will appear, let us not doubt it, he will rise up, he will hold high the sacred standard of liberty."[26] Given that Diderot, who died in 1784, could not have anticipated either the French or the Haitian revolutions, it seems anachronistic to read this passage as an incitement to revolt, but it does clearly indicate the aging philosophe's intense opposition to slavery and his impatience with half-hearted reformist measures.

Over the decades that separated *L'Esprit des lois* from the *Histoire des deux Indes*, plantation slavery in the Caribbean became a more lucrative business and a larger part of the French economy, and at the same time surfaced as a more central moral issue to the later generation of philosophes, notably the marquis de Condorcet, than it had been to their predecessors. We will return to consider Condorcet's opposition to slavery later in the chapter. First, however, we will consider the ways in which climate causality, which we have already observed in relation to the racial theory of the Enlightenment, was invoked in order to defend slavery as a "necessary evil" in the French Atlantic world.

Local Knowledge and the Colonial Enlightenment

If Montesquieu's opposition to slavery were discounted, his emphasis on climate determinism and his defense of customary law could be cited to argue that tropical colonies had to be judged by a different standard than the French metropole itself. Such was the position of the "colonial Enlightenment," in which planters, colonial officials, and their representatives sought to defend plantation slavery on rational and utilitarian grounds. Malick Ghachem has written that "Creole lawyers and publicists, relying on Montesquieu's notion of customary law, popularized an ideology of 'local knowledge' to criticize what they regarded as the high-handed application of metropolitan legal standards and practices to a Caribbean society based on radically different institutions."[27] Through this "adamantly selective" reading of Montesquieu, Ghachem argues that the defenders of slavery developed a "Creole parlementaire tradition" based upon a "veritable deification of what the colonists typically called 'local knowledge.'"[28] By emphasizing environmental determinism and the primacy of local traditions, the planters and their representatives sought to cordon off the colonies from the metropole, as separate societies requiring separate laws, between which the twain would never meet.

Hilliard d'Auberteuil, a French-born lawyer who became a spokesman for Creole interests in the period following the Seven Years' War, argued that "the difference that exists between the climate of Saint-Domingue...and the climate of interior [i.e. mainland] France...have made it clear for some time that the laws of the Metropole do not suffice for this colony."[29] Raynal, in his *Essai sur l'administration de Saint-Domingue* (a work which was heavily influenced, if not actually coauthored, by Pierre-Victor Malouet, a former colonial administrator in whose Toulon house Raynal resided while writing the *Essai*) concurred, noting that "the physical state of individuals in Saint-

Domingue influences more than is often thought the social system, the laws that are suited to [the colony], and imposes on the government at least the obligation to prevent, to moderate as much as possible the effects of these destructive causes."[30]

The defenders of slavery not only drew upon a notion of "local knowledge" derived from Montesquieu, but also cited climate-based physiological theories taken from Buffon's *Histoire naturelle*, discussed in the previous chapter. Raynal argued that, in the Americas, the European character "has degenerated in a visible way. All the Creoles, though accustomed to the climate from the cradle, are not as robust in labor or as strong in war as Europeans...Under this foreign sky, the spirit is as enervated as the body."[31] Many of Raynal's contemporaries echoed his assessment of the pernicious effects of the tropical climate on the health and vigor of European colonists. The aristocratic traveler Alexandre-Stanislas de Wimpffen reflected, "I had never better understood than I do here to what point the influence of climate can go. The sort of lassitude that excessive heat produces in the organs has the same empire over the mental faculties; one becomes as lazy in thinking as in acting, the least labor brings fatigue, the least intellectual dispute becomes an ordeal."[32] Justin Girod de Chantrans, a military engineer from Besançon who served in Saint-Domingue during the War of American Independence, wrote that in the Torrid Zone, nature "creates, perfects, and destroys in an instant," and that Europeans, accustomed to the *juste milieu* of the temperate zone and the "sweetness of its empire," can "only breathe in the American colonies by shortening their days."[33]

The high mortality of Europeans in tropical climates had become notorious by the late eighteenth century, and was frequently invoked as a justification for the enslavement of Africans, who, it was believed, were more accustomed to the intense heat of the tropics and better able to resist it. Raynal's *Histoire des deux Indes* observed that the birth rate was higher for blacks than for whites on the island of Martinique, and concluded that "the climate of America is much more favorable to the propagation of Africans than that of Europeans."[34] The shockingly high death rates for newly arrived African slaves (a third of whom died within three years of arrival, and whose working life expectancy Hilliard d'Auberteuil estimated at 15 years) do not seem to have shaken this belief, though they did contribute to a preference among planters for Creole rather than African-born laborers.[35]

The Kourou tragedy of the 1760s, in which thousands of French colonists sent to Guyana died of hunger and disease, convinced many French observers that white Europeans, born in the temperate

North, could not long survive as laborers in the tropical South. Malouet, who served as intendant of Guyana in the tragedy's aftermath, argued that slavery was essential in the Caribbean, and dismissed a proposal by the marquis de Condorcet to replace African slaves with free white colonists, writing, "This has been attempted in our time; I saw the lamentable remains of this enterprise in Guyana; I traveled the shores and deserted fields, where twelve thousand men and thirty million [livres] were buried in eighteen months." Malouet concluded that slavery was essential to the prosperity of colonies located "in a zone that does not permit any European to labor the earth."[36] Wimpffen similarly concluded that slavery was a "necessary evil," and underlined this assertion by declaring, "Your colonies, such as they are, could no longer exist without slavery, it is a truth horrible to say, but the failure to recognize it is a danger that could bring the most terrible consequences."[37] The opinion that slavery, however distasteful, was made necessary by the harsh climate of the tropics was often shared even by the purported opponents of the practice, as Raynal, describing the formation of British North America in the *Histoire des deux Indes,* faulted the drafters of Georgia's original charter for prohibiting the introduction of slavery into the colony. While he acknowledged that this error was born out of "a principle of humanity," Raynal remarked that the founders "did not foresee that colonists less favored by the metropole than their neighbors, placed upon a land more difficult to clear, under a hotter climate, would have less strength and ardor to undertake a task that demanded greater encouragement."[38] As white Europeans were unable to withstand the rigors of a torrid climate, a growing consensus maintained, the importation of African slaves became a practical necessity for the economic development of the tropical colonies.

Racial Hybridization and its Discontents

Historians of Saint-Domingue have concurred that the colony's social order, relatively fluid at the dawn of the eighteenth century, became increasingly racialized after the Seven Years' War.[39] A number of factors contributed to this development. Poor white settlers arrived from France hoping to make their fortunes, complicating the traditional correspondence of race and social status, as these new arrivals competed for land and status with upwardly mobile free colored residents who, as Stewart King has observed, were familiar with the colony's environment and connected to the planter elite by ties of patronage and kinship.[40] The failure of the socioeconomic hierarchy to correspond to normative expectations of race relations was a source of concern to many French observers, who saw in the uncertain status of free persons of color a source of potential disorder in colonial society. Writing of Hilliard d'Auberteuil, Gene Ogle has noted that the increased insistence upon racial identity after 1763 sought to engineer a new society by "reinforcing and rationalizing that visual economy" in which race and class would coincide in a clear and immutable hierarchy.[41]

As we saw in the previous chapter, the comte de Buffon presented a comprehensive description of racial "varieties" of humanity, which he attributed to the influence of climate. Buffon's portrait of Africans was generally negative, and differentiated between different ethnocultural groups primarily with regard to their benefits and drawbacks as slaves in the Americas. Citing Charlevoix's *Histoire de Saint-Domingue*, he observed that "the Senegalese are the fittest of all Negroes, the easiest to discipline and the most suited to domestic service," whereas "the Nagos are the most humane, the Mondongos the most cruel, the Mimes the most resolute, the most capricious, and the most subject to despair." He further cited Charlevoix that "the Creole Negroes, of whatever nation they originate, take from their fathers and mothers only the spirit of servitude and the color; they are more spiritual, more reasonable, more skillful, but also lazier and more libertine than those who come from Africa." Buffon further wrote that "though the Negroes have little wit, they nonetheless have a great deal of sentiment," and observed that they were happy and loyal if treated well, but melancholy and vengeful if abused, the sort of advice that one gentleman might give another regarding the treatment of a good horse or hound. At the same time, Buffon was sharply critical of greedy masters who abused their slaves, demanding, "How can men who retain some sentiment of humanity adopt these maxims, hold them as prejudice, and seek to legitimize by reason the excesses that the thirst for gold leads them to commit?"[42] Buffon's attitude toward Africans might be described as benign condescension; while he did not consider them the equals of white Europeans, he recognized their essential humanity and maintained that their owners had the obligation to treat them humanely.

Perhaps the most obsessive taxonomist of racial and cultural difference in the colonial Caribbean was Médéric-Louis-Élie Moreau de Saint-Méry, whose description of Saint-Domingue sought to define and describe the place of a wide variety of groups. He began his section on African slaves with a taxonomy based upon place of origin. This section was anything but a purely academic exercise, however, as Moreau de Saint-Méry's comments make clear his intentions of identifying the best laborers based on strength, docility, and general temperament. For example, he followed Adanson's assessment in finding the Wolof and Senegalese the most attractive of Africans, noting approvingly that they had comparatively elongated noses, "fairly similar to those of whites," and that they showed "the marks of a sort of superiority," as well as being "intelligent, good, and loyal." By contrast, Moreau de Saint-Méry described the Mandingoes as "rascals by habit," the Ibos as melancholy and prone to suicide, the Congolese as irretrievably libertine, and the Mondongues as having "the most hideous character" and being given to cannibalism.[43]

In addition to providing a taxonomy of different African ethnicities, Moreau de Saint-Méry argued for the superiority of American-born or "Creole" slaves over those born in Africa, writing that "Creole Negroes are born with physical and moral qualities that give them a real claim to superiority over those who are transported from Africa...here domesticity has improved the species...Accustomed, from their birth, to the things that proclaim the genius of man, their spirit is less obtuse than that of the African."[44] He also sought to codify a gradation of intermediate racial types, elaborating a dizzying taxonomy of 11 different categories (peoples of pure European or African descent, as well as nine intermediate categories based on their proportion of "white" or "black" blood). This highly graded taxonomy of types was combined with a "one-drop" rule that excluded all persons of African origin from holding any offices or honors. Moreau de Saint-Méry justified this exclusion, arguing that "a continuous line stretching to infinity separates the white race from all others," given that "the characteristics that had faded over two or three generations, surface and reveal the African origin."[45] Stewart King describes this taxonomic exercise as an effort "to create an invariable scheme of scientific genotypes," through which all members of colonial society would be kept in their place, and order and stability preserved. Similarly, William Max Nelson has recently argued that such discussions of racial mixing constituted a sort of protoeugenics, intended to impose order upon a notoriously libertine colonial society through state-orchestrated schemes of "large-scale selective breeding of humans."[46] While the religious sensibilities and limited resources of the eighteenth-century state made such dystopian schemes impractical, King and Nelson are surely correct that the defenders of the Caribbean plantation complex anticipated much of the "scientific racism" of the following centuries. (The degree to which these views may be considered representative of the Enlightenment as a whole is another matter entirely.)

Racial purity proved to be an elusive goal, however, as prosperous, fair-skinned persons of mixed race were often able to pass as white, especially in the first half of the eighteenth century.[47] Moreau de Saint-Méry conceded that skin color "is not always in the proportion that a purely arithmetical calculation would present" and that some persons of mixed race were so fair skinned that "one must have quite expert eyes to distinguish [them] from pure whites...only oral tradition or written evidence can serve as a guide in this respect."[48] Despite his insistence upon the "indelible stain" of African ancestry, even Hilliard d'Auberteuil recognized that "when the natural and organic character of the black race has completely disappeared, there is no longer a reason to maintain differences that are no longer real; there is a point beyond which one should no longer search, where it would become absolutely pointless."[49]

At the same time, however, race took on a multiplicity of meanings in the colonial context, encompassing more than just skin color. Debates over the status of free people of color also invoked issues such as legitimacy of birth and degrees of removal from slave status, and intermarriage across racial lines was criticized as *mésalliance,* a term used in France itself to refer to socially inappropriate marriages between nobles and commoners, or between any two people of unequal rank. In the final decade before the Revolution, the status of the fair-skinned, culturally assimilated, and economically prosperous *gens de couleur* became a topic for official debate, largely through the efforts of Julien Raimond, a wealthy mixed-race planter from southern Saint-Domingue who presented four petitions on the condition of the *gens de couleur* to the marshal de Castries, minister for the navy and colonies. Castries then invited the governor and intendant of the island to respond to Raimond's charges, and both sets of reports may be found in the French colonial archives.[50]

While the white colonists almost unanimously rejected any concessions to the *gens de couleur,* some French administrators in the Caribbean saw the latter as necessary allies, useful for the defense of the colony against both foreign enemies and rebellious or runaway slaves. The Comte d'Estaing, governor of Saint-Domingue immediately following the Seven Years' War, believed that the security and stability of the colony required increasing the ratio of free to slave inhabitants. To that end, he reduced manumission fees from 800 to 300 livres, proposed integrating white and free colored troops into single units, and suggested that all people of one-eighth African origin or less be legally recognized as white.[51] D'Estaing's contemporaries did not share his enthusiasm; white colonists condemned him as an "execrable tyrant," while his superior, the duc de Choiseul, called him a "dangerous fool."[52] Similarly, in the 1780s, the colonial administration of French Guyana, facing a dearth of white colonists, proposed relaxing the prohibitions against extending honors, commissions, and titles to the *gens de couleur* from the sixth generation removed from slavery to the fourth or fifth. This proposal, however, was vehemently rejected by the colony's legislative council, which insisted that it would lead to immorality, miscegenation, and to a shameful stigma upon the colony as a whole.[53] During times of peace and prosperity, the wealth and influence of the planter and merchant interests that benefitted from the Caribbean plantation system and the strict racial hierarchy that underpinned it were too powerful for reformers to overcome. In the age of revolution, of course, the balance of power would prove entirely different.

If many eighteenth-century observers argued that the climate, demographics, and particular traditions of the Caribbean colonies made slavery there a necessary evil, they were equally convinced that neither slavery nor slaves themselves should be admitted into mainland France, a concern eventually broadened to include the exclusion of free people of color as well. However, colonial issues began to spill over into mainland French society around mid-century, as Pierre Boulle notes, writing, "The fear of *métissage* and its supposed degenerative consequences became a commonplace among the French elite" during these years, a development which he attributes to the growing social and economic role of colonial planters and merchants in French society from the 1760s to the 1780s.[54] Diderot expressed these concerns over miscegenation in the *Histoire des deux Indes*. Even as he encouraged members of the colonial elite to retain their ties to the metropole, exhorting them, "Young Creoles, come to educate yourselves in Europe, practice there what we teach, and gather in the precious remains of our ancient manners that vigor which we have lost," he urged them, "Leave in America your Negroes, whose condition shocks our eyes, and whose blood perhaps is mingled in the leaven that alters, corrupts, and destroys our population."[55] Concerns about wealthy *gens de couleur* infiltrating the upper ranks of French society inspired the duc de Praslin, naval and colonial minister following the Seven Years' War, to issue an edict prohibiting the ennoblement of persons of mixed race on the grounds that it "would tend to destroy the difference which nature has placed between whites and blacks."[56]

The divergent paths along which the metropole and its colonies evolved over the course of the eighteenth century led to growing conflicts between the administrative and judicial powers of the French bureaucratic state, which culminated in a flurry of royal edicts issued in 1777 and 1778 in order to restrict and regulate the presence of slaves and free persons of color in mainland France itself. Sue Peabody has demonstrated that the French courts, and particularly the Parlement of Paris, were committed to a "freedom principle" according to which, as slavery was not tolerated in France, slaves who touched French soil became automatically free. Accordingly, there were not supposed to be any slaves in France itself, a legal dichotomy between the metropole and its colonies that grew ever-greater as slavery expanded in the colonial Caribbean. Royal edicts of 1716 and 1738 created exceptions to the general prohibition, which allowed colonists to take slaves to France to receive religious instruction or to learn a useful trade. These edicts, however, were never registered by the Parlement of Paris, which continued to insist that slavery was illegal in France itself. Around a hundred and fifty slaves filed petitions for freedom before the admiralty courts in the half century prior to the Revolution, with the greatest number of such lawsuits coming in the 1760s.[57] Both the Parlement of Paris and the admiralty courts under its jurisdiction consistently ruled in favor of slave plaintiffs, and following several high profile cases in the 1760s and 1770s, the minister for the navy and colonies, Antoine de Sartine, concluded that a new edict was necessary to reconcile the prohibition of slavery within France itself and the desires of colonists to preserve their property rights during visits to the metropole.

The edict of August 9, 1777, for the "police des Noirs" required all persons of color present in France, either slave or free, to be registered with the admiralty courts. Henceforth colonists were to be allowed to bring with them one slave to serve them on the voyage across the Atlantic, but were required to make a declaration and a deposit upon leaving the colony, and to consign their slave to one of eight "depots des Noirs" created for this purpose upon arrival in a French port, for return to the colony on the first available ship and at the owner's expense. Unlike its predecessors, this edict, which referred specifically to "blacks, mulattoes, and other persons of color" and did not mention slavery, was promptly registered by the Parlement of Paris and the other regional courts, and the system of depots, deposits, and registration cards was promptly put into effect, though not without a good deal of grumbling from officials in the colonies and the port cities who were to be charged with its implementation.

Port officials raised practical objections to the system of slave depots, protesting that "these prisons are so horrid that the very idea of confining the blacks there upon disembarkation offends humanity," and warning that slaves in the prisons could not be kept apart from hardened criminals who would corrupt them during their stay. [58] Colonial officials argued that exceptions should be made to the rules requiring slaves to be confined to the depots upon arrival, citing the examples of wet-nurses or nannies accompanying French women and children or caregivers accompanying those colonists whose health had been ruined by the tropical climate.[59] The ministry, by letter of May 16, 1778, approved the request to allow wet-nurses to accompany infants or pregnant women, but denied the request to allow sick colonists to keep more than one slave with them, noting that it could lead to abuses.[60] Fears over miscegenation also led to additional refinements to the August 9 edict, as the royal prosecutor Guillaume Poncet de la Grave warned of the dangers to French society posed by "bizarre marriages of black men and white women, or of white men and black women, a monstrous assemblage of the slave and the free, which procreates creatures which are neither the one nor the other." [61] A subsequent arrêt du conseil of April 5, 1778, prohibited intermarriage, observing that "it would be against good order to tolerate" it, and prohibited notaries from registering a marriage contract between persons of different races.

The edicts of 1777 and 1778 failed, however, to prevent either the passage of persons of color from the colonies to the metropole or the successful appeal to the French courts of those slaves who found themselves breathing the free air of France. Slaves continued to appeal to the admiralty courts for their freedom, and to have this freedom legally recognized by the jurists. A special legislative commission appointed by Sartine's successor as naval and colonial minister, the marshal de Castries, continued to debate the implications and interpretation of the 1777 edict several years after the fact, and failed to reach definitive conclusions regarding the status of those slaves who had not been properly registered under the terms of the edict, or who had been kept in France beyond the term designated for their repatriation to the colonies. One must therefore agree with Peabody's assertion that "the government was by its own standards not very successful in stemming either the flow of blacks to France or their acquisition of freedom once on French soil."[62] Around the same time that Sartine and his subordinates sought to cleanse France of African blood, the status of enslaved Africans in the French colonies became the topic of heated debate among metropolitan intellectuals, a debate to which we will now turn our attention.

Condorcet and Malouet on the Dilemmas of Emancipation

Even the most outspoken opponents of slavery in prerevolutionary France accepted the argument that slavery could not be immediately abolished without completely undermining the legal and economic foundations of colonial society. The marquis de Condorcet published one of the first abolitionist pamphlets to circulate in France, the *Réflexions sur l'esclavage des nègres* (1781). Adopting the persona of the Swiss pastor "Joachim Schwartz," Condorcet wrote, "I am neither a clever Parisian wit, with pretentions to the Académie Française [to which Condorcet would in fact be admitted the following year], nor an English politician, who writes pamphlets in the hopes of being elected to the House of Commons, in order to sell himself to the court at the first change of ministries. I am just a good man, who likes to speak frankly to the universe, even if the universe does not hear him."[63] Calling slavery "a crime worse than robbery," he denied that any self-interest or excuse could justify it, and blamed the European merchants who purchased slaves on the African coast rather than the local middlemen who sold them, writing, "It is the infamous commerce of the brigands of Europe that generates almost perpetual wars among the Africans, the sole motive of which is the desire to take prisoners for sale."[64]

Condorcet condemned slavery as a moral outrage that could not be justified by economic self-interest or the allegedly inferior nature of Africans, and proposed replacing slavery with free labor in the tropical colonies. Even if it were true that only Africans could endure hard labor under the tropical sun, Condorcet wrote, "the prosperity of commerce, the national wealth cannot be placed in balance against justice...The interest of the power and riches of a nation must disappear before the rights of a single man; otherwise there is no longer a difference between a regulated society and a band of thieves." Rejecting the climate determinism of Montesquieu, Buffon, and Raynal, Condorcet argued, "It is not to the climate, nor the soil, nor the physical constitution, nor the national spirit that one should attribute the laziness of certain people; it is to the bad laws that govern them." Specifically he blamed the indolence of the Creoles on their "excess of [intercourse with] Negresses and strong liquors," and called for land reform, writing that "if the islands, instead of

being divided into great estates, were divided into small proper-
ties...among the families of cultivators, it is at least very probable
that there would soon arise in these countries a race of men truly
capable of work."[65]
At the same time, however, Condorcet believed that a long tran-
sitional period was necessary to educate former slaves for their new
lives as free men, and accepted arguments that sudden and comprehensive emancipation would fatally disrupt the social and economic
order of the colony. He speculated that slaves, "by their education,
by the stupefying effects of slavery, by the corruption of their manners," might be "incapable of fulfilling the functions of free men,"
and further observed that, as the housing, clothing, and petty property of slaves belonged to their masters, freeing them immediately
would leave them in destitution. Condorcet was further concerned
about the possible impact of sudden emancipation on public order,
arguing, "As one may fear that the Negroes, accustomed to obeying
only force and caprice, could not be contained, in the first instance,
by the same laws as the whites, that they might form bands and dedicate themselves to theft, to private vengeance, and to a vagabond
life in the forests and mountains...it would be necessary to subject
the Negroes in the first times to a strict discipline, regulated by the
laws."[66] Condorcet wrote that "one cannot hide the fact that the
Negroes have in general a great stupidity, but it is not them whom
we should blame, but their masters...The sentiments natural to man
were either never born in their souls, or were smothered by oppression." He further warned that "a general emancipation would demand
expenditures and preparations...such a revolution must be the effect
of the personal will of the sovereign, supported by public opinion or
by that of a legislative body constant in spirit."[67] Condorcet, like some
latter-day historians of slavery, thus concluded that the conditions of
slaves' existence stunted their moral and intellectual development,
making them unfit, at least without long preparation, for lives as
free men. He therefore presented an elaborate blueprint under which
slave children as yet unborn would be freed upon reaching adulthood, under which, by his calculations, slavery would cease to exist
in approximately 70 years. Like the ancient Israelites, condemned to
wander for decades in the desert, the Afro-Caribbean population of
the French empire would persist for many years in limbo, until those
children whose nature had not been stunted by slavery came of age,
and finally entered the promised land of freedom.
    In the meantime, Condorcet proposed a series of humanitarian
reforms for the education and treatment of slaves, and suggested

the creation of an inspection team of medical doctors to ensure that the new laws were respected, writing, "It is only among this profession that one may find humanity, justice, and moral principles in the colonies." Under such conditions, Condorcet reassured himself, "they would no longer truly be slaves, but simply domestics engaged for a fixed term." This gradualist approach would "give the colonists the time to change gradually their method of cultivation, to obtain the means to work their lands by whites or by free blacks, and to the government, that of changing the system of police and legislation for the colonies." Over the long course of time, the unjust distinctions of the barbaric past would simply fade away, as Condorcet wrote, "After several generations, in truth, the blacks will be absolutely merged with the whites, and there will be no difference between them but their color. The mixing of races would later cause, over the long term, even this last difference to disappear."[68]

Nor was Condorcet alone in envisioning a gradual path toward emancipation. A decade earlier, the *Histoire des deux Indes* had recommended an evolutionary transition toward the production of tropical commodities by free black farmers, advising the colonists, "In giving these unfortunates their liberty, but gradually, as a reward for their economy, their conduct, their labor, take care to submit them to your laws and customs...give them a fatherland, interests to defend, productions to cultivate, consumption suited to their tastes, and your colonies will not lack manpower."[69] The Baron de Bessner made a similar, but more specific proposal with regard to the still largely undeveloped colony of French Guyana, suggesting in a memorandum to the Naval Ministry that France recruit runaway slaves from neighboring Dutch Surinam to form a population of free black cultivators.[70]

If the reform proposals of Condorcet and Bessner appear excessively timid to our eyes, their own contemporaries considered them dangerously radical and subversive to French authority in the tropical colonies. The most acerbic and persistent critic of these schemes was the colonial administrator and plantation owner Pierre-Victor Malouet, who was also a friend and close associate of Raynal, even hosting the aging abbé upon the latter's return from exile to Toulon. Malouet chose to revise and publish his *Mémoire sur l'esclavage des nègres*, written a decade earlier for the Naval Ministry, to respond to Condorcet's project for gradual emancipation.[71] Malouet cited Locke's *Treatise on Civil Government* to support the right to enslave captives taken in war, and added:

It is true that he makes this right dependent on a just and legitimate war, but how am I to judge fairly the motives that led the king of Congo to make war on his neighbors? It suffices for me to know that the prisoners of war are on the market, and that I have the obligation and the intention to treat them infinitely better than they would be treated by their victor. I may buy without scruple, as I have no other means to labor my lands, to pay my debts, to assure my subsistence and that of my family, my destiny having placed me, myself and my patrimony, in a zone that does not permit any European to labor the earth.[72]

Malouet denied that it was his intention to justify slavery on moral grounds, writing, "May God forbid that I should here attempt to consecrate slavery and to reduce it to principles! It is, it will always be a violation of the natural law to the one who knows and respects it." He declared, however, that suppressing the slave trade would bring more harm to the French than benefit to the Africans, arguing that if France were to suppress the trade unilaterally, other nations would simply take its place. "There would therefore be the same sum of slaves on the globe," he concluded. "Humanity would gain nothing from it."[73] Malouet also argued that slaves were in some respects better off than the poorest classes of Europeans, writing that "none of these Negroes, whom you consider so miserable, lack the necessities, while indigent day laborers, whom you do not pity, wander the streets and roads, vainly trying to excite our commiseration," and further contrasted the two conditions, writing, "In Europe, if a peasant steals from you, or a poacher hunts on your lands, the first is hanged, and the second sent to the galleys. In America, the Negro who steals from me is acquitted by several strokes of the whip, and he benefits, just as I do, from hunting and fishing on my lands."[74]

Malouet denounced Condorcet's humanitarian proposals as unworkable and misguided. He warned of the dangers of allowing "so long a term to the frustration of masters and the impatience of slaves, to all the disorders resulting from a condemned and hateful, yet tolerated regime," observing that the philosopher's vision of a smooth and gradual transition from slavery to freedom was hopelessly optimistic. He also ridiculed the proposal for this process to be overseen by a team of enlightened doctors and medical inspectors, and remarked that "the despotism of physicians would be as dangerous as any other."[75] He further denied that freed slaves could be assimilated, holding that a colony of free black cultivators would soon break away from French rule, noting that former slaves would be "a foreign society in our midst, which no moral or political considerations, no interest could bring into labor or commercial relations with the colonists." He argued that, if France required additional citizens and laborers, "Let us choose them preferably among those foreign societies whose race, manners, and beliefs are the most analogous to our own. Let us incorporate Spaniards, Turks, Persians, rather than Negroes. The latter are not, and can never become part of our society." Malouet thereby invoked the specter of miscegenation and national decline, should Condorcet's ideas regarding the assimilation of black freedmen into French society be allowed, declaring, "It is to the ignominy attached to an alliance with a black slave that our nation owes its legitimate descent. If this prejudice is destroyed, if the black man is assimilated to the whites among us, it is more than likely that we will regularly see mulatto noblemen, financiers, businessmen, whose wealth will soon procure them [white] wives and mothers from all orders of the state. This is how individuals, families, and nations are altered, degraded, and dissolved."[76]

If an unbridgeable chasm separated black Africans and white Europeans, Malouet nonetheless maintained that slavery could play a civilizing function with regard to the former, who, he claimed, "are brought closer to the condition of reasonable men by becoming our laborers than in remaining in their own lands, subject to all the excesses of brigandage and ferocity."[77] Malouet declared:

> Doubtless it would be a fine thing only to seek out these stupid and ferocious men in order to educate them in their rights, in their interests, and to return them to nature freer and happier. But as philosophy and humanity have never ordered such a mission...they may pardon us for taking from the altar of despotism the most absurd of its victims to convert them into laborers. The European merchant on the coast of Africa did not create servitude and is unable to destroy it; he simply purchases from a barbarous society the members who compose it, and who sell one another...and he delivers them in exchange for money to the American colonist who employs them in the cultivation of the land and who, along with the right and power to make them happy, contracts at least the obligation to treat them well.[78]

Finally, Malouet defended the continuation of slavery on the grounds of economic interest, observing that colonial products such as sugar and coffee were sold to neighboring European markets, increasing France's national revenue. In contrast to the market-oriented

Physiocrats, Malouet defended the mercantilist system of the French empire, observing that it reserved colonial markets for French goods, while requiring the colonies to sell all of their harvests, in the first instance, to the French market or to French merchant interests. Malouet argued, "If we lose our sugar islands, the result will be an enormous subtraction of national revenue," and concluded, "The colonies are thus useful, it matters to preserve them."[79]

Interestingly, both Condorcet and Malouet appealed to the experience of Turgot, the most prominent exemplar of a *philosophe* in power in the late Old Regime. Condorcet celebrated his mentor as "the only man perhaps who could say that his existence was necessary to humanity," and wrote that "never was a man possessed of a broader, deeper, and more just spirit; a purer, gentler, and braver soul."[80] Malouet, by contrast, cited Turgot's rapid downfall and the failure of his attempted free market reforms (Turgot's temporary deregulation of the grain trade had led to soaring prices and bread riots across France in 1775), as an example of the dangers of legislating from abstract philosophical principles. Malouet wrote, "If the most ardent promoters of the emancipation of the Negroes found themselves at the head of the government, they would soon recognize, like M. Turgot, the danger and the impossibility of making legislative acts all of the movements of benevolence that contradict great political interests."[81]

Malouet's arguments were echoed by other colonial defenders of slavery, such as the colonial jurists Hilliard d'Auberteuil and Moreau de Saint-Méry. Hilliard d'Auberteuil denounced philosophical humanitarianism as hypocritical, remarking, "The philosophers whisper of it, and yet they participate in this iniquity, for they have not yet retired into the deserts; do they have the right to reproach us an evil which we found already in effect? If their writings condemn its emergence and expansion, their indolence approves it." He offered a frankly utilitarian justification of slavery, writing, "I will not stop to consider if this property is legitimate; it is at least useful, and if they are treated humanely their slavery will not be unhappy. They have been pulled out of ignorance and laziness to be applied to useful works."[82] Similarly, Moreau de Saint-Méry mused upon the question of "whether the abolition of slavery in the colonies is necessary, useful, or even possible," and concluded that "it would have been better if this cause, touching as it is, had not been raised...that the recognition of the impossibility of ending slavery had given rise to efforts to soften it, to end its rigors through means that would have been supported even by the interests of the masters."[83]

As this last statement demonstrates, there was a curious convergence between the metropolitan and the colonial Enlightenments that focused on the reform of slavery in the here and now, whether this was seen as a first step toward emancipation or as a bulwark to preserve the plantation system. Jean Ehrard notes that in the final years of the Old Regime, "the idea of a humanized slavery seduced many enlightened spirits, even at Saint-Domingue...To their minds it would be an acceptable compromise between the needs of the colonial economy, so essential to the metropolitan economy, and the protests of conscience."[84] In retrospect, one cannot help feeling frustration with the naïve belief of the Enlightenment reformers that so great an injustice as slavery could ever be "humanized," and with their equally naïve self-confidence in the ability of governments and administrators to engineer a smooth transition from slavery to freedom over the course of many decades, in societies rife with social tensions and irreducible economic conflicts of interest thousands of miles away from the seat of French power and authority. But while we can and should deplore their naiveté and blindness to socioeconomic realities, we should also acknowledge the benevolence of their intentions and their inability to overcome the entrenched colonial interests defending the perpetuation of the plantation complex.

Slavery and the Value of Free Labor

In addition to the moral argument against slavery, which would be presented most forcefully by Condorcet and by the Amis des Noirs in the final years of the Old Regime, some critics of the institution made an economic argument against the practice, declaring that free labor would prove more productive than enslaved labor, as the free farmer had an incentive to work harder in order to maximize his revenue. Such arguments, typical of the Physiocratic school, challenged the institution of slavery by disputing the contention of its apologists that certain tropical commodities could only be produced by African slaves. The Physiocratic economic theorist Pierre-Samuel Dupont de Nemours calculated the costs and benefits of slavery in a series of articles appearing from 1770 to 1772 in the *Ephémerides du citoyen*, and concluded that, when one considered the cost of purchasing, maintaining, and guarding slaves and the losses produced by revolts and runaways, slavery was a less profitable economic system than was free labor.[85] Dupont de Nemours shared the view of his contemporary Adam Smith that it was self-interest that, by compelling men to labor, produced in the aggregate the economic growth of societies, and concluded, "Slaves have no motive to perform the tasks to which they are bound with the intelligence and care that could ensure their success; therefore it follows that these labors produce very little."[86] Dupont de Nemours remained consistent in this position despite the dramatic changes of the age, and a quarter-century later, under the Directory, he presented to the Institut de France a proposal to establish colonies in West Africa to cultivate sugar with free African labor.[87]

The Physiocrat and colonial administrator Pierre Poivre's relationship to the institution of slavery was a complex one. As intendant of the Isle de France, he was responsible for the island's finances and economic development. In that capacity, he lamented the persistent lack of the necessary labor that would allow the colony to flourish and achieve its full potential, and he sought to increase the supply of slaves from Madagascar and Mozambique to the island. His correspondence with French officials during his term as intendant included laments on the scarcity of slaves and requests for the trade goods that were necessary to obtain them.[88] Though his administrative correspondence was sharply critical of abuses in the slave trade, particularly the illegal importation of slaves without paying the required customs duties, it did not go so far as to criticize the institution of slavery itself.

By contrast, Poivre's main philosophical work, the *Voyages d'un philosophe*, written prior to his service as chief financial officer of a troubled colony, condemned slavery in no uncertain terms. Though not insensitive to the moral case against slavery, Poivre argued primarily on the grounds of political economy, asserting, as Dupont would also do, that the self-interest and ambition of free farmers led them to be more productive and therefore more valuable to the state than degraded, enslaved labor. Recounting his voyage to Cochinchina (present-day Vietnam), Poivre observed that sugarcane, cultivated by African slaves in the Caribbean, was in Southeast Asia raised and harvested by free peasants. Poivre wrote, "After what I have seen in Cochinchina, I cannot doubt that free cultivators, among whom one could have divided without restrictions the lands of America, would not have produced double the product that is drawn from the slaves." Poivre then asked, "What, then, has civilized Europe gained, this Europe so enlightened as to the rights of humanity, in authorizing by its decrees the daily outrages committed against human nature in our colonies, allowing itself there to so vilify men, as to regard them exclusively as beasts of burden?" Poivre concluded that free labor was not only morally superior to slavery, but economically more efficient as well, declaring, "The earth which bestows its bounty with a sort of prodigality upon free cultivators, appears to dry itself out by the very sweat of slaves. Such was the wish of the author of nature, who created men free, and who bestowed the earth upon them with the order that each man cultivate his possession by the sweat of his brow, but in freedom."[89]

Condorcet made a similar point in his *Réflexions sur l'esclavage des nègres*, which we have considered above. He cited the example given by Poivre of the cultivation of sugarcane in Asia by free peasants, and even suggested that if plantation slavery were replaced by a network of free farmers, the market, rather than a greedy planter oligarchy, would set the price of sugar and coffee. He concluded, "The destruction of slavery would ruin neither colonies nor commerce; it would make the colonies more flourishing, it would increase the volume of commerce. It would do no harm but to prevent a few barbaric men from growing fat off of the sweat and blood of their brothers."[90]

The superiority of free over slave labor is also asserted in Louis-Sebastien Mercier's futuristic novel *L'an 2440*, which as we have seen provided the French Enlightenment's most radical rejection of an Atlantic world colonial system based on plantation slavery. Mercier was not, however, categorically opposed to a different sort of colonialism, which would bring progress and mutual prosperity through the expansion of global commerce. In the course of his imaginary journey to the twenty-fifth century, Mercier's narrator learns that, although the slave trade and the plantation colonies that it supplied have been destroyed, European consumers may still indulge their sweet tooth, as sugar is now produced in Africa itself by free farmers for export, as the Physiocratic reformers Dupont and Poivre had advocated.[91] Mercier's narrator is told, "Alas! So much effort, expense, and cruelty are not necessary in order to have sugar. It suffices not to degrade the men whom Nature placed alongside the sugar cane, in their country of origin... for the earth is miserly only toward tyrants and slaves."[92]

Conclusions

The glaring contradictions between the philanthropic ideals of the Enlightenment and the utilitarian defense of slavery offered by many eighteenth-century French writers were no less apparent to contemporaries than they are to twenty-first century readers. Girod de Chantrans bitterly lamented the divide between idealism and practice, writing that "the constant harshness demanded by the disciplining of slaves, and the thirst for gold, far more ardent in America than in Europe, are enemies too powerful for weak humanity to resist."[93] The *Histoire des deux Indes* called justifications of slavery "sophisms... to ease the cries of conscience," and concluded that "the majority of men are not born wicked, and do not wish to do harm, but even among those whom nature seems to have formed good and just, there are few who have sufficient integrity, courage, and greatness of spirit to do good at the cost of some sacrifice."[94] Plantation slavery in the Caribbean played a central role to the eighteenth-century global economy, and the island colonies figured prominently in projects for French imperial renewal following the disaster of the Seven Years' War. Given the strong economic and strategic arguments in favor of the tropical colonies, even the most ardent abolitionists did not suggest abandoning them altogether.

There was, nevertheless, a sharp divide between the "colonial Enlightenment" and that of the mainland, between the great majority of the *philosophes* who condemned slavery and the planters, spokesmen, and officials of France's Caribbean colonies, who stressed the centrality of the practice to the prosperity of the empire, and consequently to France itself. By the final years of the Old Regime, denunciations of slavery became increasingly frequent and strident, particularly once Physiocrats and humanitarian reformers alike argued that slavery was not only immoral, but also inefficient compared to the greater productivity of free labor. Nevertheless, this growing force of opinion was not, by itself, sufficiently powerful to dethrone the entrenched interests of the planters and the metropolitan merchants who prospered from colonial trade. Ultimately, it was to be Diderot's "black Spartacus," rather than Malouet's benevolent planter, Condorcet's humanitarian doctor, or Hilliard d'Auberteuil's impartial jurist, who would resolve the contradictions between Enlightenment and slavery.

7
The Apotheosis of Europe

In the preceding chapters, we have observed that French Enlightenment authors used cross-cultural comparisons in a number of ways: to comment approvingly or disapprovingly on their own country's culture and institutions, to engage in debates regarding natural law and the principles governing human society, and to prove or disprove theories regarding human origins, human nature, and the causes of racial and cultural diversity. This chapter will focus on one very specific trope that developed out of these cross-cultural comparisons, which was widely though not universally shared among French Enlightenment writers, and on whose significance we have already remarked on several occasions: the idea of a space-time continuum in which all of the peoples of the world represented different stages or points along a common axis of social and cultural development. Both the anarchic "savages" of the various new worlds known to the eighteenth century and the "despotic" empires of the Orient served an important function in this multidimensional comparison, which increasingly operated to Europe's advantage as the century drew nearer to its conclusion. In the "stadial history" of the Enlightenment, Europe came to be defined as civilized (in contrast to the primitive peoples of America, Africa, and Oceania) and also as dynamic and free (as opposed to the allegedly static and despotic societies of the Orient). Together, the attributes of civilization and dynamism contributed to the apotheosis of Europe as the vanguard of human progress.

The progressive universalism of the late Enlightenment required the rejection, or at least the trivialization, both of the climate determinism that had dominated cross-cultural comparisons in the earlier part of the century, and also of the scientific racism that had been anticipated by several eighteenth-century thinkers and would come to dominate the field in the nineteenth and early twentieth centuries. Instead, it asserted the predominance of culture—laws, customs, political institutions, and belief systems—over heredity and the natural environment alike. While the proponents of stadial history asserted the present-day superiority of European society over non-European peoples and cultures, and designated Europe as the central protagonist in the emergence of a new global order, this superiority was recognized to be entirely contingent, an inheritance that could and should become the patrimony of all humanity. For this reason, many (though not all) Enlightenment authors, even as they rejected purely destructive and self-interested wars of conquest, envisioned a new, benevolent form of colonialism, which would aid the march of civilization and be mutually beneficial to Europeans and colonized peoples alike.

The Triumph of Culture

As we have seen in previous chapters, climate determinism was one of the most widely held and influential interpretations cited in eighteenth-century France to explain both the racial and cultural difference of humanity. This theory, as we have seen, enjoyed the prestige of a classical pedigree that drew upon the authority of Aristotle, Hippocrates, and Galen, and was also supported by the erudition and eloquence of two of the greatest minds of the eighteenth century, Montesquieu and Buffon. It satisfied the moderate mainstream of Enlightenment thought by reconciling empirical scientific observations on human diversity with the religious doctrine of the common origin of humanity, and flattered the vanity of contemporary Europeans by presenting the inhabitants of the temperate zone as the most beautiful, vigorous, and civilized of men, while still incorporating the less favored residents of the tropics and the poles into a common humanity.

While this synthesis held great explanatory power for the authors of the early Enlightenment, it came increasingly under fire as the eighteenth century progressed. A logical corollary of climate determinism was that savage peoples should remain savage and civilized people should remain civilized, given the relatively unchanging nature of the environments in which they lived. The historically conscious authors of the Enlightenment, however, recognized that this was not the case. In voluminous works of macrohistory, Montesquieu and Gibbon contemplated the decline of the Roman Empire, while Voltaire sought to chart the reemergence of European culture from alleged medieval barbarism and to introduce French readers to the great civilizations of the ancient Orient. After noting the contrast between the past glory and present decadence of Egypt, Voltaire commented, "This is an irrefutable proof that if climate influences the character of men, governments have a still greater influence than does climate."[1] At the same time that they contemplated the rise and fall of past empires, eighteenth-century Europeans also witnessed dramatic shifts in the balance of power between existing states, as the once-mighty Persian and Mughal empires collapsed, while the Ottoman and Chinese empires showed clear signs of relative decline *vis-à-vis* the West.[2] Henry Laurens has described the cultural consequences of this shift, writing that "at the start of the eighteenth century, stability still reigns. The Oriental states still appear strong, and western thought is not yet revolutionary. This stability is expressed in climate theory... Around 1750, everything changes... and an inexorable determinism gives way to the possibility of political transformation."[3] The relatively stable worldview that had characterized the early Enlightenment thereby gave way to a more dynamic tableau of the epic rise and fall of empires, which climate theory proved entirely inadequate to explain.

One of the first French thinkers to note the unsuitability of climate theory to explain a rapidly changing world was the materialist philosopher Claude-Adrien Helvétius, whom we have already encountered in the context of Enlightenment opposition to slavery. In his treatise *De l'esprit,* Helvétius took issue with Montesquieu's use of climate determinism to explain "Oriental despotism" and the successive waves of barbarian invasions from north to south. While Helvétius recognized the pattern of conquests of decadent southern empires by northern barbarians cited by Montesquieu (noting the Germanic invasions of the Roman Empire, the Mughal conquest of India, and the Mongol and Manchu conquests of China), he also cited counterexamples in which the south invaded the north, as in the Arab conquest of Spain and the Roman conquest of Britain, and wrote that "victory has flown alternatively from south to north and from north to south [and] all peoples have been successively conquerors and conquered."[4] Helvétius elaborated this point further in an extended discussion of the rise and fall of nations, which he denied could be attributed to the influence of climate:

> If the different temperatures of climates had such influence over souls and minds, why are these Romans, so generous and bold under a republican government, today so weak and effeminate? Why are these Greeks and Egyptians, once so admirable for their

genius and their virtue, who were then the admiration of the world, why are they now the object of its scorn?... Why have the sciences and the arts, alternately cultivated and neglected among different peoples, successively traveled through almost all climates?

Why has philosophy passed from Greece to Italy, from Italy to Constantinople and Arabia, and why, returning from Arabia to Italy, has it found refuge in France, England, and even in the north of Europe?... The temperature of these climates has not changed. To what then should we attribute the transmigration of the arts and sciences, of courage and virtue, if not to moral causes?[5]

Helvétius further likened the rise and decline of nations to the life cycle of individuals. If the condition of the American savages marked the infancy of humanity, the despotism of Asia, by contrast, marked the decrepitude of old age, and Helvétius suggested that a society that had fallen into despotism and decadence could not recover its former vigor. By contrast, the freer, more dynamic societies of Europe marked the vigor and health of young adulthood. Helvétius wrote, "If the peoples of the South are the most long enslaved, and if the nations of Europe...may be regarded as free nations, it is because these nations are more newly civilized...It is not before a long sequence of centuries...that tyrants can smother in the hearts [of their subjects] the virtuous love which all men naturally have for freedom." He further noted that "if the nations of Asia are the scorn of Europe, it is because time has submitted them to a despotism incompatible with a certain elevation of the soul."[6] However, Helvétius cautioned that Europeans should not simply look down scornfully on the oppressed subjects of Oriental despots, but should rather learn the lessons of history and struggle to defend their liberties, lest their descendants should suffer the same fate.

Only under free societies, Helvétius maintained, could the full potential of the human mind be realized. In the contemporary world, he argued, these conditions were present only in parts of northern and western Europe. In the once-great societies of Asia, by contrast, the arts and sciences were crushed under the heel of despotism, where "citizens cannot, without displeasing the despot, dedicate themselves to the study of the laws of nature, of public law, or of morals and politics. They do not dare to trace these sciences to their first principles, nor to rise to great ideas."[7] Helvétius further wrote that "great talents are always suspicious to unjust governments," and that "an enslaved people must necessarily cast ridicule upon bravery, generosity, disinterestedness...on all of the virtues founded upon an extreme love of freedom and fatherland."[8] Despotism led inevitably to the decline and fall of empires, Helvétius argued, because "in order to exercise arbitrary power with impunity, the despot is forced to weaken the spirit and courage of his subjects."[9]

It was not climate, therefore, but rather bad government that had weakened the peoples of the Orient and made them easy prey for their more vigorous neighbors. Michèle Duchet has written that, in the work of Helvétius, "Oriental despotism ceases to appear as a phenomenon specific to Asian societies, and becomes the abyss into which any society risks falling, if it departs from the principles which can preserve it."[10] Helvétius warned that France would suffer a similar fate if it abandoned its traditional institutions in favor of despotic rule, writing that "in a country as bounded as our own, surrounded by powerful and enlightened nations, souls could not be debased with impunity. France, depopulated by despotism, would soon be the prey of these nations."[11] As despotism led inexorably to the corruption and decay of nations, Helvétius insisted, the more vigorous citizens of free societies would inevitably conquer and destroy those made soft and indolent under despotic rule.

A very similar conclusion was reached a generation later by Constantin-François de Chasseboeuf, comte de Volney. While Volney concurred with Montesquieu in associating the Orient with despotism and decadence, he disagreed sharply with him regarding its causes, rejecting climate determinism to conclude that political and cultural factors were to blame for the decline of the Arab world from its days of past glory. Volney criticized Montesquieu for naturalizing Oriental despotism as a function of hot climates, the inhabitants of which "must be indolent, inert in body, and by analogy, inert in spirit and character," and for whom despotic rule was "as natural and necessary as their own climate." Volney further declared, "It would seem that the harshness, or better said, the barbarity of this conclusion should have cautioned spirits against the error of these principles, but they have had a brilliant fortune in France, and even in all of Europe, and the opinion of the author of the *Esprit des lois* has become for a great many minds an authority against which it is fearful to rebel." Highlighting the absurdity of climate determinism, Volney asked, "At what degree of the thermometer may one recognize one's aptitude for freedom or slavery?"[12] He argued that a more extensive study of history belied such facile conclusions, observing, as Helvétius had previously done, that the same climates, over the course of centuries, had seen both dynamism and decadence, servitude and freedom. Contrasting the past splendor of ancient Mesopotamian civilizations with the region's contemporary torpor, Volney asked:

> If the men of these nations were inert men, what then is activity? If they were active, where is the influence of climate? Why in the same countries where once there was such activity, does so profound an inertia now reign? Why are the modern Greeks so debased amid the ruins of Sparta and Athens, in the fields of Marathon and Thermopylae? Will one say that the climate has changed? Where is the proof? And if it were the case, it must have changed by leaps and bounds...did the climate of Persia then change from Cyrus to Xerxes? Did the climate of Athens change from Aristides to Demetrius, that of Rome, from Scipio to Scylla, and from Scylla to Tiberius? Has the climate of Portugal changed since Albuquerque, and that of the Turks, since Suleiman?[13]

Volney argued that it was the dead hand of despotism that had caused the decadence and desolation that he witnessed in his travels through Egypt and Syria. Citing the bombastic proclamations of the Ottoman sultans, Volney considered what contempt such conquerors must have for the unfortunate peoples who fell under their rule. "With so much grandeur," Volney asked, "what will the Sultan perceive when he lowers his gaze toward the rest of humanity?...How will he perceive these peoples whom he has conquered, but as slaves devoted to his service?" Volney concluded, "One may compare the Empire to a plantation on our sugar islands, where a crowd of slaves work for the luxury of a great proprietor under the surveillance of several employees who profit from it."[14] Volney's case against despotism thus closely paralleled the arguments that the Physiocrats and other Enlightenment reformers had made against slavery; namely, that it retarded the progress and development of society by removing one of its mainsprings: the hope of free citizens to enjoy the fruits of their labors.

Volney also attributed what he presented as the degraded state of the contemporary Near East to the lack of education and circulation of information. He wrote that "barbarity is complete in Syria as in Egypt...The centuries of the Caliphs have passed for the Arabs, and they have not yet been born for the Turks."[15] He blamed this state of ignorance on the shortage of books, noting that books were rare and prohibitively expensive in the region, as those that existed were still copied by hand as had been done for centuries. By contrast, he praised the role of the printing press in the flourishing of European culture since the Renaissance, and wrote, "One perceives, in thinking about it, that it alone is perhaps the true cause of the revolutions that have occurred in the last three centuries in the moral system of Europe." The power of the written word, Volney recognized, had allowed "isolated men, by the sole power of their writings, to produce moral revolutions upon entire nations, and form an empire of opinion which has imposed itself even upon the empires of armed power."[16] If the pen was not always mightier than the sword, he implied, the printing press frequently was, and Europe's growing superiority over the rest of the world was in no small part a function of the ever-increasing circulation of information.

However, even as he sang the praises of European civilization Volney recognized that there was nothing essential, inevitable, or irreversible about Europe's progress or its growing predominance in world affairs. Were it to abandon its free institutions or erect barriers to the pursuit of commerce and the advances of the arts and sciences, it could suffer the same consequences as the fallen empires of the past. At the conclusion of his *Voyages*, Volney wrote of his sense of disorientation upon his return to France after three years in the Middle East, noting that the beauty and abundance of its landscapes moved him to "admiration and tenderness." These sentiments, however, were soon followed by the fear that one day his beloved France might, to borrow Kipling's phrase from a century later, become one with Nineveh and Tyre. Volney speculated that, had the ancient empires of the Orient been warned of the destructive consequences of their actions, they would have reformed their ways, and concluded:

> What they did not do, we can do; their example may serve as a lesson to us. This is the benefit of history, which through the memory of past events, offers to the present times the precious fruits of experience. Voyages in this sense lead to the same goal as history...the traveler's account can become an indication of the causes of greatness and decadence, a means to appreciate the present term of any empire. From this vantage point Turkey is a very instructive country; that which I have revealed demonstrates how much the abuse of authority, in provoking the misery of private citizens, becomes ruinous to the prosperity of a state.[17]

We have seen that eighteenth-century missionaries and learned travelers from Lafitau to La Pérouse, as well as the philosophers such as Rousseau and Diderot who drew upon their observations, considered the observation of "primitive" peoples to be a window into the past, a means through which they could witness firsthand how the remote ancestors of civilized Europeans had once lived, and a necessary corrective to false or superfluous social institutions that alienated man from his true nature. In this passage from the *Voyages,* and even more explicitly in *Les Ruines,* Volney perceives in the debris of the once-mighty empires of the Orient a frightening glimpse into Europe's possible future, to the ruin that awaited it should the forces of despotism and obscurantism gain the upper hand.

Volney's subsequent work, *Les Ruines,* published in 1791, took as its point of departure his visit to the imposing ruins of Palmyra, a once-great city now lost in the deserts of Syria, which he had already described at length in the second volume of his *Voyages.* In *Les Ruines,* however, Volney abandoned the detached and analytical tone that characterized the former work in favor of a rhapsodic romanticism, which soon led him to meditate upon the transience of all human achievements. He wrote, "These solitary places, this peaceful night, this majestic scene, inspired in my spirit a religious meditation. I sat upon the trunk of a column, and there, with my elbow resting on my knee and my head upon my hand, gazing first into the desert, and then upon the ruins, I abandoned myself to a profound reverie."[18] "Here, I told myself," he continued, "once flourished an opulent city, here was the seat of a powerful empire. Yes! These places now so deserted, were once animated by a lively multitude, an active crowd once circulated in these abandoned streets...And now behold what remains of this powerful city, a lugubrious skeleton! Behold what remains of a vast dominion, a shadowy and vain memory!...The silence of the tomb has replaced the murmur of the public square."[19] Volney was moved to reflect, "How such glory has been eclipsed! How many labors have been annihilated! So perish the works of man! So empires and nations disappear!"[20] Recalling the glory of ancient Persia, Phoenicia, and Babylon, he asked, "What has become of these ages of abundance and life? What has become of so many brilliant creations of the hand of man? Where now are those ramparts of Nineveh, those walls of Babylon, that palace of Persepolis, these temples of Balbeck and Jerusalem?"[21] Volney's thoughts then turned from ancient Asia to contemporary Europe, and to "the course of vicissitudes that one by one transmitted the scepter of the world among peoples so different in religion and manners." He recalled the homeland he had left behind, "its richly cultivated fields, its well-built roads, its cities inhabited by a numerous people, its fleets spread over all the seas, its ports covered with tributes from both Indies," and after placidly contemplating the parallels between "the past splendor of Asia" and the glory of contemporary Europe, he was suddenly troubled by a nagging anxiety. "Who knows, I told myself, if such will not one day be the abandon of our own countries? Who knows if upon the shores of the Seine, the Thames, and the Zuidersee...one day a traveler like me will sit upon the mute ruins, and in solitude weep over the ashes of these peoples and the memory of their greatness?"[22]

Volney's comparison between Western dynamism and Oriental decadence draws the same contrast as that of Montesquieu, but reaches entirely different conclusions as to its cause, attributing the divide not to the "empire of climate," but rather to the power of social institutions, primarily government and religion. The implications of this conclusion are far reaching, in that Volney suggests that Europe's superiority over Asia is contingent rather than essential, and that even the most enlightened nations of Europe will decay and disappear if they fail to heed the lessons of the past. On the other hand, Volney argues that the decadence and immobility that he and other Enlightenment observers perceived in the Orient and elsewhere were in no way foreordained. If other peoples would cultivate the arts and sciences and embrace free institutions and a more rationalized religion, the benefits that progress had brought to Europe would flow to them as well. As a matter of culture and institutions rather than climate (or race, for that matter), civilization was not confined to the temperate latitudes, as Buffon had suggested, but could spread eventually to encompass the entire earth.

Future Perfect: Mercier's Enlightenment Utopia

One of the key historical innovations of the eighteenth century in France was a new progressive and linear concept of time. The classical view of history, dating from Hesiod, had represented the early prehistory of humanity as an idyllic "golden age," which was followed by the successively less idyllic ages of silver, bronze, and iron.[23] This Greek concept of history was easily merged in the medieval and early modern mind with the Christian legend of the Garden of Eden and the expulsion of man from Paradise. We have had frequent occasion to witness the enduring power of this vision of the primeval innocence of humanity, which was evoked by many eighteenth-century French writers, such as Lahontan, Rousseau, Adanson, and Bougainville. Like Thomas More, who in the sixteenth century situated his Utopia on a distant island, these writers displaced the myth of a primitive golden age of man onto the supposedly primitive societies of America, Africa, and Oceania.[24]

In both the classical and the Judeo-Christian traditions, however, the golden age of humanity's innocence is not to be recovered here on earth. While the Christian tradition offered believers the hope of a future paradise, the "new Jerusalem" to which they aspired was not of this world. As we have already observed, the tragic undercurrent of Rousseau's evocation of the state of nature is his awareness that, once man has left this state of pure nature, developed his passions and acquired a taste for the forbidden fruits of civilization, he can never return to his previous condition. In the eighteenth century, however, growing faith in human perfectibility led to a radical break from the previous traditions that placed the golden age in an unrecoverable past. Some Enlightenment authors instead displaced utopia onto a distant but attainable future, in which the progress of science and the arts and a better understanding of human nature and of the true principles of good government would lead to the emergence of a better, more just, and more refined social order. The very connotation of the word "futuristic" in our own lexicon is a product of this Enlightenment displacement of ancient dreams of the golden age from the past to the future. In his final work, the *Esquisse d'un tableau historique des progrès de l'esprit humain,* the marquis de Condorcet argued, "If man can predict, with almost entire assurance, the phenomena of which he knows the laws, if…he can, with the experience of the past, predict with great probability the events of the future, why should it be seen as a chimerical enterprise to trace, with some plausibility, the portrait of the future destiny of the human race, according to the results of its history?"[25]

The clearest Enlightenment expression of this utopian vision of the future was the novel *L'an 2440, rêve s'il en fut jamais* (The Year 2440, A Dream If There Ever Was One) by Louis-Sebastien Mercier, a man of letters and critical observer of eighteenth-century French society whom contemporaries dubbed *le singe de Jean-Jacques* (the ape of Jean-Jacques) for his fervent admiration of Rousseau.[26] In the novel, a contemporary French observer, modeled on Mercier himself and born in the same year (1740) falls asleep in 1768, and in his dreams finds himself projected seven centuries into the future, to a world without the abuses of Old Regime society. Guided around twenty-fifth-century Paris by a learned man of the future, Mercier's narrator is informed of the changes that have been made over the intervening centuries.

Given that, over the course of the nineteenth and twentieth centuries, "futuristic" has come to imply the transformation of the world through the advance of science and technology, new inventions are strikingly absent from Mercier's utopia. His narrator is informed that the lavish carriages that cluttered the streets of eighteenth-century Paris have been banned, and that twenty-fifth century Parisians walk everywhere, thereby maintaining themselves fit and healthy. The only technological wonders that are described in the novel (actually in the second edition, published in 1786) are hot-air balloons, the first of which had been pioneered by the Montgolfier brothers in 1783, and which in the future are depicted carrying travelers to and fro between Europe and Asia.[27]

Mercier's future France remains a monarchy, but rather than the absolutism of the earlier Bourbons, Louis XXXIV reigns over a mixed system, "reasonable and made for men," in which revitalized provincial estates and a rationalized, codified legal system leave him with "all the necessary power and authority to do good, and his arms tied for doing evil." Religious dogmatism and the mutual hatred between Catholics and Protestants has been replaced with a refined, vaguely Deist religion of the supreme being, whose ministers live simply, travel about without pomp, and dedicate themselves to the service of the needy. Rather than abstract and incomprehensible theological doctrines, the youth of the future are taught to venerate the majesty of God in nature through a "ceremony of the two infinities," which Mercier describes as replacing the first communion, in which a young initiate is led to an observatory to contemplate the heavens through a powerful telescope, and to a laboratory to observe the minute invisible world through a microscope.[28]

Mercier's future world has no use for history, and the narrator is informed by his guide that the subject is not taught to children at all, "because history is the shame of humanity, and each page is a tissue of crimes and follies. God forbid that we should put before their eyes these examples of brigandage and ambition." The guide went on to denounce historians for "elevating kings into gods" and writing panegyrics to honor wicked tyrants, and declared, "It is only a grown man who can regard this panorama without blanching, even feeling a secret joy in seeing the ephemeral triumph of crime and the eternal fate that should belong to virtue. But this picture should be hidden from children." The guide further declares that children are no longer taught the "useless" dead languages Greek and Latin, but rather the modern languages English, German, Italian, and Spanish, and study science and logic rather than "metaphysics... a chimerical and always useless system."[29] Another scholar of the future justifies this choice to the narrator by exclaiming, "Remember your érudits! They knew Latin, Greek, and Hebrew, but they did not reason!"[30]

In fact, there are a number of features of Mercier's future utopia that appear rather dystopian to the contemporary reader. His narrator proudly announces that the majority of the collection of the *Bibliothèque du Roi* had been condemned as useless or harmful and burned in an enormous bonfire. These condemned works included not only the devout Bossuet, whose universal history is condemned as "a poor chronological skeleton, without life or color," and the Jansenist Pascal, but also the majority of the writings of Voltaire, who had dared to mock the great Jean-Jacques Rousseau.[31] The scholar of the future also reports that eighteenth-century France had been too indulgent toward the Jews (an assertion that surely would have surprised Mercier's Jewish contemporaries), and that their successors had been forced to demonstrate "great wisdom, constancy, and firmness" in order to "repress the ferocious fanaticism of some of them," though he does not elaborate on what precisely this entailed.[32] Mercier's utopia also entails a dramatic reduction in the status of women; on several occasions, his characters report that dowries have been suppressed to curtail women's pride and that the women of the future are valued for their modesty and virtue rather than their wealth, wit, or beauty.[33] In this patriarchal vision, which strongly echoes the views that Rousseau articulated in *Emile* and the *Lettre à M. d'Alembert sur les spectacles*, one of Mercier's guides declares that "the husband has again become what he was in the order of nature, and what he should be for the subordination, order and peace of the household, a master and an absolute judge."[34]

By displacing utopia from the past to the future, Mercier suggested that humanity could hope to achieve an ideal society once this process of progressive evolution had run its course. Robert Darnton has written that, while Plato, More, and Bacon "had imagined societies located far away in space and cut off from the real world by impossible journeys or extravagant shipwrecks...Mercier made his seem inevitable, because he presented it as the outcome of a historical process already at work and he placed it in Paris...*L'An 2440* demanded to be read as a serious guidebook to the future."[35] Similarly, Simon Collier argues that *L'an 2440* is "the classic Enlightenment utopia," justifying this assertion with the observation that the book "represents a projection into the future of virtually every aspect of the Enlightenment programme of reform: equality of rights, political liberalism, administrative simplification, scientific advance, humanitarian justice—they are all there."[36] While Mercier's novel is fanciful fiction, it captured the philosophical hopes and expectations that many of his contemporaries expressed in learned treatises. We will now consider the "stadial" theories of history of Turgot and Condorcet, the French Enlightenment's most explicit presentation of universal history as the march of progress.

Stadial History and the March of Progress

If there is a single idea that is often taken as central to the alleged "Enlightenment project," it is the notion of universal history as humanity's steady progress toward a rational new world order. This hoary cliché is at most half true; not all of the social and political thinkers of the Enlightenment embraced the idea of history as a narrative of progress. Peter Gay has observed that "Locke, Montesquieu, Hume, Diderot had no theory of progress; Rousseau's thought stressed the fact of man's retrogression and the hope for man's regeneration; Voltaire saw human history as a long string of miseries broken by four happy ages. Only Kant, with his speculative world history, Turgot with his three stages, and Condorcet with his ten epochs, may be said to have held a theory of progress, and these three thinkers stood not at the center but at the bright end of the spectrum of Enlightenment thought."[37] Nevertheless, a view of universal history as a narrative of progress is often associated with the Enlightenment, and was indeed characteristic of one of the period's principal contributions to social thought. The Enlightenment concept of stadial history, which holds that societies progress by passing through a series of evolutionary stages, would have a foundational impact on the subsequent development of the human sciences. Although, as Ronald Meek and Karen O'Brien have shown, this view was elaborated most explicitly and consistently by the "conjectural historians" of the Scottish Enlightenment, it was first suggested in an early, unpublished manuscript by Turgot, and its most elaborate and extreme expression was composed by Turgot's protégé and successor, the marquis de Condorcet.

Turgot's "Plan for Two Discourses on Universal History," composed in 1751, classified the peoples of the world into hunting, pastoral, and agricultural societies, and argued that it was the quest to secure means of subsistence that drove the advance of society. Turgot imagined that the first men, "without subsistence in the middle of the forest," turned to hunting, which led to the broad diffusion of small bands of peoples, without fixed domicile, who "wandered aimlessly wherever the hunt took them." He then supposed that these first peoples discovered that certain useful animals could be domesticated, and "the pastoral life was soon introduced wherever such animals were found: cattle and sheep in Europe, camels and goats in the Orient, horses in Tartary, and reindeer in the North." Peoples who found themselves in fertile lands became farmers, Turgot further speculated, but he argued that this transition was necessarily "through infinitely slow advances."[38] Robert Nisbet has praised the "utter originality" of this formulation, which held that "such differences, far from being mere adaptations to terrain or climate, are most fundamentally differences of degree of social development."[39] Turgot argued that a people must pass through each of these stages in succession, observing that hunters, lacking the livestock to pull plows and produce manure for their fields, could not become farmers without first becoming herdsmen. Turgot's insight that a society's structure and ways of life were determined in the first instance by its means of subsistence would go on to exercise a great influence over the development of anthropology in the nineteenth and twentieth centuries. Turgot also developed this insight to argue (as the Jesuit missionary-scholar Joseph-François Lafitau had claimed a generation earlier) that contemporary "primitives" could be taken as exemplars of how prehistoric peoples of the remote past had once lived. Observing that the contemporary world offered examples of peoples in each stage of development, Turgot called geography "the cross-section of history," and declared in a 1750 lecture at the Sorbonne that "all ages are linked together by a chain of causes and effects which unite the present state of the world with everything that has preceded it... The present state of the world, in presenting every shade of barbarism and civilization, gives us at a single glance all the monuments, the vestiges, of each step taken by the human mind, the likeness of each stage it has passed through, the history of all ages."[40] Nisbet writes that "modern anthropology came into existence as a self-conscious discipline in the middle of the nineteenth century largely around a broad-gauged use of this method."[41]

Turgot also went much further than his contemporaries in theorizing a law of historical progress. Although he noted periods of retrogression in the area of high culture, he argued that "one should not believe that the mechanical arts suffer the same eclipse as do letters and the speculative sciences. An art, once invented and established, becomes an object of trade which sustains itself." Even the more intangible abstract knowledge of societies tended toward ever greater perfection, he argued, noting that "as long as the language in which books are written endures and it is conserved among a few men of letters, one will not forget what has been known...Thus the Greek scholars who came to Italy after the fall of Constantinople knew everything that had been known in ancient Greece."[42] Turgot also drew a contrast between Western dynamism and the imposing but allegedly static societies of the Orient. He compared China to "those trees whose stem has been cut at their branches close to the ground. They will never go past mediocrity. They have too much respect for sciences barely begun, and for ancestors who made the first steps, that they believed that there was no more to be added." Turgot further argued that "a precocious maturity, in science and letters, is not an advantage to be envied. Europe, developing later than Asia, has produced more numerous and more nourishing fruits."[43]

The marquis de Condorcet, one of Turgot's most fervent admirers, incorporated his mentor's insights regarding stadial history and cross-cultural comparisons into his final work, the *Esquisse d'un tableau historique des progrès de l'esprit humain*, which was composed over several months in 1793, at which time the author was in hiding from the Jacobin Committee of Public Safety, just before his arrest and death in prison the following year. In it, Condorcet articulated the most stark and unambiguous statement of universal history as the progress of human reason that the age had yet witnessed, presenting history as the progressive advancement of humanity through a series of ten stages. Condorcet's narrative of progress began with Turgot's three-stage theory of the development of early societies, but built upon it to incorporate the progress of advanced civilizations, with Western Europe of his own times passing through the ninth stage, and the tenth stage as a utopia of perfect reason and justice to be achieved in the future.

Condorcet's "sketch" of universal history drew a sharp contrast between progressive, dynamic Europe and both the decadent Orient and the still barbaric savages of Africa and America. In fact, while the first three stages of Condorcet's history are presented as universal and depicted in the most general terms, from the fourth stage (the rise of classical Greek civilization) to the ninth (Europe since the Scientific Revolution), the advance of civilization is a purely Western affair. He wrote that China "seems to have preceded the others in sciences and arts only to see itself subsequently surpassed by all. These people, whose knowledge of artillery did not prevent them from conquest by barbaric nations, where the sciences...alone lead to all honors, and where nonetheless, subjected to absurd prejudices, they are condemned to an eternal mediocrity; where finally the very invention of printing remained useless to the progress of the human spirit."[44] He condemned the contemporary Near East as "presenting the hideous spectacle of a people degenerated to the final stage of servitude, corruption, and misery," writing that "the religion of Mohammed...seems to condemn to an eternal slavery and an incurable stupidity all the vast portion of the earth where it has established its empire."[45] If Condorcet was dismissive of the civilizations of Asia, he was even harsher of his assessment of "those who occupy the rest of the globe," who, he asserted, "have been halted in their progress, and still depict for us the age of the childhood of humanity, or have been carried by events through the later stages [of history]." By contrast, Condorcet wrote that Greece was "the benefactor and the guide of all nations and all ages, an honor which, until today, no other people has shared."[46]

After summarizing the portrait of the "noble savage" and of the decadence of civilization that Rousseau presented in his *Discourses*, Condorcet himself, as a prophet of civilization, rejected Rousseau's thesis that the advancement of the arts and sciences led to the decadence of morals, and declared that "these eloquent declamations against the sciences and arts are based upon a false application of history." Instead, he wrote, "the stormy and painful passage of a barbaric society to the state of civilization of enlightened and free peoples is not a degeneration of the human race, but a necessary crisis in its gradual march towards its absolute perfection. We will see that it is not the spread of enlightenment, but its decadence, which has produced the vices of civilized peoples, and finally, far from corrupting men, it has refined them, where it has not been able to correct or transform them."[47] Condorcet further denied that primitive peoples were as virtuous as Rousseau had argued, writing that, where men had not acquired the more elevated pleasures of learning and the arts, they "have adopted with a sort of fury the physical means of acquiring sensations that can be repeated ceaselessly, such as the habits of fermented liquors, of hot drinks, of opium, tobacco, or betel," mindless escapes that, Condorcet lamented, prolonged the "childhood and inactivity" of these peoples. [48]

Reflecting upon the differences between savagery and civilization, Condorcet considered the rights and duties of civilized Europe with regard to the "primitive" peoples of the non-European world, noting that "some philosophers have pitied these nations, others have praised them; the latter have called wisdom and virtue that which the former called stupidity and laziness." Condorcet observed that many "savages" remained attached to their traditional ways despite contact with European explorers, colonists, and missionaries, which, he said, had given them "some knowledge, some industry, and particularly a great many vices, but they have not been able to lift them out of this sort of immobility." Condorcet blamed the failure of the civilizing process partly on "climate, customs. . . . the laziness of the body and especially that of the spirit. . . [and] the empire that superstition already wields over the first societies," but partly also on the poor example presented by the Europeans themselves, who "showed themselves to these nations more powerful, richer, more educated, more active, but also more vicious and especially less happy than they were. The latter must have often been less struck by the superiority of the former than frightened by the multiplicity and extent of their needs, the torments of their greed, the eternal agitation of their always active, always insatiable passions."[49] Condorcet's comments reflect one of the pressing debates of the late Enlightenment, which we have already encountered in the previous chapters: could (and should) "savages" be civilized in Europe's image?

The "Black Legend" of the Spanish Conquest

Sankar Muthu has argued that "the latter half of the eighteenth century is an anomalous period in modern European political thought, for it is only then that a group of significant thinkers attacked the very foundations of imperialism."[50] While, as we shall see, Enlightenment thinkers were not categorically opposed to all forms of colonial expansion, there was a strong consensus that violent acts of imperial conquest leading to the subjugation and systematic oppression of defenseless peoples were immoral and unworthy of a civilized society. In particular, anticolonialism and anticlericalism came together in frequent denunciations of the sixteenth-century Spanish conquest of the Americas. The "black legend" of the conquest of America, though inspired by Spanish colonial sources such as Bartolomé de las Casas and Garcilaso de la Vega, was largely a creation of the Enlightenment. Some of the most vehement passages that Diderot contributed to the *Histoire des deux Indes* dealt with this conquest and the abuses that followed. Diderot described the conquistadores as "brigands without lineage, without education, and without principles" and predicted a coming revolution, leading to "the massacre of all the race of the murderers of Atahualpa, and the priests who sacrificed him will in turn be the victims of all of the blood which they have spilled over the altar of a god of peace."[51] Speaking more generally about the conduct of European colonizers in the New

World, Diderot wrote, "He is a domestic tiger returning to the forest; the thirst of blood takes hold of him once more."[52] Similarly, Condorcet, while praising the boundless energy and curiosity that led explorers such as Columbus and Vasco da Gama to discover new worlds, sharply condemned the cruelty and fanaticism of their countrymen who went on to conquer the Americas, writing:

> If a noble curiosity animated the heroes of navigation, a base and cruel greed, a stupid and ferocious fanaticism directed the kings and brigands that would profit from their labors. The unfortunate beings who inhabited these new countries were not treated as men, because they were not Christians. This prejudice, more debasing for the tyrants than for the victims, smothered all form of remorse, abandoned without restraint to their inexhaustible thirst for gold and blood the greedy and barbaric men that Europe vomited forth from its breast. The bones of five million men covered these unfortunate lands, where the Portuguese and the Spanish transported their greed, their superstitions, and their fury.[53]

Many other Enlightenment authors expressed similar revulsion at the brutality of the Spanish conquest of America. Cornelius de Pauw called the discovery of America "the greatest misfortune which humanity has known," and wrote that the "cruel and atrocious character" of the Spanish conquistadores "surpasses anything that had been seen or imagined of the most denatured of men." He further asked whether "Europe in general would not have been happier, if two Italians had not, in the fifteenth century, revealed the route to the New World."[54] Similarly, Charles de Brosses unambiguously condemned the brutality of the Spanish conquest, writing in the preface to his *Histoire des navigations aux terres australes* that the Spaniards "slaughtered with disdain, like vile animals of another color, the millions of Indians whom they could have made into men." De Brosses further argued that this gratuitous brutality was counterproductive to the goal of spreading civilization, writing, "One could not believe that the Indians would have remained until the present in their brutish nature in the sight of Spaniards, if the poor treatment that the latter burdened them with had not led them wisely to escape as soon as possible."[55]

While their condemnation of the Spanish conquest of America was virtually universal, the position of French Enlightenment thinkers with regard to colonialism more broadly defies easy categorization.

Some eighteenth-century writers extended their rejection of the Spanish conquest to denounce all forms of European imperialism. Voltaire's indifference to the overseas colonies is well known; most famously, he wrote in *Candide* that France and Britain were "warring over a few acres of snow in Canada and... expending on this fine war much more than all Canada is worth."[56] Grimm's *Correspondance littéraire*, in reviewing Pierre Poivre's 1768 work *Voyages d'un philosophe*, concluded that "God did not grant the French nation the talent and the spirit to form colonies. This people, gifted with so many precious and admirable qualities, has nothing of what is needed to succeed in this enterprise; its vivacity leads it to do in a day what should only be done in a year... No patience, no perseverance in a plan; setbacks deter it and lead it to attempt something else."[57] Similarly, in the aftermath of France's defeat in the Seven Years' War, the abbé Mably argued against future colonial ventures, writing, "There is no doubt that this kingdom can be very happy and very powerful without colonies... It is not then in the interest of France to aggravate the weight of her debts in order to recapture useless lands from the English."[58]

The learned traveler and Orientalist scholar Abraham-Hyacinthe Anquetil-Duperron, who witnessed the collapse of the Mughal Empire and the rise of British hegemony over South Asia, invoked the example of the Spanish conquest of America to condemn more recent acts of aggressive imperialism, writing, "We tremble still as we read of the horrors committed against the Americans after the discovery of this new part of the world. We doubtless consider ourselves more just, and our rights over the Indians better established. Interest and ambition, these are the motives of all conquests; the manifestoes come afterwards."[59] While acknowledging the decline of the Mughal Empire, he retorted that "its weakness gives no rights to Europeans who are absolutely foreign to the country." Anquetil-Duperron also observed that "the majority of Europeans who go to India, full of these declamations against Asiatic government, believe that they follow the established order in these countries in imitating the rapacity and cruelty of some Indian rulers... It is difficult to be just and humane, when on the one hand interest dictates acts of blood, and on the other, one believes oneself to be dealing only with slaves, with beings scarcely elevated above the brutes."[60] He further elaborated that "it seems that Europeans in India believe themselves in a country belonging to the first who can seize control of it, and thereby consider that everything is permitted them. Personal interest determines their conquests."[61] Finally, Anquetil-Duperron questioned the moral status of Europeans to accuse Indians of barbarism, writing, "I acknowledge that the Indians neglect certain means of enriching themselves that self-interest could suggest to them. For example, they have not yet attempted to establish in regular commerce this sale of human flesh that in Europe is known as the slave trade. In this they are less advanced than we are."[62]

Perhaps more surprisingly, Cornelius de Pauw, whom we encountered as a champion of the superiority of Europe in the "dispute of the New World," combined an absolute and utter scorn for the "primitive" peoples of the non-European world with a steadfast rejection of colonialism. Not only did de Pauw condemn past instances of abusive imperialism in the Americas, as we have just seen, but he also urged his fellow Europeans to refrain from colonizing the newly discovered islands of the South Pacific. "Distant peoples have already too much to complain of Europe," he wrote, "she has, in their regard, greatly abused her superiority. Now prudence, if not equity, demands that she leave the southern lands alone, in order to better cultivate her own." He went on to implore his contemporaries, "Let us not massacre the Papous, in order to introduce Reaumur's thermometer to the climate of New Guinea." De Pauw further declared, "If those who preach virtue in the civilized countries are themselves too vicious to instruct the savages without tyrannizing them, let us allow these savages to vegetate in peace, let us pity them, if their misfortunes surpass our own, and if we cannot contribute to their happiness, let us not increase their misery."[63] Ironically, de Pauw's racism and his sense of the infinite superiority of Europeans over the "primitives" of America and Oceania informs and directs his rejection of colonialism: if the "savages" are incapable of becoming civilized in the Western sense, and the great disparity of power and civilization between the two worlds can only lead to exploitation, then the only moral and ethical choice for Europeans is to leave them alone.

Such categorical rejection of colonialism was not the only response of the Enlightenment to the ethical dilemmas produced by cross-cultural encounters. Several eighteenth-century French authors explicitly distinguished between a "bad" form of purely destructive colonialism, of which the Spanish conquest of the Americas was held up as the most prominent example, and a "good" constructive colonialism, which would spread the benefits of European civilization and integrate previously isolated peoples into global networks of commerce for the mutual advantage of all. One noteworthy example of this contrast is Jean-François Marmontel's historical novel *Les Incas* (1777), a fictionalized account of the Spanish conquest of Peru. While Marmontel condemns the historical conquest as it happened, he laments that a more rational, peaceful colonization did not occur in its place. His rather fanciful account presents the most prominent sixteenth-century critic of the conquest of the Americas, the Spanish Dominican friar Bartolomé de las Casas, as a sort of benign patriarch revered by the noble savages of the Americas. This fictional Las Casas laments the abuses of his countrymen, declaring, "Alas! If they had only managed their conquest, the Indies would be happy, and Spain would be rich, but because of the shameful abuse they made of their victory, they will have exhausted Spain and ruined the Indies fruitlessly."[64] Marmontel's novel, while sharply critical of the sixteenth-century conquistadores, offers the hope for a more humane and enlightened form of cultural exchange. Such a vision, which not subtly implied that Enlightenment France would be a better colonizer than was golden age Spain, was characteristic of one strain of Enlightenment thinking about the future relationship between Europe and the non-European world.

The Mission to Civilize

Nearly a century ago Carl Lokke, observing that "repugnance to the West Indies never developed into general opposition to the holding of colonies" in eighteenth-century France, juxtaposed the growing antislavery sentiment of the late Enlightenment with the desire for "colonies in other parts of the world which could produce necessary tropical commodities without wounding the delicate sensibilities of the age." Liberal guilt and enlightened self-interest intermingled in odd ways in the later Enlightenment, as Lokke further notes that "contemporaries were anxious to expiate handsomely their crimes of past centuries in dealing with subject, non-white races." [65] The hope for a kinder and gentler sort of empire, which Sunil Agnani has described as *douce colonisation*, gained broad popularity among Enlightened French authors and policymakers in the 1770s and 1780s. This "sweet colonization" was seen as preferable to the old, exploitative kind, Agnani suggests, because it implied a consensual and mutually beneficial relationship, in which "savage" peoples would themselves come to see the advantages of European civilization and seek to emulate their more advanced benefactors. Diderot suggested this approach in a letter to Catherine the Great of Russia, writing, "If I had to civilize savages, what would I do? I would do useful things in their presence, without saying or prescribing anything to them...I would leave the remainder to time and to the force of example."[66]

The contrast between the "bad," exploitative imperialism of the past and the "good," mutually beneficial colonialism that enlightened Europe could now consider is a recurring motif in the *Histoire des deux Indes*, the most extensive discussion of empire produced by the late Enlightenment. While the *Histoire des deux Indes* is sometimes considered an anticolonial text, I would argue that it is better understood as an antimercantilist one, as it condemns colonial abuses, but not colonialism itself. Among many other things, the *Histoire des deux Indes* can be read as a sort of capitalist manifesto, which celebrates the dynamism and the civilizing potential of international trade, while denouncing mercantilism, religious intolerance, national hatred, and the spirit of conquest. A classic example of the eighteenth-century "enlightened narrative," the *Histoire des deux Indes* credits commerce for Europe's rise from the chaos and barbarism of the Middle Ages, and suggests that the Turks would have overrun the rest of Europe, as they overran Constantinople, had the discovery of the Americas and the expansion of trade not made Europe richer and stronger.[67] The authors of the *Histoire des deux Indes* contrasted purely destructive conquests, like that of the Americas in the sixteenth century, with a more peaceful and constructive commercial colonialism, writing that warlike savage peoples "may be exterminated, but not subdued by force. It is only humaneness, the attractions of riches or of freedom, the example of virtue and moderation, a gentle administration, which can civilize them."[68] Considering the practical difficulties of conquering the interior of Africa, long coveted by Europeans for its riches of gold, the authors of the *Histoire des deux Indes* observed, "It would be difficult to bring to a country so distant from the seas sufficient forces to invade it, and Europeans would soon die in its burning sands, which are pestilent and barren. Seduction appears to be the only path open to them. The most certain means to win over this nation would be to furnish it with the merchandises it draws from the Moors, but at a better price, and to acquaint it with new pleasures. At this price, the Bambaras might cede the right to exploit their mines."[69]

In Mercier's ideal future of the year 2440, this transition had already happened, as the seductions of commerce and the power of mutual self-interest led Africans willingly to produce the tropical commodities that French consumers coveted. Rejecting both climate and heredity as causes for human inequality, Mercier's guide to the future told him, "The apostles of reason and the arts, in taking our discoveries and our knowledge to these peoples debased under the most atrocious despotism, have regenerated the greater part of

Africa... For stupidity is not an inherent characteristic of the peoples of Africa. The climate, the land, the waters are the same; the laws have changed, and men have changed with them."[70]

In the years prior to the Revolution, one of the focal points for this *douce colonisation* was French Guyana, an imperial backwater that never lived up to the expectations of its proponents. Baron Alexandre-Ferdinand de Bessner, a longtime colonial officer and governor of Guyana from 1781 until his death in 1785, argued that indigenous labor was the key to the colony's chronic labor shortages, and suggested a program of sponsoring Catholic missions (citing the Jesuits of Paraguay as an example), establishing French forts in the interior of the colony to offer both protection and surveillance to these communities, and providing tools, trade goods, and incentives for them to cultivate cash crops desired by European markets.[71] A very similar proposal was made in the 1780s by Bessner's successors, who suggested that the colony's indigenous population could be drawn into the market economy and encouraged to raise cash crops and tend livestock. Recognizing that "Men in the state of pure nature like the Indians only have industry in proportion to their needs," they concluded that "wise policy demands that they be inspired to adopt our needs... that they be given a taste for a certain luxury in their clothing as in their lodging and furnishings, then they will work to satisfy these new desires."[72] By contrast, the former intendant of the colony, Pierre-Victor Malouet, whom we have already encountered as Condorcet's antagonist in the debate over the abolition of slavery, argued that Bessner's proposals to attract and assimilate Native Americans were utopian and impractical. In a letter to the minister, the maréchal de Castries, Malouet wrote that "Their civilization, so often proposed, is, if I am not mistaken, an old chimera that is impossible to achieve. The Indians neither can nor wish to be civilized, and if they ever were, their character leads them so much to inertia that it would be necessary to award them pensions for their nourishment."[73]

Malouet's antagonist in the prerevolutionary debates over slavery, the marquis de Condorcet, credited the philosophy of the Enlightenment with bringing a new humanitarian spirit to Europe's relations with the non-European world, and especially praised the growth of the abolitionist Société des Amis des Noirs, in which he had played a principal role. Condorcet wrote, "Animated by the sentiment of universal philanthropy, they combated injustice... they roused themselves in Europe against the crimes for which greed soiled the shores of America, Africa, and Asia. The philosophers of

England and France did honor to their name, fulfilling the duties as 'friends' of the same blacks that their stupid tyrants refused to count among the number of men."[74] He lamented, however, that the Enlightenment had only just begun to transform human society, writing, "We see at the same time knowledge only occupying a small part of the globe, and the number of those who truly have it disappear before the mass of men abandoned to prejudice and ignorance. We see vast countries trembling in slavery, presenting only nations, here degraded by the vices of a civilization whose advance is hindered by corruption, there still vegetating in the childhood of the first ages."[75] However, Condorcet imagined that, in the tenth and final stage of history, the wisdom of the enlightened West would spread to the rest of the globe:

> These vast countries offer it numerous peoples, who seem only to await, to become civilized, to receive from us the means, and to find in Europeans brothers, in order to become their friends and their disciples. There, nations enslaved under sacred despots or stupid conquerors, who have called for liberators for many centuries; there, still savage tribes, the hardness of whose climate distances them from the sweetness of a perfected civilization, as this same harshness repels those who wish to share with them its advantages, or hordes of conquerors, who know no law but force, no occupation but brigandage. The progress of these two last classes of people will be slower and accompanied by more storms; perhaps even, reduced to a lesser number, to the extent that they find themselves driven back by the civilized nations, they will finish by imperceptibly disappearing, or being absorbed into them.[76]

Although Condorcet imagined that the unredeemable savage peoples of the most distant lands would disappear almost naturally and bloodlessly, and certainly without the cruelty and fanaticism that accompanied the Spanish conquest of the Americas, the contemporary reader cannot help but be shocked at the equanimity with which he considered this disappearance, without even the ambivalent lament that Diderot had articulated in the *Histoire des deux Indes* regarding the loss of the corrective example of the savage for the instruction of the civilized men of the future.[77] Believing that the spread of civilization from advanced to primitive societies was in the interest of the latter, Condorcet therefore articulated and justified the civilizing mission of Europe toward the non-European world, a theme that was to recur in the following centuries.

The clearest contrast between the "bad" imperialism of Counter-Reformation Spain and the "good" imperialism of Enlightenment France was drawn by Charles de Brosses, president of the Parlement of Dijon and, as we saw in chapter 4, an advocate of a renewed French colonialism in the South Pacific and Indian Ocean. Although, as we have seen above, de Brosses was sharply critical of Spanish brutality in the New World, he did not condemn colonialism in principle, but rather argued that a more humane and enlightened power, such as eighteenth-century France, could in some way expiate the crimes of Europe's past by spreading the benefits of civilization to the remote corners of the earth. "Supposing that so great a fortune as that which Christopher Columbus procured for our neighbors allowed us ever to make the full discovery of the southern world," de Brosses wrote, "their example would serve to instruct us, we would avoid the two vices that the Spaniards then held: avarice and cruelty."[78] Indeed, de Brosses argued, French colonialism would prove beneficial to the yet-to-be discovered natives of the South Seas. "The *Australiens*," he wrote, "could only benefit in giving any goods whatsoever in exchange for a shovel, for a saw, or for a pair of scissors, but this gain would be nothing at all in comparison to that which they would obtain from the instruction which they could receive from us." Enlightened French tutelage, he maintained, "would mollify their savage manners, and would make of them men, out of so many beings who have only the form [of humanity]." Appealing to Louis XV to pursue the colonization of the yet undiscovered lands of the southern hemisphere, de Brosses asked the king, "What more noble expense can a sovereign make, what greater object can he propose himself, than that of creating nations, so to speak, and giving them the greatest possible good?"[79]

De Brosses also stressed the glory of the great lawgivers of antiquity, and praised Peter the Great as the greatest of modern rulers for civilizing the Russian people. He also reminded his readers that their own ancestors were once barbarians, before receiving the precious gift of civilization from the ancient Phoenicians and Greeks:

> The Europeans of those first centuries were hardly less brutish than the *Australiens* may be. Like them they inhabited caves and forests, living as isolated families, or ran about as vagabond bands, living from hunting and pillaging, ignorant of agriculture and the arts... This is from whence we departed to arrive, through education, good example, and commerce with more advanced foreigners, to the point where we now find ourselves. Any other people

can arrive as we did. If there are wild nations in the climates of the south, those of Scotland, Ireland, Russia, Scandinavia, were they not similar, as previously were also the Germans?...Could one do a greater service to humanity than that of bringing humanity itself to fruition? And is there any occupation more worthy of mankind than that of forming and developing one's own species?[80]

During the century that separated the collapse of France's Caribbean empire and the Third Republic's "mission to civilize" West Africa and Indochina, North Africa exercised the greatest pull on French colonial ambitions, with Napoleon's short-lived invasion of Egypt and the conquest of Algeria under Charles X and Louis-Philippe as the most significant instances of this trans-Mediterranean imperial venture. As we saw in the first chapter, the Ottoman Empire's decline, made particularly apparent by its defeat in the Russo-Turkish War of 1768–1774, led to a series of proposals for French colonial ventures in the region. French diplomatic envoys to Constantinople, such as the baron de Tott and the comte de Saint-Priest, came to see the French conquest of Egypt and the Maghreb as both possible and desirable, while French statesmen, writers, and merchants, including such luminaries as Charles-Maurice de Talleyrand and Frédéric-Melchior Grimm, spoke enthusiastically of the possibility, with the former playing a pivotal role in launching Bonaparte's expedition to Egypt in 1798.[81] Mercier's utopian novel presented a future world transformed by benevolent colonialism, in which France has established its rule over Egypt and Greece, contributing to the revival of civilization in these lands, and has constructed a canal in the Egyptian desert that links the Mediterranean and Arabian seas, the Russians rule in Constantinople, and the Barbary States of North Africa have been conquered and administered jointly by the European maritime powers.[82]

As early as 1770, however, a plan for the conquest, colonization, and cultural transformation of the Maghreb appeared in the *Histoire des deux Indes*. The eleventh book of the *Histoire*, which discusses Africa, begins with a discussion of the North African coast, which had been known to Europeans since antiquity and which was integrated into a trans-Mediterranean network of commerce. Lamenting the decadence of Egypt, "which was the cradle of the arts, sciences, and government," but was now "bent under the yoke of despotism, ignorance, and superstition which the Turks have imposed upon it," and condemning the depredations of the Barbary pirates on

European shipping, the *Histoire* observed that the Habsburg emperor Charles V had considered conquering North Africa in the sixteenth century, but renounced the project due to more pressing rivalries in Europe itself. However, the *Histoire* continued, the time to pursue this imperial vision had now arrived, as "the peoples that inhabit Barbary tremble under a yoke which they are eager to break." Recognizing the rivalries between the European colonial powers and the certain opposition that a new French expedition in the Mediterranean would generate from Britain, Spain, and other rivals, the author of this proposal suggested that "it must therefore be the work of a universal league. It is necessary that all the maritime powers cooperate in the execution of a design that equally interests all of them."[83] The subsequent discussion of this design suggested that this conquest would be swift, sure, and irreversible, as "this people of pirates, these monsters of the sea, would be transformed into men with good laws and examples of humanity," who "would always remember tenderly the memorable epoch which drew us to their shores." The proposal goes on to suggest that this conquest would lead to "commerce, mutually beneficial to both countries," which would "roll back the barriers of the world," and concludes that such a benevolent form of colonialism "would be a precious recompense for those which for so many centuries have been the misfortune of humankind."[84]

However, the authors of the *Histoire des deux Indes* insisted that this ambitious plan should only be pursued if Europeans were to change their ways and to become true agents of enlightenment and progress, and further declared:

> If the reduction and disarmament of the Barbary pirates is not to be a source of happiness for them as for us; if we do not wish to treat them as brothers; if we do not aspire to make them our friends; if we wish to maintain and perpetuate slavery and poverty among them; if fanaticism may still renew these odious crusades that philosophy has long condemned to the indignation of all centuries; if Africa is now to become the theater of our barbarity, as Asia and America have been, and so remain; may this project, dictated by our heart for the good of our fellow men, fall into eternal oblivion! Let us remain in our ports. It matters not whether it is Christians or Muslims who suffer. Only man is worthy of being of interest to man.[85]

There are unmistakable echoes between this proposal and Napoleon's 1798 expedition to Egypt, which Edward Said has rightly signaled as marking an important turning point in the relationship between Europe and the Islamic Orient.[86] Juan Cole has observed that the leaders of the Directory used similar language of decadence and civilizing mission to justify their intervention, writing that "degeneration allowed the French to appropriate classical civilization for their own, displacing its splendor into the distant past and positioning its present heirs as unworthy, so that the mantle of these glories fell on the French instead...This attempt at restoring the Egyptians to greatness and curing their degeneracy through liberty and modernity was central to the rhetoric of the invasion."[87] Similar sentiments would be used to justify French republican imperialism in the nineteenth century and beyond, and Cole's book on the Napoleonic expedition to Egypt, written against the backdrop of the American occupation of Iraq, strongly suggests that they have not yet run their course.

Conclusions

If such promises that the armed vanguard of progress will be greeted as a liberating force by the downtrodden subjects of despotism have a familiar echo to today's readers, it is because the "progressive universalism" born out of the Enlightenment's encounter with human difference still holds great sway over our collective imagination. Belief in the superiority of a dynamic and civilized Europe over both the static, decadent Orient and the benighted savages of both hemispheres, and the legitimization of colonial conquest in the name of the spread of "civilization" are undoubtedly characteristic of one strain of French Enlightenment thought. The connections between such attitudes and the expansionist, ethnocentric policies of the following centuries are sufficiently clear as to need no further elaboration. Nevertheless, if this "civilizing mission" later provided a useful alibi to proponents of imperialism in subsequent years (whose own motives were generally political or economic rather than cultural in nature), this fact should not blind us to the progressive intentions of Condorcet, Raynal, and de Brosses, for whom the spread of enlightened civilization to encompass the globe was the natural culmination of an evolutionary historical process.

The "apotheosis of Europe" in the late Enlightenment resulted from a heightened sense of the factors that distinguished the modern West from the rest of the world, factors which, being cultural rather than physical in nature, could be transmitted to contemporary "savages," in much the same way, de Brosses argued, as the ancient

Greeks and Romans had spread civilization to the barbaric ancestors of the now civilized French. These advocates of "enlightened
colonialism" took the mission to civilize quite seriously, and made
the improvement of the well-being of colonized peoples an essential
condition of the legitimization of colonial expansion. Throughout
this period, however, there were always discordant voices who argued
against such ventures. Enlightenment critics of empire, most prominently Diderot, argued passionately in defense of the autonomy of
"primitive" peoples and sought to temper progressive universalism
with tolerance and respect for human differences. The same ethical
dilemma remains with us to this day.

Conclusion

This book has explored the importance of cross-cultural comparisons to the social and political thought of the French Enlightenment. Cross-cultural comparisons, and the *sciences humaines* for which they stood as foundations, served as a powerful double-edged sword for Enlightenment-era French writers and cultural critics, defining a discourse that was simultaneously universalist and relativist, Eurocentric and cosmopolitan. Eighteenth-century French philosophers, scientists, and men of letters, as we have seen, sought to build a universal science of humanity through empirical observation of particular peoples and societies, which would encompass both the underlying unity of humankind and its remarkable diversity. The comparative method that they elaborated could be used to decry the barbarism of non-European peoples and to advocate their assimilation to enlightened Western norms, but could also be invoked to condemn the abuses of contemporary European society and to advocate alternative "possible worlds," even radically different ones, modeled upon the examples of non-European societies and cultures. Above all, the comparative method, by presenting a broad panorama of human diversity, emphasized the accidental, contingent nature of all cultural practices and social institutions.

A persistent latter-day stereotype asserts that Enlightenment universalism rejected and effaced human difference.[1] One of the harshest critics of the alleged "Enlightenment project," the British social philosopher John Gray, has written that the "philosophical anthropology of the Enlightenment" saw cultural differences as "ephemeral, or at least developmental, phases in the history of the species," which were destined "to flow irresistibly into the great ocean of universal humanity."[2] I would argue, on the contrary, that Gray's definition of the "Enlightenment project" as the creation of a "universal civilization grounded in generic humanity and a rational morality,"[3] is a gross oversimplification of one strand of Enlightenment thought, which I have labeled "progressive universalism." Expressed most polemically and unambiguously by Condorcet, this progressive universalism assumed a relatively constant human nature and a linear, evolutionary narrative of progress through successive stages of development, and held that the differences among nations and societies were primarily the result of the contingent factors of culture, customs, and institutions, rather than of the more immutable forces of climate and heredity. Condorcet's theory of progress cannot, however, be said to characterize the Enlightenment as a whole, and several prominent figures, most notably Rousseau, maintained exactly the opposite position. Judith Shklar has written that Condorcet's boundless optimism "was far from being the only mood of the age" and that "the very skepticism, eclecticism and self-awareness" that characterized Enlightenment discourse "inspired doubt, pessimism, and self-criticism among some of the boldest prophets of the new age."[4] As I have shown throughout this book, French Enlightenment thinkers vigorously debated a wide range of questions regarding the unity and diversity of humanity, the relative merits of civilization and "primitivism," the legitimacy of slavery and colonialism, and the ethics of cross-cultural encounters. Their debates reached no definitive conclusion, but rather defined the contours of the "discursive field" that the human sciences would contest over the following centuries.

Perhaps most surprisingly, given contemporary assumptions regarding the allegedly homogenizing impact of Enlightenment universalism, a number of the eighteenth-century French authors whose works examined these questions argued that the advance of civilization would *increase*, rather than decrease, the diversity of human customs and institutions. For these thinkers, human beings were similar to one another in their physical constitution, but became differentiated from one another by culture, a formulation that allowed them to explain the diversity of customs without sacrificing the underlying unity of humankind. Both Voltaire and Diderot asserted that savage man, dominated by natural instincts and in thrall to a hostile environment, was more or less the same everywhere, but that culture, manners, and customs, which varied greatly between societies, made civilized men (a Frenchman and a Persian, for example) increasingly different from one another. The epistemology of Locke and his French imitators, by denying the existence of innate ideas and maintaining that all forms of cognition were the result of sensory inputs from the surrounding environment, implied that culture was entirely a human creation, appearing and developing differently in different places and times.[5] This juxtaposition of nature and culture (or *moeurs*, to use the term favored by most Enlightenment authors) allowed eighteenth-century thinkers to explain and accommodate the most striking diversity of cultural expressions within an overarching panorama of the unity of humankind. Voltaire concluded his massive *Essai sur les moeurs* by observing:

> All that derives from human nature is the same from one end of the world to the other, while everything that depends upon custom is different, and any resemblances are a matter of chance. The empire of custom is much vaster than that of nature; it extends itself over manners and practices and spreads variety across the stage of the universe. Nature spreads unity; it establishes everywhere a small number of invariable principles. The soil is therefore everywhere the same, while cultivation produces different fruits.[6]

The agricultural metaphor that Voltaire used to express the development of human civilization was a popular one among Enlightenment authors, as the French term *culture* originally referred to the cultivation of crops, and was only subsequently applied to the cultivation of manners and customs. Despite his romantic evocation of the primitive condition in the "Supplement to the Voyage of Bougainville," Diderot's views on the civilizing process were strikingly similar to those of Voltaire. Diderot discussed the relationship between civilization and cultural difference most explicitly in one of his many contributions to the abbé Raynal's *Histoire des deux Indes*. After a brief but sweeping ethnographic catalog of the different peoples and cultures of the West African coast, he asserted that "there are not such pronounced differences between these peoples and their conditions" as existed between the civilized nations of Europe. Diderot explained this discrepancy as follows:

> The more that men distance themselves from nature, the less they should resemble one another. The multiplicity of civil and political institutions necessarily creates in their moral character and physical customs nuances unknown to less complex societies...In Europe, an extensive and diverse commerce, varying and multiplying pleasures, fortunes, and conditions, adds still more to the differences that climate, laws, and beliefs have established among these active and laborious peoples.[7]

Far from ignoring human diversity, the French Enlightenment was virtually obsessed with it. The theorists and compilers of the age struggled to make sense of the vast body of ethnographic data accumulated by travelers, missionaries, colonists, and administrators from all corners of the globe, and used that diversity to advance a wide range of political, social, and philosophical arguments. As we have seen, Voltaire, Quesnay, and Poivre suggested that the French monarchy should imitate China by creating a rationalized, bureaucratic form of enlightened absolutism, in harmony with what they perceived as the laws of nature, in order to clear away the barriers to social and economic progress. Conversely, Lahontan, Rousseau, and (more ambiguously) Diderot maintained that Europeans should instead learn from the primitive peoples of America and Polynesia, not to abandon civilized life to live in a primeval forest or on a tropical island (which all recognized was an impossible retrogression of an evolutionary historical process), but rather to use the savage as a sort of magic mirror in which to recognize the absurdity and artificiality of many of their own customs and institutions, in order to build a new and better social order upon the debris of the old. Finally, Helvétius, Tott, and Volney argued that the decadence of once-mighty Near Eastern empires should serve as a warning to modern Europe of the ultimate consequences of the dead hand of despotism, and asserted that progress and happiness could only be achieved and maintained by free peoples.

As these examples suggest, the French Enlightenment perspective on human diversity was far more varied, complex, ambivalent, and self-critical than the straw man that has been constructed by the contemporary culture wars. For every de Brosses who advocated colonial expansion and the acculturation of native peoples, there was a Diderot who denounced colonialism and defended the autonomy of indigenous societies such as Tahiti. For every Condorcet who celebrated the march of progress, there was a Rousseau who argued that primitive man was happier and freer than civilized man. For every Quesnay who championed enlightened despotism as a force for the improvement of society, there was a Volney who countered that despotism of any sort stifled the creative genius of free peoples. While many eighteenth-century French thinkers believed that they lived in "an enlightened century" and made their own society the key protagonist in the unfolding drama of human progress, most of them also believed that this progress must be universal in scope, and should shower its benefits upon all the peoples of the world. Even the defenders of slavery, such as Malouet, were compelled to argue that the institution benefited the African slaves themselves by removing them from savagery and bringing them into the universal advance of civilization. While such assertions could hardly have comforted the slaves themselves, they did establish a utilitarian criterion for judging slavery (the happiness, well-being, and moral and intellectual advancement of "primitive" Africans), against which the practice could be evaluated and found wanting. Late Enlightenment figures, such as Condorcet, the abbé Henri Grégoire, and their colleagues in the Société des Amis des Noirs, would later contest the institution of slavery on the universalist grounds of a common human nature and inalienable human rights.[8]

In arguing that cross-cultural comparisons were fundamental to the emergence of historical, political, and social thought in eighteenth-century France, I do not wish to suggest that Enlightenment travel-writers and theorists were in any way objective or scrupulously accurate observers of the non-Western societies they depicted. On the contrary, as I have noted throughout, many of these observers studied the mandarin and the savage, the despot and the slave, for the lessons which these figures could offer contemporary Europe regarding universal human nature and the natural law of societies. We have already considered the thesis, famously presented in Edward Said's classic study *Orientalism*, that European depictions of the Orient (and those of other non-European zones and peoples) drew upon existing stereotypes and presumptions to generate a closed and self-referential discourse, erecting what Michael Keevak has called the "great wall of Europe," which obscured and distorted eighteenth-century perceptions of the world beyond.[9] While there is much to be said for this view, the examples of Enlightenment writing about the non-European world we have examined in this book demonstrate that this discourse was neither monolithic nor entirely solipsistic, nor were French visions of non-European realities completely blinkered by discursive or cultural barriers. If Enlightenment observers perceived the non-European world through a glass darkly, as it were, they nonetheless saw it, and sometimes what they saw was sufficiently striking or surprising to force changes to their *idées reçues*. Rather than a vicious circle of self-referential textual representations, I contend that a dialectical relationship developed between existing tropes, stereotypes, and frameworks of interpretation, on the one hand, and newly discovered ethnographic or historical data, on the other, which drove forward a continual process of incorporation and reevaluation of both the parts (specific peoples, cultures, and societies) and the whole (human nature and natural law) that together constituted the object of study of the emerging human sciences.

The discursive field of the *sciences humaines* shifted substantially over the course of the eighteenth century. I would argue that what most distinguishes the Enlightenment human sciences is their lack of a unifying paradigm comparable to the providential theism of the seventeenth century or the scientific racism of the nineteenth. As Sankar Muthu has observed, "In eighteenth-century debates about human diversity, no single category, classificatory scheme, or set of explanations of cultural difference was hegemonic in the manner that racial typologies of non-European peoples dominated post-Enlightenment anthropological and political thought."[10] At the dawn of the eighteenth century, secular interpretations of human diversity and the rise and fall of civilizations had to contend with biblical literalism and with theological arguments predicated on the fall from Paradise, the post-Babel dispersion of peoples, and the common descent of humanity from Adam and Eve. Over the course of the century, stadial theories of progress were challenged by neo-classical, Stoic celebrations of cultural primitivism and of a primeval golden age of humanity, of which Rousseau was the most prominent eighteenth-century advocate.[11]

As the eighteenth century neared its close, progressive universalism was contested less by such theological or metaphysical discourses than by a new discourse that claimed to be scientific, and which held that inherent and inexorable biological differences divided humanity into separate and unequal races. Such theories of human difference, which were most fully developed in the nineteenth century, drew upon the ideas of eighteenth-century philosophers and scientists such as Voltaire, Buffon, and Maupertuis, but elaborated their arguments in directions that the *philosophes* neither anticipated nor intended. Marvin Harris notes that, while racial determinism became prevalent in the nineteenth-century human sciences, "throughout the eighteenth century, the balance on the nature-nurture continuum remained well over on the nurture side."[12] The Enlightenment's nuanced discussions of human difference, which invoke the interplay of biological, environmental, and cultural factors, appear closer to our own views than does the monocausal racial determinism of the nineteenth century.[13] The reasons for the hardening of racial categories from the eighteenth to the nineteenth century lie outside the scope of the present work, but I would argue that this shift has more to do with the changing political and economic relationships between Europe and the non-European world than it does with the unfolding dialectic of Enlightenment thought. Furthermore, as Colin Kidd has demonstrated, the rationalist secularism of the Enlightenment was not a necessary prerequisite for the development of modern racism, and Scripture was invoked as often as science to justify the racial hierarchies of the nineteenth century.[14]

There is throughout the eighteenth century an unresolved tension between progressive universalism, predicated on the assumption of *both* an underlying human nature common to all peoples *and* a process of ever-greater cultural differentiation and diversity, and the taxonomic impulse to classify human beings into a hierarchy of fixed racial categories. Both of these intellectual paradigms are recognizable progeny of the Enlightenment. It would be a great tragedy, however, were we to throw out the baby of progressive universalism with the bathwater of scientific racism, for it is precisely the former that provided the intellectual tools (far more powerful than those that an equivocating cultural relativism could ever furnish) and the moral imperative to combat and to convincingly refute the latter.

As a complex and often contradictory cultural moment, the Enlightenment contributed to creating the conditions of possibility for a wide variety of different outcomes. It is, however, the contention of this author that the progressive, emancipatory face of the Enlightenment was its most important and enduring legacy. In an age in which slavery was generally accepted as legitimate, many Enlightenment writers challenged its legitimacy. In a political and economic system in which colonies were believed to exist only for the good of the metropole, they argued that the well-being of colonial subjects had to be taken into account as well, with some authors going so far as to question Europe's right to conquer weaker, more "primitive" peoples, even when this was done in the name of the advance of civilization. In a society in which religious persecution remained widespread, they called for tolerance and mutual understanding, even as they not infrequently failed to practice what they preached. While it is certainly true that some Enlightenment thinkers, especially those with personal or professional ties to the Caribbean plantation colonies, defended slavery, racial stratification, and colonial conquest as integral parts of the eighteenth-century world economic system, these evils were frequently contested in the name of other parts of the same heritage, such as equality, tolerance, and humanitarianism, and cannot without great distortion be seen as the only or inevitable result of Enlightenment.

The Enlightenment, in short, was an incomparably fertile period for the expansion of knowledge and the elaboration of competing theories regarding human nature, the causes and significance of racial and cultural differences, and the factors governing the advance and decline of human societies. This was a pivotal moment in the emergence of the *sciences humaines*, the development of a conceptual imaginary to represent, classify, and interpret human difference, and the rise of commercial, political, and cultural networks integrating nearly all the world into a Europe-centered system of global relations. This process, though indisputably constitutive of the modern world, was far too complex and contested to be reduced to a unitary "Enlightenment project." The Enlightenment was not, as Clemenceau famously said of the Revolution, *un bloc*, which subsequent generations of scholars are compelled to endorse or oppose in its entirety.[15] Instead, I would argue, it is appropriate for *nous autres philosophes*, as children of the world the eighteenth century made, to preserve and expand upon the best elements of the Enlightenment legacy, while drawing upon its critical, reflective spirit to denounce and to combat those social and intellectual ills that it either failed to destroy or helped to create.

Notes

Introduction

1. For the eighteenth-century fascination with travel literature, see René Pomeau, "Voyages et lumières dans la littérature française du XVIIIe siècle" *Studies on Voltaire and the Eighteenth Century* 57 (1967), 1269–1289; Percy G. Adams, *Travelers and Travel Liars, 1660–1800* (Berkeley, CA: University of California Press, 1962); and the essays in Larry Wolff and Marco Cipollini, eds., *The Anthropology of the Enlightenment* (Stanford, CA: Stanford University Press, 2007).
2. On this point, see the essays in Christopher Fox, Roy Porter, and Robert Wokler, *Inventing Human Science: Eighteenth Century Domains* (Berkeley and Los Angeles: University of California Press, 1995).
3. For a summary and refutation of this argument, see Peter Gay, *The Party of Humanity* (New York: Norton, 1971), especially 262–290.
4. Edward W. Said, *Orientalism* (New York: Vintage, 1979), 3, 204.
5. An overview of the historiographical and theoretical debates can be found in a recent review essay: Karen O'Brien, "The Return of the Enlightenment," *American Historical Review* 115:5 (December 2010), 1426–1435.
6. For example, John Gray has charged the Enlightenment with an "assault on cultural difference," leading to the "cultural impoverishment" of humankind through globalization. See John Gray, *Enlightenment's Wake: Politics and Culture at the Close of the Modern Age* (London and New York: Routledge, 1995), viii, 106.
7. Kathleen Glenister Roberts, *Alterity and Narrative: Stories and the Negotiation of Western Identities* (Albany, NY: State University of New York Press, 2007), 4.
8. Jean-Jacques Rousseau, "Discourse on the Origins of Inequality" [1755], in *The First and Second Discourses,* trans. Roger D. Masters (Boston, MA: Bedford St. Martin's, 1964), 212–213.
9. Anne-Robert-Jacques Turgot, "Reflexions sur les *Pensées philosophiques* de Diderot," in Gustav Schelle ed., *Oeuvres* (Paris: Felix Alcan, 1913), 95.
10. Jürgen Habermas, *The Philosophical Discourse of Modernity* (Cambridge, MA: MIT Press, 1987); David Harvey, *The Condition of Postmodernity: An Enquiry into the Origins of Cultural Change* (Oxford: Blackwell, 1990).

11. Richard Wolin, *The Seduction of Unreason: The Intellectual Romance with Fascism from Nietzsche to Postmodernism* (Princeton, NJ: Princeton University Press, 2004), 312–313.

12. James Schmidt, "What Enlightenment Project?" *Political Theory* 28:6 (2000), 737–738. See also Lynn Festa and Daniel Carey, "What Is Postcolonial Enlightenment?" in Daniel Carey and Lynn Festa, eds., *The Postcolonial Enlightenment: Eighteenth-Century Colonialism and Postcolonial Theory* (Oxford and New York: Oxford University Press, 2009), 1–33.

13. For the importance of national distinctions, see O'Brien, "The Return of the Enlightenment." For the distinction between "moderate" and "radical" Enlightenment, see Jonathan Israel, *Radical Enlightenment: Philosophy and the Making of Modernity, 1650–1750* (Oxford and New York: Oxford University Press, 2001). For the distinctiveness of the "colonial Enlightenment," see Malick Ghachem, *Sovereignty and Slavery in the Age of Revolution: Haitian Variations on a Metropolitan Theme* (Stanford University Dissertation, 2001).

14. Daniel Gordon, "On the Supposed Obsolescence of the French Enlightenment," in Daniel Gordon, ed., *Postmodernism and the Enlightenment: New Perspectives in Eighteenth-Century French History* (New York: Routledge, 2001), 212. For this distinction between the "spirit of system" and the "systematic spirit," see Ernst Cassirer, trans. Fritz Koellns and James Pettegrove, *The Philosophy of the Enlightenment* (1932; repr., Boston: Beacon Press, 1955), especially vi–viii, 8–9, and 104–108.

15. Robert Wuthnow, *Communities of Discourse: Ideology and Social Structure in the Reformation, the Enlightenment, and European Socialism* (Cambridge, MA: Harvard University Press, 1989), 13.

16. Sankar Muthu, *Enlightenment against Empire* (Princeton, NJ: Princeton University Press, 2003), 260.

17. Ursula Vogel, "The Skeptical Enlightenment: Philosopher Travellers Look Back at Europe," in Norman Geras and Robert Wokler, eds., *The Enlightenment and Modernity* (Basingstroke and London: Macmillan, 2000), 4.

18. On these topics, see Jeremy Popkin, *News and Politics in the Age of Revolution: Jean de Luzac's Gazette de Leyde* (Ithaca, NY: Cornell University Press, 1989); Robert Darnton, *The Literary Underground of the Old Regime* (Cambridge, MA: Harvard University Press, 1982); and Arlette Farge, *Subversive Words: Public Opinion in Eighteenth-Century France* (University Park, PA: Pennsylvania State University Press, 1995), respectively.

19. The title of a recent edited volume makes the point: Felicity Nussbaum, ed. *The Global Eighteenth Century* (Baltimore, MD: Johns Hopkins University Press, 2003). A recent survey text that emphasizes the importance of globalization to Enlightenment philosophy and culture is Dorinda Outram, *The Enlightenment* (Cambridge: Cambridge University Press, 2005).

20. For the enduring relevance of the Enlightenment to contemporary cultural debates, see David A. Hollinger, "The Enlightenment and the Genealogy of Cultural Conflict in the United States," in Keith Michael

Baker and Peter Hanns Reill, eds., *What's Left of Enlightenment: A Postmodern Question* (Stanford: Stanford University Press, 2001), 7–18.

1 Philosophy in the Seraglio: Orientalism and the Enlightenment

1. Thomas Kaiser, "The Evil Empire? The Debate on Turkish Despotism in Eighteenth-Century French Political Culture," *The Journal of Modern History* 72:1 (2000), 7.
2. For these contacts, see Ian Coller, "East of Enlightenment: Regulating Cosmopolitanism between Istanbul and Paris in the Eighteenth Century," *Journal of World History* 21:3 (2010), 447–470.
3. Robert Darnton, *The Great Cat Massacre and Other Episodes in French Cultural History* (New York: Vintage, 1985), 89.
4. Constantin-François de Chasseboeuf, comte de Volney, *Voyage en Syrie et en Egypte, pendant les années 1783, 1784, et 1785* (Paris: Volland, 1787), 2:419.
5. Jean Chardin, *Sir John Chardin's Travels in Persia*, ed. Sir Percy Sykes (1686; repr. London: The Argonaut Press, 1927), 125; François Bernier, *Evénemens particuliers, ou ce qui s'est passé de plus considérable après la guerre pendant cinq ans, ou environ, dans les Etats du Grand Mogol* (Paris : Claude Barbin, 1670), 2:248.
6. Henry Laurens, *Aux sources de l'orientalisme : La Bibliothèque Orientale de Barthélemy d'Herbelot* (Paris: Maisonneuve et Larose, 1978), 25.
7. Antoine Galland, Preface to Barthélemy d'Herbelot, *Bibliothèque orientale* (Paris : Compagnie des Libraires, 1697), n.p. See also Laurens, *Aux sources de l'orientalisme*, 28.
8. Galland, Preface to Herbelot, *Bibliothèque orientale*, n.p.
9. Henri de Boulainvilliers, *La Vie de Mahomed* (London, 1730), 5, 7.
10. Voltaire, *Essai sur les moeurs et l'esprit des nations* (1756; repr., Paris: Garnier Frères, 1963), 1:196, 1:55.
11. Voltaire's anti-Semitism is a complex and much-debated topic. For a harsh view, see Arthur Hertzberg, *The French Enlightenment and the Jews* (New York: Columbia University Press, 1968); and Léon Poliakov, *The Aryan Myth: A History of Racist and Nationalist Ideas in Europe* (New York: Basic Books, 1971), both of whom condemn Voltaire as an anti-Semite. For the argument that Voltaire's diatribes against the Jews reflect his rejection of Christian monotheism and intolerance, see Peter Gay, *The Party of Humanity* (New York: Norton, 1971). For a more recent and balanced view, see Ronald Schechter, *Obstinate Hebrews: Representations of Jews in France, 1715–1815* (Berkeley, CA: University of California Press, 2003).
12. Edward W. Said, *Orientalism* (New York: Vintage, 1979), 3.
13. Henry Laurens, *Les origines intellectuelles de l'expédition d'Egypte: L'Orientalisme islamisant en France (1698–1798)* (Paris and Istanbul: Editions Isis, 1987), 2.
14. Nicholas Dew, *Orientalism in Louis XIV's France* (Oxford and New York: Oxford University Press, 2009), 7.

15. Galland, Preface to Herbelot, *Bibliothèque orientale*, n.p.
16. Charles Sécondat de Montesquieu, tr. Anne Kohler, *The Spirit of the Laws* (1749; repr., Cambridge: Cambridge University Press, 1989), 235.
17. Volney, *Voyage*, 1:vi.
18. Robert Irwin, *Dangerous Knowledge: Orientalism and Its Discontents* (Woodstock, NY: The Overlook Press, 2008), 76, 82–83.
19. Laurens, *Aux sources de l'orientalisme*, 34–35.
20. Cited in Laurens, *Aux sources de l'orientalisme*, 7. For Racine's role as royal historiographer, and the origins of historical scholarship in the France of Louis XIV, see Orest Ranum, *Artisans of Glory: Writers and Historical Thought in Seventeenth-Century France* (Chapel Hill, NC: University of North Carolina Press, 1980).
21. Laurens, *Aux sources de l'orientalisme*, 92.
22. Laurens, *Aux sources de l'orientalisme*, 8–9.
23. Anthony Grafton, "Joseph Scaliger and Historical Chronology: The Rise and Fall of a Discipline," *History and Theory* 14:2 (1975), 179.
24. Herbelot, *Bibliothèque orientale*, 598, 599–600.
25. Herbelot, *Bibliothèque orientale*, 86, 88.
26. Dew, *Orientalism*, 172–173.
27. Dew, *Orientalism*, 204.
28. On this point, see Poliakov, *Aryan Myth*, 24.
29. Irwin, *Dangerous Knowledge*, 116–117.
30. Boulainvilliers, *Vie de Mahomed*, 226.
31. Boulainvilliers, *Vie de Mahomed*, 248.
32. Voltaire, *Zaïre* [1732], in *Œuvres complètes de Voltaire*, ed. Louis Moland, (Paris, 1877).
33. Voltaire, *Le fanatisme, ou Mahomet le prophète* (Amsterdam: Estienne Ledet et Cie, 1753), 36.
34. Voltaire, *Le fanatisme*, 36, 63, 104.
35. On this point, see Magdy Gabriel Badir, *Voltaire et l'Islam (Studies on Voltaire and the Eighteenth Century)*, Vol. *CXXV* (Oxford: Voltaire Foundation, 1974), 127.
36. Voltaire, "A Sa Majesté le roi de Prusse," in *Le fanatisme*, n.p.
37. Badir, *Voltaire*, 98.
38. Voltaire, *Essai sur les mœurs*, 1:256–257, 1:275.
39. Voltaire, *Essai sur les mœurs*, 1:560, 1:599, 1:822.
40. Chardin, *Chardin's Travels*, 139. See also Stephen F. Dale, *The Muslim Empires of the Ottomans, Safavids, and Mughals* (Cambridge and New York: Cambridge University Press, 2010), 124.
41. Charles-Louis de Sécondat, baron de Montesquieu, Jacques Roger ed., *Lettres persanes* (1721; repr., Paris: Garnier-Flammarion, 1964), 143.
42. Montesquieu, *The Spirit of the Laws*, 61, 462.
43. For an overview of the Enlightenment discourse on "Oriental despotism," see Franco Venturi, "Oriental Despotism," *Journal of the History of Ideas* 24:1 (1963), 133–142; and Thomas A. Kaiser, "The Evil Empire? The Debate on Turkish Despotism in Eighteenth-Century French Political Culture," *The Journal of Modern History* 72:1 (2006), 6–34. For Montesquieu's indebtedness to early modern travel literature, see David Young, "Montesquieu's

View of Despotism and His Use of Travel Literature," *The Review of Politics* 40:3 (1978), 392–405.

For a recent critique of Eurocentric biases in the construction of Oriental despotism, see Asli Çirakman, "From Tyranny to Despotism: The Enlightenment's Unenlightened Image of the Turks," *International Journal of Middle East Studies* 33:1 (2001), 49–68.

44. Chardin, *Chardin's Travels*, 130, 187, 192.
45. Galland, Preface to Herbelot, *Bibliothèque orientale*, n.p.
46. Bernier, *Evénemens*, 2:189–190; 2:63–67.
47. Bernier, *Evénemens*, 2 :220–222.
48. Chardin, *Chardin's Travels*, 138.
49. Montesquieu, *The Spirit of the Laws*, 61.
50. Dew, *Orientalism*, 133.
51. Bernier, *Evénemens*, 2:277–280.
52. Çirakman, "Despotism," 59.
53. Montesquieu, *Lettres persanes*, 73.
54. Montesquieu, *Lettres persanes*, 316, 278.
55. For the ancient roots of the climate theory, see Benjamin Isaac, *The Invention of Racism in Classical Antiquity* (Princeton, NJ: Princeton University Press, 2004), especially 56–82.
56. Chardin, *Chardin's Travels*, 249.
57. Anne-Robert-Jacques Turgot, "Recherches sur les causes des progrès et de la decadence des sciences et des arts," in *Oeuvres*, ed. Gustave Schelle (Paris: Felix Alcan, 1913), 1:120.
58. Hans Wolpe, *Histoire des deux Indes* (Stanford, CA: Stanford University Press, 1957), 1:63.
59. Chardin, *Chardin's Travels*, 216.
60. Boulainvilliers, *Vie de Mahomed*, 43.
61. Boulainvilliers, *Vie de Mahomed*, 154, 158–159.
62. Voltaire, *Zaïre*, 557, 593.
63. Voltaire, *Essai sur les mœurs*, 1 :269–270.
64. Voltaire, *Essai sur les moeurs*, 2:807.
65. Montesquieu, *Lettres persanes*, 59.
66. Montesquieu, *Lettres persanes*, 173–174.
67. Montesquieu, *Lettres persanes*, 75.
68. Diana J. Schaub, *Erotic Liberalism: Women and Revolution in Montesquieu's Persian Letters* (Boston, MA: Rowman and Littlefield, 1995), 17.
69. Montesquieu, *The Spirit of the Laws*, 104, 270, 272.
70. Cited in Fatma Göçek, *East Encounters West: France and the Ottoman Empire in the Eighteenth Century* (Oxford and New York: Oxford University Press, 1987), 45.
71. Göçek, *Encounters*, 44.
72. François de Tott, *Memoirs of Baron de Tott*, ed. John E. Woods, (1785; repr., New York: Arno Press, 1973), 1: 13, 74.
73. Tott, *Baron de Tott*, 1:163.
74. Volney, *Voyage*, 2:442, 446.
75. Volney, *Voyage*, 2 :441.
76. Information on Anquetil-Duperron's life is taken from Raymond Schwab, *La Renaissance orientale* (Paris: Payot, 1950), and Abraham-Hyacinthe

Anquetil-Duperron, *Voyage en Inde 1754–1762: Relation du voyage en preliminaire à la traduction du Zend-Avesta* (1771; repr., Cahors: Maisonneuve et Larose, 1997).

77. Abraham-Hyacinthe Anquetil-Duperron, *Législation orientale* (Amsterd am: Marc Michel Rey, 1778), 1.
78. Anquetil-Duperron, *Législation orientale*. 61, 66.
79. Anquetil-Duperron, *Législation orientale*, 75, 114, 175.
80. Anquetil-Duperron, *Législation orientale*, 32, 37.
81. Anquetil-Duperron, *Législation orientale*, iv–v.
82. Anquetil-Duperron, *Législation orientale*, v.
83. Anquetil-Duperron, *Législation orientale*, 31–32.
84. Anquetil-Duperron, *Législation orientale*, 181, 195.
85. Laurens, *Les origines intellectuelles de l'expédition d'Egypte*, 63.
86. Laurens, *Les origines intellectuelles de l'expédition d'Egypte*, 64.
87. On these events, see Dale, especially 247–280.
88. Laurens, *Les origines intellectuelles de l'expédition d'Egypte*, 174–175. For French policy debates regarding the Ottoman Empire and the "eastern question," see also Kaiser, "The Evil Empire."
89. Tott, *Baron de Tott*, 3:49, 3:172, 3:86.
90. Tott, *Baron de Tott*, 1:4, 1:234.
91. Tott, *Baron de Tott*, 1:167–168.
92. Tott, *Baron de Tott*, 1:31–32, 1:xxix.
93. Tott, *Baron de Tott*, 2:13, 1:189.
94. *Correspondance littéraire*, November 1784, 225–226.
95. Tott, *Baron de Tott*, 4:35–36.
96. Volney, *Voyage*, 2:434, 2 :432.
97. Volney, *Voyage*, 1 :179, 2 :340–341.
98. Çirakman, "Despotism," 49.
99. Irwin, *Dangerous Knowledge*, 128–129.

2   The Wisdom of the East: Enlightenment Perspectives on China

1. Michael Keevak, *The Story of a Stele: China's Nestorian Monument and its Reception in the West, 1625–1916* (Hong Kong: Hong Kong University Press, 2008), 63.
2. Voltaire, *Essai sur les moeurs et l'esprit des nations* (1756; repr., Paris: Garnier Frères, 1963), 2:398–399.
3. Voltaire, *Essai*, 2:785–786.
4. For an excellent recent survey of the Jesuit mission to China, see Liam Matthew Brockey, *Journey to the East: The Jesuit Mission to China, 1579–1724* (Cambridge, MA: Harvard University Press, 2007).
5. Alvarez Semedo, *The History of that Great and Renowned Monarchy of China* (London, 1655), 108–109.
6. Jean-Baptiste du Halde, *Description géographique, historique, chronologique, politique, et physique de l'Empire de la Chine et de la Tartarie chinoise* (Paris : P. G. Le Mercier, 1735).

7. For more information on the Kangxi emperor, see Jonathan Spence, *Emperor of China: Self Portrait of K'ang-Hsi* (New York: Vintage, 1988).

8. Jean-Baptiste du Boyer, marquis d'Argens, *Lettres Chinoises, ou correspondance philosophique, historique, et critique, entre un Chinois voyageur à Paris et ses correspondans à la Chine, en Moscovie, en Perse et au Japon* (The Hague: Pierre Paupie, 1740), 1:29, 2:20.

9. D'Argens, *Lettres*, 1:26, 1:163.

10. D'Argens, *Lettres*, 2:130.

11. D'Argens, *Lettres*, 3:242.

12. D'Argens, *Lettres*, 5:2–3.

13. Cited in Basil Guy, *The French Image of China before and after Voltaire* (Geneva: Publications de l'Institut et Musée Voltaire, 1963), 40.

14. Guy, *French Image*, 49–50.

15. Colin Mackerras, *Western Images of China* (Oxford: Oxford University Press, 1999), 30.

16. Keevak, *Story of a Stele*, 29.

17. For the Chinese rites controversy and the end of the Jesuit mission to China, see Brockey, *Journey to the East*, especially pages 184–203.

18. Cited in Guy, *French Image*, 124–125.

19. Cited in Mackerras, *Western Images*, 33.

20. Voltaire, *Essai*, 2:396; Voltaire, tr. Martyn Pollack, *The Age of Louis XIV* (1751; repr., London: J. M. Dent, 1961), 456.

21. Voltaire, *Essai*, 2:791.

22. Voltaire, *Essai*, 1:69.

23. D'Argens, *Lettres*, 4 :49–51; 1:59.

24. D'Argens, *Lettres*, 5:264, 5:288.

25. D'Argens, *Lettres*, 4:276, 4:311; 4:318–320.

26. D'Argens, *Lettres*, 5:23, 5:26.

27. Virgile Pinot, *La Chine et la formation de l'esprit philosophique en France, 1640–1740* (1932; repr. Geneva: Slatkine Reprints, 1971), 190–191.

28. Brian Curran, *The Egyptian Renaissance: The Afterlife of Ancient Egypt in Early Modern Italy* (Chicago, IL: University of Chicago Press, 2007), 18.

29. For Kircher's theory, see Paula Findlen, ed., *Athanasius Kircher: The Last Man Who Knew Everything* (New York: Routledge, 2004); Erik Iversen, *The Myth of Egypt and its Hieroglyphs in European Tradition* (1961; repr., Princeton, NJ: Princeton University Press, 1993), and Curran, *Egyptian Renaissance*. For the eighteenth-century revival of this theory, see Joseph de Guignes, *Mémoire dans lequel on prouve, que les chinois sont une colonie égyptienne, lu dans l'Assemblée publique de l'Académie Royale des Inscriptions et Belles Lettres, le 14 novembre 1758*.

30. P. J. Marshall and Glyndwr Williams, *The Great Map of Mankind: Perceptions of New Worlds in the Age of Enlightenment* (Cambridge, MA: Harvard University Press, 1982), 108.

31. Etienne Fourmont, *Réflexions sur l'origine, l'histoire, et la succession des Anciens Peuples, Chaldéens, Hébreux, Phéniciens, Egyptiens, Grecs, etc., jusqu'au tems de Cyrus* (Paris: De Bure, 1747), 2:399.

32. Fourmont, *Réflexions*, 2:398.

33. Paul-Yves Pezron, *L'Antiquité des Temps rétablie et défendue, contre les Juifs et les Nouveaux Chronologistes* (Paris: Veuve d'Edme Martin, 1687), 241–242.

34. Cited in Claudine Pouloin, *Le temps des origines: L'Eden, le Déluge, et les 'temps reculés' de Pascal à l'Encyclopédie* (Paris: Honoré Champion, 1998), 473.

35. Anthony Grafton, "Joseph Scaliger and Historical Chronology: The Rise and Fall of a Discipline," *History and Theory* 14:2 (1975), 170.

36. Quoted in Pinot, *La Chine*, 223.

37. Voltaire, *Essai*, 1:186–187.

38. Voltaire, *Essai*, 1:69; Letter of Voltaire to Leroux-Deshauterayes, December 21, 1760, in Voltaire, *Voltaire: Correspondance choisie*, edited by Jacqueline Hellegouarch. Librairie Générale Française (1990), 585–586.

39. D'Argens, *Lettres*, 5:250–251.

40. Voltaire, dedication to "L'Orphelin de la Chine," [1755] in *Théatre classique des Français*, Vol. IV, (1831), 212.

41. Voltaire, "L'Orphelin de la Chine," 289–291.

42. Guy, *French Image*, 285, 267.

43. J. H. Brumfitt, *Voltaire, Historian* (Westport, CT: Greenwood Press, 1985), 77.

44. On the Physiocrats, see Elizabeth Fox-Genovese, *The Origins of Physiocracy: Economic Revolution and Social Order in Eighteenth-Century France* (Ithaca, NY: Cornell University Press, 1976).

45. François Quesnay, "Despotisme de la Chine," [1767] in Christine Théré, Loïc Charles, et Jean-Claude Perrot, eds., *François Quesnay : Œuvres Economiques Complètes et Autres Textes* (Paris: Institut National d'Etudes Démographiques, 2005), 1091, 1015, 1017.

46. Quesnay, "Despotisme," 1014, 1019.

47. Guy, *French Image*, 350–351.

48. Quesnay, "Despotisme," 1031, 1079.

49. Quesnay, "Despotisme," 1065.

50. Quesnay, "Despotisme," 1059.

51. Biographical reference in ANOM F2C 10.

52. Pierre Poivre, *Voyages d'un philosophe, ou observations sur les mœurs et les arts des peuples de l'Afrique, de l'Asie, et de l'Amérique* (Yverdon, 1768), 9, 44.

53. Poivre, *Voyages d'un philosophe*, 110, 118–119.

54. Poivre, *Voyages d'un philosophe*, 111–112.

55. Poivre, *Voyages d'un philosophe*, 72–73, 77.

56. Poivre, *Voyages d'un philosophe*, 121–122, 124–125, 126–127.

57. Mackerras, *Western Images*, 36.

58. *Correspondance littéraire*, July 1, 1768, 459–460.

59. Mackerras, *Western Images*, 39.

60. Montesquieu, *Spirit of the Laws*, [1749], trans. by Anne Kohler (Cambridge: Cambridge University Press, 1989), 126–128.

61. Voltaire, *Essai*, 2:398–399.

62. Brumfitt, *Voltaire*, 79.

63. Voltaire, *Essai*, 1:223. For the singular relics of the Dalai Lama, see Voltaire, *Lettres chinoises, indiennes, et tartares, à M. de Paw, par un Bénédictin* (London, 1776), 59.
64. Voltaire, *Essai*, 1:223–224.
65. Voltaire, *Essai*, 2:399.
66. Quesnay, "Despotisme," 1100.
67. Quesnay, "Despotisme," 1112.
68. Jean-François de Galaup de La Pérouse, *Voyage de La Pérouse autour du monde* (Paris: Imprimérie de la République, 1797), 2:315, 321.
69. Chrétien-Louis-Joseph de Guignes, *Réflexions sur les anciennes observations astronomiques des Chinois, et sur l'état de leur empire dans les temps les plus reculés, lues a l'Institut de France.* (Paris, n.d.), 438.
70. Guignes, *Réflexions*, 13, 22–23.
71. *Correspondance littéraire*, September 15, 1766, 151.
72. *Correspondance littéraire*, September 15, 1766, 153.
73. *Histoire de l'Académie des Sciences* (1759), 45.
74. Guillaume-Thomas Raynal, *Histoire philosophique et politique des établissements et du commerce des Européens dans les deux Indes* (Amsterdam, 1770), 1:99.
75. Jean-Jacques Rousseau, "Discourse on the Sciences and Arts" [1750], in *The First and Second Discourses*, trans. Roger D. Masters (Boston, MA: Bedford St. Martin's, 1964), 41.
76. Rousseau, "Discourse," 41.
77. Cited in Guy, *French Image*, 321.
78. Cornelius De Pauw, *Recherches philosophiques sur les Egyptiens et les Chinois* (London: Thomas Johnson, 1774), 2:401.
79. De Pauw, *Recherches philosophiques*, 1:9, 1:75.
80. De Pauw, *Recherches philosophiques*, 2:408, 1:440.
81. Cited in Guy, *French Image*, 337.
82. Letter of Denis Diderot to Sophie Volland, October 28, 1760, in Diderot, *Diderot. Tome V: Correspondance*, ed. Laurent Versini (Paris: Robert Laffont, 1997), 290.
83. Cited in Guy, *French Image*, 352.
84. Cited in Henry Vyverberg, *Human Nature, Cultural Diversity, and the French Enlightenment* (New York: Oxford University Press, 1989), 130.
85. *Correspondance littéraire*, September 1773, 233.
86. Karen O'Brien, *Narratives of Enlightenment: Cosmopolitan History from Voltaire to Gibbon* (Cambridge: Cambridge University Press, 1997), 50.
87. Voltaire, dédicatoire, "L'Orphelin de la Chine," [1755], *Théatre classique des Français* (Paris, 1831), 217.
88. Voltaire, *Essai*, 2:412.
89. *Correspondance littéraire*, August 1773, 213.
90. Keevak, *Story of a Stele*, 17.
91. J. J. Clarke, *Oriental Enlightenment: The Encounter between Asian and Western Thought* (London: Routledge, 1997), 26.
92. Keevak, *Story of a Stele*, 77.
93. Clarke, *Oriental Enlightenment*, 54.

3 The New World and the Noble Savage

1. Michel de Montaigne, "Des Cannibales" [1580] in *Essais*, ed. Charles Louandre (Paris: Charpentier, 1862), 1:307.
2. Montaigne, *Essais*, 1:307–309.
3. Montaigne, *Essais*, 1:313–314.
4. Alain Beaulieu, "Introduction," Réal Ouellet and Alain Beaulieu, eds., *Lahontan: Oeuvres complètes* (Montreal: Presses Universitaires de Montreal, 1990), 91.
5. Louis-Armand de Lom d'Arce, baron de Lahontan, *Dialogues de Monsieur le Baron de Lahontan et d'un Sauvage, dans l'Amérique* (Amsterdam: Veuve de Boeteman, 1704), 53.
6. Lahontan, *Dialogues*, 54.
7. For a more thorough analysis of Lahontan's life and work, and the political and intellectual motives behind his construction of the noble savage, see David Allen Harvey, "The Noble Savage and the Savage Noble: Philosophy and Ethnography in the *Voyages* of the Baron de Lahontan," *French Colonial History* 11 (2010), 161–191.
8. Beaulieu, "Introduction," *Lahontan: Oeuvres complètes*, 11–198.
9. *Mémoires de Trévoux*, July 1703, 1111–1112.
10. Lahontan, *Oeuvres Complètes*, 1009–1010.
11. Jonathan Israel, *Radical Enlightenment: Philosophy and the Making of Modernity, 1650–1750* (Oxford and New York: Oxford University Press, 2001), 582.
12. Sankar Muthu, *Enlightenment against Empire* (Princeton, NJ: Princeton University Press, 2003), 7.
13. Jean-Jacques Rousseau, "Discourse on the Origins of Inequality" [1755], in *The First and Second Discourses*, trans. Roger D. Masters (Boston, MA: Bedford St. Martin's, 1964), 93.
14. Arthur Lovejoy and George Boas, *Primitivism and Related Ideas in Antiquity* (1935; repr., New York: Octagon Books, 1965); Ter Ellingson, *The Myth of the Noble Savage* (Berkeley, CA: University of California Press, 2001).
15. Rousseau, *First and Second Discourses*, 223.
16. Rousseau, *First and Second Discourses*, 151.
17. For critiques of the common association of Rousseau with the idea of the noble savage, see Giuliano Gliozzi, "Rousseau: Mythe du bon sauvage ou critique du mythe des origines?" in *Primitivisme et mythes des origines dans la France des Lumières, 1680–1820*, ed., Chantal Grell and Christian Michel, (Paris : Presses de l'Université de Paris-Sorbonne, 1989), 193–203; and Ellingson, *The Myth*, xiii-xvi.
18. Cited in Maurice Cranston, *The Noble Savage: Jean-Jacques Rousseau, 1754–1762* (Chicago, IL: University of Chicago Press, 1991), 9.
19. Charles Palissot, *Les Philosophes* (Paris : Duchesne, 1760), 84–85.
20. Rousseau, *First and Second Discourses*, 20, 201.
21. Rousseau, *First and Second Discourses*, 202.
22. Jean-Jacques Rousseau, *Du contrat social* (1762; repr., Paris: Union Générale d'Editions, 1963).

23. Muthu, *Enlightenment,* 20, 30, and 23.
24. Joseph-François Lafitau, *Mœurs des sauvages amériquains, comparés aux mœurs des premiers temps,* (Paris: Saugrain, 1724), 1:111.
25. Lafitau, *Mœurs des sauvages,* 1:113.
26. For a more extensive discussion of the religious roots of Lafitau's anthropology, see David Allen Harvey, "Living Antiquity: Lafitau's *Moeurs des sauvages amériquains* and the Religious Roots of the Enlightenment Science of Man." *Proceedings of the Western Society for French History* 36 (2008), 75–92; as well as Andreas Motsch, *Lafitau et l'emergence du discours ethnographique* (Sillery, PQ: Septentrion, 2001).
27. Lafitau, *Mœurs des sauvages,* 1:12.
28. For Lafitau as a forerunner of modern anthropology, see Christian Feest, "Father Lafitau as Ethnographer of the Iroquois" *European Review of Native American Studies* 15:2 (2001); William N. Fenton, "J. F. Lafitau, Precursor of Scientific Anthropology," *Southwestern Journal of Anthropology* 25:2 (1969), 173–187; and Mary E. Fleming Mathur, "The Iroquois in Ethnography...A Time-Space Concept," *The Indian Historian* 2:3 (1969), 12–18.
29. Anthony Pagden, *European Encounters with the New World: From Renaissance to Romanticism* (New Haven, CT: Yale University Press, 1993), 24.
30. Lafitau, *Mœurs des sauvages,* 2:222, 257–258, 325.
31. Voltaire, *Essai sur les moeurs et l'esprit des nations* (1756; repr., Paris: Garnier Frères, 1963), 1:30.
32. Pierre-François Xavier Charlevoix, *Histoire de la Nouvelle France* (Paris, 1744), 3:265.
33. Charlevoix, *Histoire,* 1:27, 1:124, 1:183.
34. Charlevoix, *Histoire,* 1:280.
35. Charlevoix, *Histoire,* 2:264, 2:453.
36. Charlevoix, *Histoire,* 1:309.
37. Charlevoix, *Histoire,* 1:316–317, 334.
38. Charlevoix, *Histoire,* 3:82.
39. Charlevoix, *Histoire,* 1: 345.
40. Charlevoix, *Histoire,* 1:344.
41. Charlevoix, *Histoire,* 2:98.
42. Charlevoix, *Histoire,* 1:497.
43. Charlevoix, *Histoire,* 2:247.
44. Charlevoix, *Histoire,* 2:29–30.
45. Charlevoix, *Histoire,* 3:37.
46. On this point, see Ronald L. Meek, *Social Science and the Ignoble Savage* (Cambridge: Cambridge University Press, 1976).
47. For more information on the La Condamine expedition, see Charles-Marie de La Condamine, *Relation abrégée d'un voyage fait dans l'intérieur de l'Amérique Méridionale, depuis la côte de la Mer du Sud, jusqu'aux Côtes de Brésil et de la Guyane* (1745; repr., Maastricht: Dugour & Roux, 1778); Neil Safier, *Measuring the New World : Enlightenment Science and South America* (Chicago, IL: University of Chicago Press, 2008) ; and Roger Mercier, "Les Français en Amérique du Sud dans le XVIIIe siècle : La

Mission de l'Académie des Sciences, 1735–1745," *Revue Française d'Outre-Mer* 56:205 (September 1969), 327–374.
48. Safier, *Measuring the New World*, 71–73.
49. La Condamine, *Relation*, 50.
50. La Condamine, *Relation*, 50–51.
51. De Pauw, *Défense des Recherches Philosophiques sur les Américains* (Berlin: Georges Jacques Decker, 1770), 34–35.
52. Cited in Safier, *Measuring the New World*, 106–107.
53. *Journal des Sçavans*, January 1746, 51.
54. Safier, *Measuring the New World*, 99, 259.
55. Cited in Safier, *Measuring the New World*, 166.
56. Mercier, *Revue Française*, 349.
57. Claude-Adrien Helvétius, *De l'esprit* (Paris: Durand, 1758), 21.
58. Helvétius, *De l'esprit*, 315.
59. Louis-Antoine de Bougainville, "Journal de l'expédition d'Amérique commencée en l'année 1756, le 15 mars," in Bougainville, *Ecrits sur le Canada : Mémoires, journal, lettres* (Sillery, PQ : Septentrion, 2003), 137.
60. Denis Diderot, letter of November 2, 1760 to Sophie Volland, in Diderot, ed. Laurent Versini, *Diderot. Tome V: Correspondance* (Paris: Robert Laffont, 1997), 303.
61. For Diderot's contribution to the essay that launched Rousseau's notoriety, see Raymond Trousson, *Jean-Jacques Rousseau* (Paris: Taillandier, 2003), 210–211.
62. Diderot, letter of September 15, 1755, to the abbé Le Monnier, in Diderot, *Correspondance*, 51.
63. Diderot, letter of March 30, 1769, to Falconet, in Diderot, *Correspondance*, 939.
64. Cited in Jacques Roger, *Buffon* (Paris: Fayard, 1989), 400.
65. Antonello Gerbi, *The Dispute of the New World: The History of a Polemic, 1750–1900*, trans. Jeremy Moyle (Pittsburgh: University of Pittsburgh Press, 1973), 55.
66. Cornelius de Pauw, *Recherches Philosophiques sur les Américains* (London, 1770), 1:126.
67. De Pauw, *Défense*, 136. The passage in question reads as follows: "What is most admirable about them, and should lead them to be regarded as true philosophers, is that the sight of our commodities, of our riches, of our magnificence hardly affects them, and they are perfectly willing to do without them. Some Iroquois who were brought to Paris in 1666, and who were shown all of the royal houses and all the beauties of this great city, admired nothing, and would have preferred their villages to the capital of the most flourishing kingdom of Europe, had they not seen the rotisserie shops in the rue de la Huchette, which they found always adorned by meats of all kinds, which charmed them greatly." Charlevoix, *Histoire*, 3:322.
68. De Pauw, *Recherches*, 1 :23.
69. De Pauw, *Recherches*, 1:30.
70. De Pauw, *Recherches*, 1:171.

71. Antoine-Joseph Pernety, *Dissertation sur l'Amérique et les Américains, contre les recherches philosophiques de M. de Pauw* (Berlin, 1770), 4, 8.
72. Pernety, *Dissertation,* 12.
73. Pernety, *Dissertation,* 15.
74. Pernety, *Dissertation,* 87.
75. Pernety, *Dissertation,* 91.
76. Antoine-Joseph Pernety, *Histoire d'un voyage aux isles Malouines, fait en 1763 et 1764, avec des observations sur le détroit de Magellan et sur les Patagons* (Paris: Saillant et Nyon, 1770), 1 :298.
77. De Pauw, *Défense,* 6–7.
78. Rollin, "Mémoire physiologique et pathologique sur les Américains," in Jean-François de Galaup de La Pérouse, *Voyage de La Pérouse autour du monde* (Paris: Imprimérie de la République, 1797), 4:42.
79. Cited in Meek, *Ignoble Savage,* 22.
80. *Mémoires de Trévoux,* September 1724, 1569.
81. *Mémoires de Trévoux,* November 1724, 2001–2003.
82. Cited in Pagden, *European Encounters,* 118.
83. Harry Liebersohn, *The Travelers' World: Europe to the Pacific* (Cambridge, MA: Harvard University Press, 2006), 299.
84. Roger Mercier, "L'Amérique dans l'*Histoire des Deux Indes* de Raynal," *Revue française d'histoire d'outre-mer* 65:3 (1978), 316.
85. *Histoire des Deux Indes,* Vol. VI, 41–44.
86. Muthu, *Enlightenment,* 23.

4   The Last Frontiers

1. Jean-Jacques Rousseau, "Discourse on the Origins of Inequality" [1755], in *The First and Second Discourses,* trans. and ed. Roger D. Masters (Boston, MA: Bedford St. Martin's, 1964), 212–213.
2. For more information on Maupertuis's remarkable life and scientific career, see Mary Terrall, *The Man Who Flattened the Earth: Maupertuis and the Sciences in the Enlightenment* (Chicago, IL: University of Chicago Press, 2002).
3. Pierre Moreau de Maupertuis, *Lettre sur le progrès des sciences* (n. p., 1752), 6–7.
4. Maupertuis, *Lettre,* 7–8.
5. Maupertuis, *Lettre,* 15–16.
6. Maupertuis, *Lettre,* 18.
7. Maupertuis, *Lettre,* 47–50.
8. Maupertuis, *Lettre,* 27.
9. Maupertuis, *Lettre,* 28–29.
10. Maupertuis, *Lettre,* 29.
11. Maupertuis, *Lettre,* 55–56.
12. Madeleine V. David, "Le Président de Brosses historien des religions et philosophe," in *Charles de Brosses, 1777–1977 : Actes du colloque organisé à Dijon du 3 au 7 mail 1977,* ed., Jean-Claude Garreta (Geneva: Slatkine, 1981), 129.

234 Notes to Pages 100–110

13. Charles de Brosses, *Histoire des navigations aux terres australes* (Paris : Durand, 1756), 1:2.
14. De Brosses, *Histoire*, 1:13.
15. De Brosses, *Histoire*, 1 :10.
16. De Brosses, *Histoire*, 1 :16.
17. De Brosses, *Histoire*, 1:20–21.
18. De Brosses, *Histoire*, 1:28.
19. De Brosses, *Histoire*, 1:31.
20. Louis-Antoine de Bougainville, *Voyage autour du monde* (1771; repr., Paris: Gallimard, 1982), 225–6. For a brief biographical sketch of Louis-Antoine de Bougainville, see the introduction to this edition by Jacques Proust.
21. Matt Matsuda, *Empire of Love: Histories of France and the Pacific* (Oxford and New York: Oxford University Press, 2005).
22. Harry Liebersohn, *The Travelers' World: Europe to the Pacific* (Cambridge, MA: Harvard University Press, 2006), 86.
23. Bougainville, *Voyage*, 235.
24. Bougainville, *Voyage*, 19.
25. Bougainville, *Voyage*, 22.
26. P. J. Marshall and Glyndwr Williams, *The Great Map of Mankind: Perceptions of New Worlds in the Age of Enlightenment* (Cambridge, MA: Harvard University Press, 1982), 259.
27. Bougainville, *Voyage*, 259, 257.
28. Louis-Antoine de Bougainville, *Écrits sur le Canada : Mémoires—Journal—Lettres,* ed. Etienne Taillemite (Sillery: Septentrion, 2003), 93.
29. Bougainville, *Écrits*, 73.
30. Bougainville, *Écrits*, 109, 181, 209.
31. Bougainville, *Écrits*, 211.
32. Bougainville, *Voyage*, 254.
33. Bougainville, *Voyage*, 46–47.
34. Bougainville, *Voyage*, 192.
35. Bougainville, *Voyage*, 192–193.
36. Liebersohn, *Travelers' World*, 44.
37. Denis Diderot, "Supplement to the Voyage of Bougainville" [1772], in *Diderot: Political Writings,* trans. and ed., John Hope Mason and Robert Wokler (Cambridge: Cambridge University Press, 1992), 42.
38. Larry Wolff, "Discovering Cultural Perspective: The Intellectual History of Anthropological Thought in the Age of Enlightenment," in *The Anthropology of the Enlightenment,* ed., Larry Wolff and Marco Cipolloni, *The Anthropology of the Enlightenment* (Stanford, CA: Stanford University Press, 2007), 22.
39. Diderot, "Voyage of Bougainville," 74.
40. Claudia Moscovici, "An Ethics of Cultural Exchange: Diderot's *Supplément au Voyage de Bougainville,*" *Clio* 30:3 (2001), 290, 307.
41. Diderot, "Voyage of Bougainville," 71–72. It is interesting and instructive to juxtapose this analysis of civilized man's unhappiness to that offered by Freud in *Civilization and Its Discontents.*
42. Diderot, "Voyage of Bougainville," 40–41.
43. Diderot, "Voyage of Bougainville," 66–67.

44. Tzvetan Todorov, *On Human Diversity: Nationalism, Racism, and Exoticism in French Thought* (Cambridge, MA: Harvard University Press, 1993), 280.
45. Liebersohn, *Travelers' World,* 18.
46. Cited in Sankar Muthu, *Enlightenment against Empire* (Princeton, NJ: Princeton University Press, 2003), 149.
47. Cited in Marshall and Williams, *Great Map,* 286.
48. Jean-François de Galaup de La Pérouse, *Voyage de La Pérouse autour du monde* (Paris: Imprimérie de la République, 1797), 3:191.
49. Cited in Jordan Kellman, *Discovery and Enlightenment at Sea: Maritime Exploration and Observation in the Eighteenth-Century French Scientific Community* (Princeton University Dissertation, 1998), 408.
50. Letter of La Pérouse to Fléurieu, February 7, 1788, reprinted in Jean-François de Galaup de La Pérouse, *Voyage de La Pérouse autour du monde* (Paris: Imprimérie de la République, 1797), 4:239.
51. Letter of La Pérouse to Fléurieu, February 7, 1788, reprinted in La Pérouse, 4:239.
52. La Pérouse, *Voyage de La Pérouse,* 2 :192, 195.
53. La Pérouse, *Voyage de La Pérouse,* 2 :193–194.
54. La Pérouse, *Voyage de La Pérouse,* 2:67.
55. La Pérouse, *Voyage de La Pérouse,* 2:93.
56. La Pérouse, *Voyage de La Pérouse,* 2:95.
57. La Pérouse, *Voyage de La Pérouse,* 3:20–21.
58. La Pérouse, *Voyage de La Pérouse,* 3:39.
59. La Pérouse, *Voyage de La Pérouse,* 3:88–89.
60. Daniel Headrick, *The Tools of Empire: Technology and European Imperialism in the Nineteenth Century* (Oxford: Oxford University Press, 1981).
61. C. Becker and V. Martin, eds., "Mémoires d'Adanson sur le Sénégal et l'île de Gorée," *Bulletin de l'Institut fondamental de l'Afrique noire* 42:4 (1980), 725–726.
62. Michel Adanson, *Voyage au Sénégal,* ed. Denis Reynaud and Jean Schmidt (1757; repr., Saint-Etienne: Publications de l'Université de Saint-Etienne, 1996), 44.
63. Adanson, *Sénégal,* 40.
64. Adanson, *Sénégal,* 45.
65. Adanson, *Sénégal,* 50–51.
66. Adanson, *Sénégal,* 120.
67. Editor's footnote, Adanson, *Sénégal,* 120.
68. *Mémoires de Trévoux,* January 1758, 123–124.
69. Adanson, *Sénégal,* 45.
70. Adanson, *Sénégal,* 46–47.
71. Adanson, *Sénégal,* 105.
72. *Mémoires de Trévoux,* January 1758, 122.
73. Biographical information taken from Auguste Chevalier, *Michel Adanson: Voyageur, naturaliste, et philosophe* (Paris: Larose, 1934). On Adanson's contribution to the fields of natural history and biology, see Robert Huxley, ed., *The Great Naturalists* (London: Thames & Hudson, 2007), 153–158

74. Cited in Chevalier, *Michel Adanson,* 88–89.
75. Cited in Chevalier, *Michel Adanson,* 31.
76. Chevalier, *Michel Adanson,* 10.
77. David Diop, "La mise à l'épreuve d'un *régime de véridiction* sur 'la paresse et la négligence des Nègres' dans le *Voyage au Sénégal* d'Adanson,'" in *L'Afrique du siècle des Lumières : savoirs et représentations,* ed. Catherine Gallouët et. al. (Oxford : Voltaire Foundation, 2009), 22.
78. Abbé Demanet, *Nouvelle histoire de l'Afrique française, enrichie de cartes et d observations astronomiques et géographiques, de remarques sur les usages locaux, les mœurs, la Religion, et la nature du commerce général de cette Partie du Monde* (Paris: La Veuve Duchesne, 1767), 1:226–227.
79. Demanet, *Nouvelle histoire,* 2:7–8.
80. Demanet, *Nouvelle histoire,* 1:1–2.
81. Demanet, *Nouvelle histoire,* 2:194–195.
82. Charles de Brosses, *Du culte des dieux fétiches* (Paris, 1760), 182.
83. De Brosses, *Du culte,* 193–194.
84. David Bindman, *Ape to Apollo: Aesthetics and the Idea of Race in the Eighteenth Century* (Ithaca, NY: Cornell University Press, 2002).
85. Bougainville, *Voyage,* 252.
86. Bougainville, *Voyage,* 286, 311.

5   The Varieties of Man: Racial Theory between Climate and Heredity

1. George Mosse, *Toward the Final Solution: A History of European Racism* (New York: Howard Fertig, 1978), 1. See also George M. Fredrickson, *Racism: A Short History* (Princeton, NJ: Princeton University Press, 2002); and Leon Poliakov, *The Aryan Myth: A History of Racist and Nationalist Ideas in Europe,* trans. Edmund Howard (New York: Basic Books, 1971).
2. On these points, respectively, see Benjamin Isaac, *The Invention of Racism in Classical Antiquity* (Princeton, NJ: Princeton University Press, 2004); David Nirenberg, "Was there race before modernity? The example of 'Jewish' blood in late medieval Spain" in *The Origins of Racism in the West,* ed. Miriam Eliav-Feldon, et. al. (Cambridge and New York: Cambridge University Press, 2009), 232–264; and Anthony Pagden, *The Fall of Natural Man: The American Indian and the Origins of Comparative Ethnology* (Cambridge: Cambridge University Press, 1982).
3. Emmanuel Chukwudi Eze, *Race and the Enlightenment* (Malden, MA: Blackwell, 1997), 5.
4. Colin Kidd, *The Forging of Races: Race and Scripture in the Protestant Atlantic World, 1600–2000* (Cambridge and New York: Cambridge University Press, 2006), 85. For the most prominent examples of prerevolutionary French polygenism, see Isaac La Peyrère, *A Theological System, upon that Presupposition that Men Were Before Adam* (London, 1655); Voltaire, *Traité de Métaphysique (1734), Reproduced from the Kehl Text* (Manchester: Manchester University Press, 1937). For the debate between monogenism and polygenism more generally, see Poliakov, *The Aryan Myth.*

5. Pierre Boulle, "François Bernier and the Origins of the Modern Concept of Race," in *The Color of Liberty: Histories of Race in France*, ed. Sue Peabody and Tyler Stovall (Durham, NC: Duke University Press, 2003), 12.

6. François Bernier, "Une nouvelle division de la Terre," *Journal des Sçavans* (1684), 133–134.

7. Bernier, "Une nouvelle, " 134–136.

8. Bernier, "Une nouvelle, " 137.

9. Boulle, *Color of Liberty*, 15–16, 19.

10. Isaac, *Invention of Racism*, 30.

11. Kidd, *Forging of Races*, 8–9.

12. David Bindman, *Ape to Apollo: Aesthetics and the Idea of Race in the Eighteenth Century* (Ithaca, NY: Cornell University Press, 2002), 16.

13. Kidd, *Forging of Races*, 27.

14. Giuliano Gliozzi, *Adam et le Nouveau Monde* (Lecques: Théétète, 2000), 14.

15. Cited in Gliozzi, *Adam*, 161.

16. Cited in Gliozzi, *Adam*, 28–29.

17. Poliakov, *The Aryan Myth*, 131.

18. Cited in David Livingstone, "The Pre-Adamite Theory and the Marriage of Science and Religion," *Transactions of the American Philosophical Society* 82:3 (1992), 4.

19. Cited in Gliozzi, *Adam*, 257.

20. La Peyrère, *Theological System*, 2–4. For a discussion of the "natural religion" thesis in early modern Europe, see D. P. Walker, *The Ancient Theology: Studies in Christian Platonism from the Fifteenth to the Eighteenth Century* (Ithaca, NY: Cornell University Press, 1972).

21. Richard Popkin, "The Philosophical Basis of Eighteenth-Century Racism," in *Racism in the Eighteenth Century*, ed., Harold Pagliaro (Cleveland, OH: Case Western Reserve University Press, 1973), 252.

22. Livingstone, "Pre-Adamite Theory," 7.

23. La Peyrère, *Theological System*, prologue, 113, 152, 250.

24. La Peyrère, *Theological System*, 86.

25. Isaac La Peyrère, *Lettre de la Peyrère a Philotime, dans laquelle il expose les raisons qui l'ont obligé a abjurer la secte de Calvin qu'il professait, et le Livre des Preadamites qu'il avait mis au jour* (Paris: Augustin Courbé, 1668), 123–131.

26. Louis-Armand Lom d'Arce, baron de Lahontan, *Nouveaux voyages de M. le Baron de Lahontan dans l'Amérique Septentrionale* (The Hague: Frères l'Honoré, 1703), 249–250.

27. Lahontan, *Nouveaux voyages*, 252.

28. *Journal de Trévoux*, July 1703, 1112.

29. Fredrickson, *Racism*, 45.

30. I am grateful to April Shelford for sharing with me her unpublished paper on the dispute between Malfert and Tournemine, "Racializing Scripture in Eighteenth-Century France."

31. R. P. Auguste * * *, "Mémoire sur l'Origine des Nègres et des Américains," *Mémoires de Trévoux* (1733), 1935.

32. Auguste, *Mémoires de Trévoux*, 1939–1941, 1948.
33. Auguste, *Mémoires de Trévoux*, 1953–1955.
34. Tournemine, "Remarques du Père Tournemine Jésuite sur le mémoire touchant l'origine des Nègres et des Américains, inséré dans ce Journal au mois de Novembre 1733," *Mémoires de Trévoux* (1734), 621.
35. Cited in Jean Ehrard, *Lumières et esclavage: L'esclavage colonial et l'opinion publique en France au XVIIIe siècle* (Brussels: André Versaille, 2008), 106.
36. Voltaire, "Traité de Métaphysique," 3–5.
37. Voltaire, *Essai sur les mœurs et l'esprit des nations* (1756; repr., Paris: Garnier Frères, 1963), 1:6.
38. Voltaire, *Essai*, 1:233.
39. Isaac, *Invention of Racism*, 60, 86, 57.
40. Margaret T. Hodgen, *Early Anthropology in the Sixteenth and Seventeenth Centuries* (Philadelphia, PA: University of Pennsylvania Press, 1971), 214.
41. Bindman, *Ape to Apollo*, 59.
42. Jean-Baptiste du Bos, *Réflexions critiques sur la peinture et la poésie* (n.d.), 252–254.
43. Pierre-François-Xavier Charlevoix, *Histoire de la Nouvelle France* (Paris, 1744), 3:310–311.
44. Charlevoix, *Nouvelle France*, 1:19–20.
45. Bindman, *Ape to Apollo*, 59.
46. Du Bos, *Réflexions*, 155–156.
47. Isaac, *Invention of Racism*, 85.
48. Bruce Baum, *The Rise and Fall of the Caucasian Race: A Political History of Racial Identity* (New York: New York University Press, 2006), 68–69.
49. Cited in Philip Sloan, "The Idea of Racial Degeneracy in Buffon's *Histoire naturelle*" in Harold Pagliaro, ed., *Racism in the Eighteenth Century* (Cleveland, OH: Case Western Reserve University, 1973), 294.
50. Michèle Duchet, *Anthropologie et histoire au siècle des Lumières* (Paris: François Maspéro, 1971), 232–233.
51. George-Louis Leclerc, comte de Buffon, "Des variétés de l'homme," *Histoire naturelle générale et particulière* (Paris: Imprimerie Royale, 1750–1804), 3 : 401.
52. Charlevoix, *Nouvelle France*, 1:20.
53. Jean-François de Galaup de La Pérouse, "Questions proposées par la Société de Médicine, à MM. Les voyageurs qui accompagnent M. de La Pérouse, lues dans la séance du 31 mai 1785," in *Voyage de La Pérouse autour du monde* (Paris: Imprimérie de la République, 1797), 1:184–185.
54. Rollin, "Mémoire physiologique et pathologique sur les Américains," in Jean-François de Galaup de La Pérouse, *Voyage de La Pérouse autour du monde* (Paris: Imprimérie de la République, 1797), 4:42.
55. Buffon, "Des variétés," 433.
56. Buffon, "Des variétés," 446–448.
57. Buffon, "Des variétés," 473.
58. Buffon, "Des variétés," 448–449, 454.
59. Buffon, "Des variétés," 480–481.
60. On this point, see Robert Huxley, *The Great Naturalists* (London: Thames and Hudson, 2007), 140–148.

61. Claude Blanckaert, "Buffon and the Natural History of Man: Writing History and the 'Foundational Myth' of Anthropology," *History of the Human Sciences* 6:1 (1993), 39.
62. Buffon, "Des variétés," 482–483.
63. Buffon, "Des variétés," 487.
64. Buffon, "Des variétés," 510–511.
65. Buffon, "Des variétés," 515.
66. Buffon, "Des variétés," 528.
67. Buffon, "Des variétés," 529–530.
68. Buffon, "Des variétés," 530.
69. Pierre Moreau de Maupertuis, *La Vénus physique* (n.p., 1745), 147.
70. For the terms of the debate, and Maupertuis's position within it, see Jacques Roger, *Les sciences de la vie dans la pensée française du XVIIIe siècle* (Paris: Armand Colin, 1963).
71. Maupertuis, *La Vénus,* 140.
72. Maupertuis, *La Vénus,* 155–156.
73. Maupertuis, *La Vénus,* 131.
74. Maupertuis, *La Vénus,* 141. Although Maupertuis uses the word "espèce" to describe the new and exotic races of women he imagines here, his advocacy of monogenesis would seem to exclude the notion of different "species," in a Darwinian sense, of humanity.
75. Mary Terrall, *The Man Who Flattened the Earth: Maupertuis and the Sciences in the Enlightenment* (Chicago, IL: University of Chicago Press, 2002), 337.
76. Leon Poliakov notes that Maupertuis was recognized as "one of the creators of genetics" by Jean Rostand in a preface to a 1964 edition of the scientist's works. See Poliakov, *The Aryan Myth,* 163.
77. Maupertuis, *La Vénus,* 128.
78. Maupertuis, *La Vénus,* 158–159.
79. Sloan, *Racism,* 299–300.
80. Maupertuis, *La Vénus,* 164–165.
81. Maupertuis, *La Vénus,* 160–161.
82. Maupertuis, *La Vénus,* 152.
83. Buffon, "Des variétés," 501–503.
84. Abbé Demanet, *Nouvelle histoire de l'Afrique française* (Paris: La Veuve Duchesne, 1767), xxvii–xxviii.
85. Demanet, *Nouvelle histoire,* 2:209. The comparison between the Dane and the African is an almost word-for-word plagiarism of Maupertuis's *La Vénus physique.*
86. Demanet, *Nouvelle histoire,* 2:217–220.
87. Demanet, *Nouvelle histoire,* 2:221–222.
88. Demanet, *Nouvelle histoire,* 2:223, 225–227.
89. Demanet, *Nouvelle histoire,* 2:240.
90. Cornelius De Pauw, *Recherches Philosophiques sur les Américains.* (London, 1770), 1:178.
91. De Pauw, *Recherches,* 1:187.
92. De Pauw, *Recherches,* 2:68–69, 154.
93. Antoine-Joseph Pernety, *Dissertation sur l'Amérique et les Américains, contre les recherches philosophiques de M. de Pauw* (Berlin, 1770), 74–75.

94. Voltaire, "Traité de métaphysique," 135.
95. Voltaire, *Essai*, 2:319.
96. Voltaire, *Essai*, 2:305–306, 335.
97. Cited in Duchet, *Anthropologie*, 384.
98. Helvétius, *De l'esprit* (Paris: Durand, 1758), 458.
99. Helvétius, *De l'esprit*, 290.
100. Anne-Robert-Jacques Turgot, "Recherches sur les causes des progrès et de la décadence des sciences et des arts," in *Œuvres*, ed. Gustave Schelle (Paris : Felix Alcan, 1913), 1:139. Quoted in Daniel Droixhe, "Le primitivisme linguistique de Turgot," in Chantal Grell and Christian Michel, *Primitivisme et mythes des origines dans la France des Lumières, 1680–1820* (Paris: Presses de l'Université de Paris—Sorbonne, 1989), 71–72.
101. Cited in Droixhe, "Le primitivisme, " 72.
102. Marvin Harris, *The Rise of Anthropological Theory* (Lanham, MD: Rowman & Littlefield, 2001), 82–83, 98.

6 "An Indelible Stain": Slavery and the Colonial Enlightenment

1. Michel-René Hilliard d'Auberteuil, *Considérations sur l'Etat présent de la colonie française de Saint-Domingue* (Paris: Grangé, 1776), 2:73.
2. Louis Sala-Molins, *Dark Side of the Light: Slavery and the French Enlightenment*, trans. John Conteh-Morgan, (Minneapolis, MN: University of Minnesota Press, 2006), 8–9.
3. Michèle Duchet, *Anthropologie et histoire au siècle des Lumières* (Paris: François Maspéro, 1971), 18.
4. Jean Ehrard, *Lumières et esclavage: L'esclavage colonial et l'opinion publique en France au XVIIIe siècle* (Brussels: André Versaille, 2008), 214.
5. Philip P. Boucher, *France and the American Tropics to 1700: Tropics of Discontent?* (Baltimore, MD: Johns Hopkins University Press, 2008), 116.
6. Boucher, *American Tropics*, 229.
7. John Garrigus, *Before Haiti : Race and Citizenship in French Saint-Domingue* (New York: Palgrave Macmillan, 2006), 39.
8. Boucher, *American Tropics*, 4.
9. Doris Garraway, *The Libertine Colony: Creolization in the Early French Caribbean* (Durham, NC: Duke University Press, 2005), 240.
10. For an extensive survey of white colonial society and the "patriot" movement, see Charles Frostin, *Les revoltes blanches à Saint-Domingue au XVIIe et XVIIIe siècles* (Paris : Editions de l'Ecole, 1975).
11. Ehrard, *Lumières*, 141.
12. Montesquieu, *The Spirit of the Laws*, trans. Anne Cohler, et.al. (1749, repr., Cambridge: Cambridge University Press, 1989), 250.
13. On this point, see Ehrard, *Lumières*, 26, 166.
14. Helvétius, *De l'esprit* (Paris: Durand, 1758), 25.
15. Duchet, *Anthropologie*, 404–405.
16. Voltaire, "Candide, or Optimism," [1759], in *The Portable Voltaire*, ed. Ben Ray Redman (New York: The Viking Portable Library, 1977), 282.

17. Helvétius, *De l'esprit*, 278–279.
18. Jean-Jacques Rousseau, *Du contrat social* (1762; repr., Paris: Union Générale d'Editions, 1963), 50, 55–59.
19. Sue Peabody, *"There Are No Slaves in France"*: *The Political Culture of Race and Slavery in the Ancien Regime* (Oxford: Oxford University Press, 1996), 96.
20. Voltaire, "Candide," 282.
21. Voltaire, *Essai sur les moeurs et l'esprit des nations*, (1756; repr., Paris: Garnier Frères, 1963), 2:805.
22. Voltaire, *Essai*, 2:805.
23. Louis-Sebastien Mercier, *L'an 2440, rêve s'il en fût jamais* (n.p., 1786), 1:194.
24. Mercier,, *L'an 2440*, 1:194–195.
25. Mercier,, *L'an 2440*, 1:196.
26. Cited in Ehrard, *Lumières*, 201–202.
27. Malick Ghachem, *Sovereignty and Slavery in the Age of Revolution: Haitian Variations on a Metropolitan Theme* (Stanford University Dissertation, 2001), xxv.
28. Ghachem, *Sovereignty*, 223, 221.
29. Hilliard d'Auberteuil, *Considérations*, 1:5.
30. Guillaume-Thomas Raynal, *Essai sur l'administration de Saint-Domingue* (n. p., 1785), 5. There are numerous and extensive passages in Raynal's *Essai sur l'administration de Saint-Domingue* and Malouet's *Mémoire sur l'esclavage* that are virtually identical. Although Raynal's text was published three years before Malouet's, it seems far more likely that Raynal, who employed a legion of ghostwriters and borrowed heavily from other works without attribution, should have copied Malouet's unpublished manuscript, rather than the other way around. Raynal wrote his *Essai sur l'administration de Saint-Domingue* while a guest at Malouet's home in Toulon, and undoubtedly drew heavily upon his host's experience as an official in that colony. Malick Ghachem credits Malouet as the true author of Raynal's *Essai*, while Girolamo Imbruglia writes that it was "surely a work if not written, at least envisioned in common." Girolamo Imbruglia, "Da Raynal a Burke. Il tradizionalismo philosophique di Malouet e il 1789," *Studi Settecenteschi* 10 (1987), 108. See also Anatole Feugère, *Un précurseur de la Révolution: l'abbé Raynal, 1713–1796* (1922; repr., Geneva: Slatkine Reprints, 1970).
31. Guillaume-Thomas Raynal, *Histoire philosophique et politique des établissements et du commerce des Européens dans les deux Indes* (Amsterdam, 1770), 6 :376.
32. Alexandre-Stanislas de Wimpffen, *Haïti au XVIIIe siècle : Richesse et esclavage dans une colonie française*, ed. Pierre Pluchon (1797; repr., Paris: Editions Karthala, 1993), 75. This work was originally published under the title *Voyage à Saint-Domingue, pendant les années 1788, 1789, 1790*.
33. Justin Girod de Chantrans, *Voyage d'un Suisse dans les colonies d'Amérique*, ed. Pierre Pluchon (1785; repr., Paris: Librairie Jules Tallandier, 1980), 174.
34. Raynal, *Histoire*, 5:61.
35. On this point, see Médéric-Louis-Élie Moreau de Saint-Méry, *Description topographique, physique, civile, politique, et historique de la partie française*

de d'Isle Saint-Domingue, ed. Blanche Maurel and Etienne Taillemite (1797; repr., Paris: Société de l'Histoire des Colonies Françaises, 1958), 58–59; and Girod de Chantrans, *Voyage d'un Suisse,* 134. For estimates of the death rates of slaves in the Caribbean, see Hilliard d'Auberteuil, *Considérations,* 1:54; and Ghachem, *Sovereignty,* 20.

36. Pierre-Victor Malouet, *Mémoire sur l'esclavage des nègres* (Neufchâtel, 1788), 94, 10. For the Kourou tragedy, see Emma Rothschild, "A Horrible Tragedy in the French Atlantic," *Past and Present* 192 (August 2006), 67–108.

37. Wimpffen, *Haïti au XVIIIe,* 87.

38. Raynal, *Histoire,* 6:350.

39. On this point, see Garrigus, *Before Haiti;* and Garraway, *Libertine Colony;* as well as Gene Ogle, "'The Eternal Power of Reason' and 'The Superiority of Whites': Hilliard d'Auberteuil's Colonial Enlightenment," *French Colonial History* 3 (2003); and Stewart King, *Blue Coat or Powdered Wig: Free People of Color in Pre-Revolutionary Saint-Domingue* (Athens, GA: University of Georgia Press, 2001).

40. King, *Blue Coat,* 124.

41. Ogle, "The Eternal Power," 43.

42. Georges-Louis Leclerc, comte de Buffon, "Des variétés de l'homme," *Histoire naturelle, générale et particulière* (Paris: Imprimerie Royale, 1750–1804), 3:467–470.

43. Moreau de Saint-Méry, *Description topographique,* 48, 53.

44. Moreau de Saint-Méry, *Description topographique,* 59.

45. Moreau de Saint-Méry, *Description topographique,* 99–100.

46. King, *Description topographique,* 159; William Max Nelson, "Making Men: Enlightenment Ideas of Racial Engineering," *American Historical Review* 115:5 (December 2010), 1364–1394.

47. On this point, see Garrigus, *Before Haiti,* 30.

48. Moreau de Saint-Méry, *Description topographique,* 102, 93.

49. Hilliard d'Auberteuil, *Considérations,* 2:94.

50. ANOM F3 91. Raimond's four memoirs constitute folios 174 through 196 of the file, while the response from the Saint-Domingue administrators La Luzerne and Marbois are in folios 197 through 205.

51. Frostin, *Les revoltes,* 308; Garrigus, *Before Haiti,* 86, 123.

52. Garrigus, *Before Haiti,* 122–3.

53. This debate and its outcome are discussed at length in a July 25, 1787 report entitled "Resultat de l'assemblée du conseil supérieur et des notables de cette colonie relativement aux gens de couleur," ANOM C14 61.

54. Pierre Boulle, *Race et esclavage dans la France de l'Ancien Régime* (Paris : Perrin, 2007), 28.

55. Raynal, *Histoire ,* 4:201.

56. Cited in Boulle, *Race,* 73.

57. Sue Peabody, *There Are No Slaves in France,* 55.

58. Correspondence between ministry and Le Moyne, port official of Bordeaux, contained in ANOM F1B 3, folio 220–222, 260.

59. December 23, 1777 letter of d'Argout and de Vaivre to Sartine, ANOM F1B 4, folio 631–633.

60. May 16, 1778, letter to d'Argout and de Vaivre, ANOM F1B 4, folio 644–645.

61. December 19, 1777, letter of Poncet de la Grave to Sartine, ANOM F1B 4.
62. Peabody, *No Slaves in France*, 136.
63. Pasteur Schwartz [Condorcet], *Réflexions sur l'esclavage des nègres* (Neufchatel: Société Typographique, 1781), viii.
64. Condorcet, *Réflexions*, 6.
65. Condorcet, *Réflexions*, 18–22.
66. Condorcet, *Réflexions*, 16–17, 33.
67. Condorcet, *Réflexions*, 35–36.
68. Condorcet, *Réflexions*, 57–59, 49, 52, 63.
69. Raynal, *Histoire*, 4 :173–4.
70. On the Baron de Bessner, see Duchet, *Anthropologie*, 154; Ghachem, *Sovereignty*, 143; and Pierre-Victor Malouet, *Mémoires de Malouet* (Paris: Plon, 1874), 76–84.
71. Malouet, *Mémoire sur l'esclavage*.
72. Malouet, *Mémoire*, 10.
73. Malouet, *Mémoire*, 20–21, 23.
74. Malouet, *Mémoire*, 26, 33.
75. Malouet, *Mémoire*, 77–78, 81.
76. Malouet, *Mémoire*, 105, 39–40.
77. Malouet, *Mémoire*, 21–22.
78. Malouet, *Mémoire*, 21–22.
79. Malouet, *Mémoire*, 51–53.
80. Condorcet, *Réflexions*, 87.
81. Malouet, *Mémoire*, 54.
82. Hilliard d'Auberteuil, *Considérations*, 1:131–2.
83. Moreau de Saint-Méry, *Description topographique*, 46.
84. Ehrard, *Lumières*, 186.
85. Cited in Duchet, *Anthropologie*, 165.
86. Dupont de Nemours, cited in Yves Benot, *Diderot, de l'athéisme à l'anticolonialisme* (Paris: François Maspero, 1981), 157.
87. Carl Ludwig Lokke, *France and the Colonial Question: A Study of Contemporary French Opinion, 1763–1801* (1932; repr., New York: AMS, 1968), 177.
88. On this topic, see Poivre's letters to the duc de Praslin, minister for the navy and colonies, in ANOM C4 27 and C4 29.
89. Pierre Poivre, *Voyages d'un philosophe, ou observations sur les mœurs et les arts des peuples de l'Afrique, de l'Asie, et de l'Amérique* (Yverdon, 1768), 93–95.
90. Condorcet, *Réflexions*, 26.
91. Mercier, *L'an 2440*, 2:356–361.
92. Mercier, *L'an 2440*, 2:359.
93. Girod de Chantrans, *Voyage d'un Suisse*, 226–227.
94. Raynal, *Histoire*, 6:384.

7   The Apotheosis of Europe

1. Voltaire, *Essai sur les moeurs et l'esprit des nations*, (1756; repr., Paris: Garnier Frères, 1963), 2:416.

2. For an overview of this transition, see Stephen F. Dale, *The Muslim Empires of the Ottomans, Safavids, and Mughals* (New York and Cambridge: Cambridge University Press, 2010).

3. Henry Laurens, *Les origines intellectuelles de l'expédition d'Egypte: L'Orientalisme islamisant en France (1698–1798)* (Paris and Istanbul: Editions Isis, 1987), 190.

4. Helvétius, *De l'esprit* (Paris: Durand, 1758), 452.

5. Helvétius, *De l'esprit,* 442–444.

6. Helvétius, *De l'esprit,* 457–458.

7. Helvétius, *De l'esprit,* 127–128.

8. Helvétius, *De l'esprit,* 201, 398.

9. Helvétius, *De l'esprit,* 405.

10. Michèle Duchet, *Anthropologie et histoire au siècle des Lumières* (Paris: François Maspéro, 1971), 392, 397.

11. Helvétius, *De l'esprit,* 378–379.

12. Constantin-François de Chasseboeuf, comte de Volney, *Voyage en Syrie et en Egypte, pendant les années 1783, 1784, et 1785* (Paris: Volland, 1787), 2:422–423, 2:427.

13. Volney, *Voyage en Syrie,* 2:424–426.

14. Volney, *Voyage en Syrie,* 2:343.

15. Volney, *Voyage en Syrie,* 2:405.

16. Volney, *Voyage en Syrie,* 2:413.

17. Volney, *Voyage en Syrie,* 2:457–458.

18. Constantin-François Volney, *Les Ruines, ou Méditation sur les Révolutions des Empires* (1791; repr., Paris: Decembre-Alonnier, 1869), 7.

19. Volney, *Ruines,* 8.

20. Volney, *Ruines,* 9.

21. Volney, *Ruines,* 9.

22. Volney, *Ruines,* 11–12.

23. For classical notions of the primeval "golden age" of humanity, see Arthur O. Lovejoy and George Boas, *Primitivism and Related Ideas in Antiquity* (1935; repr., New York: Octagon Books, 1965), especially 23–47.

24. For early modern utopian thought, see Raymond Trousson, *Voyages aux pays de nulle part: histoire littéraire de la pensée utopique* (1975; repr., Brussels: Editions de l'Université de Bruxelles, 1999).

25. Jean-Antoine-Nicolas de Caritat, marquis de Condorcet, *Esquisse d'un tableau historique des progrès de l'esprit humain* (1793; repr., Paris: Flammarion, 1988), 265.

26. Simon Collier, "Mercier's Enlightenment Utopia: Progress and Social Ideals," in *The Enlightenment and Its Shadows,* ed., Peter Hulme and Ludmilla Jordanova (London: Routledge, 1990), 89.

27. Louis-Sebastien Mercier, *L'an 2440, rêve s'il en fût jamais* (n.p., 1786), 1:34, 2:304.

28. Mercier, *L'an 2440,* 2:126, 1:173.

29. Mercier, *L'an 2440,* 1:84–87.

30. Mercier, *L'an 2440,* 2:251–252.

31. Mercier, *L'an 2440,* 1:346, 362.

32. Mercier, *L'an 2440*, 3:181–182.
33. Mercier, *L'an 2440*, 2:150–162, 3:19–29.
34. Mercier, *L'an 2440*, 3:23.
35. Robert Darnton, *The Forbidden Best-Sellers of Pre-Revolutionary France* (New York: Norton, 1996), 120.
36. Collier, "Utopia," 89, 99.
37. Peter Gay, *The Party of Humanity*, (New York: Norton, 1971), 271.
38. Anne-Robert-Jacques Turgot, "Plan de deux discours sur l'histoire universelle," in *Oeuvres*, ed. Gustave Schelle, (Paris: Felix Alcan, 1913), 1:278–282.
39. Robert Nisbet, "Turgot and the Contexts of Progress," *Proceedings of the American Philosophical Society* 119:3 (1975), 217.
40. Turgot, "Plan d'un ouvrage sur la géographie politique," in Turgot, *Oeuvres*, 1:258; Nisbet, "Progress," 218.
41. Nisbet, "Progress," 218.
42. Turgot, "Recherches sur les causes des progrès et de la decadence des sciences et des arts," in Turgot, *Oeuvres*, 1:118–120.
43. Turgot, "Plan de deux discours," 1:320–321.
44. Condorcet, *Esquisse*, 119–120.
45. Condorcet, *Esquisse*, 174.
46. Condorcet, *Esquisse*, 120–121.
47. Condorcet, *Esquisse*, 137, 102–103.
48. Condorcet, *Esquisse*, 113.
49. Condorcet, *Esquisse*, 101–102.
50. Sankar Muthu, *Enlightenment against Empire* (Princeton, NJ: Princeton University Press, 2003), 259.
51. Guillaume-Thomas Raynal, *Histoire philosophique et politique des établissements et du commerce des Européens dans les deux Indes* (Amsterdam, 1770), 3 :139, 144.
52. Cited in Muthu, *Enlightenment*, 74.
53. Condorcet, *Esquisse*, 192.
54. Cornelius de Pauw, *Recherches philosophiques sur les Américains* (London, 1770), 1:89, 1:84.
55. Charles de Brosses, *Histoire des navigations aux terres australes* (Paris: Durand, 1756), 1:17.
56. Cited in Carl Ludwig Lokke, *France and the Colonial Question: A Study of Contemporary French Opinion, 1763–1801* (1932; repr., New York: AMS, 1968), 40.
57. *Correspondance littéraire*, July 1, 1768, 452–453.
58. Cited in Lokke, *Colonial Question*, 37–38.
59. Abraham-Hyacinthe Anquetil-Duperron, *Législation orientale* (Amsterdam: Marc Michel Rey, 1778), 178.
60. Anquetil-Duperron, *Législation*, 18.
61. Anquetil-Duperron, *Législation*, 175.
62. Anquetil-Duperron, *Législation*, 29.
63. De Pauw, *Recherches*, 1:v–viii.
64. Jean-François Marmontel, *Les Incas, ou la destruction de l'empire du Pérou* (1777; repr., Tours : André Mame et Cie, 1847), 59.

65. Lokke, *Colonial Question*, 7–8, 110.
66. Cited in Sunil Agnani, "Doux commerce, douce colonisation: Diderot and the Two Indies of the French Enlightenment," In *The Anthropology of the Enlightenment*, ed. Larry Wolff and Marco Cipollini (Stanford, CA: Stanford University Press, 2007), 78.
67. Raynal, *Histoire des deux Indes*, 1:61–62. I borrow the term "enlightened narrative" from Karen O'Brien, *Narratives of Enlightenment: Cosmopolitan History from Voltaire to Gibbon* (Cambridge: Cambridge University Press, 1997).
68. Raynal, *Histoire des deux Indes*, 1:73.
69. Raynal, *Histoire des deux Indes*, 4:140.
70. Mercier, *L'an 2440*, 2:361.
71. Bessner's multiple unpublished memoirs to this effect are conserved in manuscript in the French colonial archives, especially in ANOM C14 35 and F3 95.
72. Thomas Fitz-Maurice and Daniel Lescallier, "Instructions relatives à la civilisation des Indiens dans la Guiane française," ANOM F3 95.
73. Letter of Pierre-Victor Malouet, March 17, 1787, ANOM C14 60.
74. Condorcet, *Esquisse*, 230–231.
75. Condorcet, *Esquisse*, 260.
76. Condorcet, *Esquisse*, 269–270.
77. Raynal, *Histoire des deux Indes*, 6:41–44.
78. De Brosses, *Histoire des navigations*, 1:17.
79. De Brosses, *Histoire des navigations*, 1:17.
80. De Brosses, *Histoire des navigations*, 1:19–20.
81. On this point, see Lokke, *Colonial Question*, as well as Laurens, *Origines intellectuelles*.
82. Mercier, *L'an 2440*, 2:356–361.
83. Raynal, *Histoire des Deux Indes*, 4:113.
84. Raynal, *Histoire des Deux Indes*, 4:114.
85. Raynal, *Histoire des Deux Indes*, 4:115–116.
86. Edward Said, *Orientalism* (New York: Vintage, 1978), 42.
87. Juan Cole, *Napoleon's Egypt: Invading the Middle East* (New York: Palgrave Macmillan, 2007), 29.

Conclusion

1. For a good discussion of this issue, which convincingly refutes the claim of a binary opposition in Enlightenment thought between universalism and diversity, see Sankar Muthu, *Enlightenment against Empire* (Princeton, NJ: Princeton University Press, 2003), 260–266.
2. John Gray, *Enlightenment's Wake: Politics and Culture at the Close of the Modern Age* (London and New York: Routledge, 1995), 125.
3. Gray, *Enlightenment's Wake*, 2.
4. Judith N. Shklar, "Politics and the Intellect," in *Political Thought and Political Thinkers*, ed. Stanley Hoffmann (Chicago, IL: The University of Chicago Press, 1998), 95. On this point, see also Peter Gay, *The Party of Humanity* (New York: Norton, 1971).

5. The foundational text for this interpretation of human nature is John Locke, *An Essay Concerning Human Understanding* (London: William Tegg & Co, 1879 [1690]). For the centrality of Locke's *Essay* to the development of the human sciences in the eighteenth century, see Marvin Harris, *The Rise of Anthropological Theory* (Lanham, MD: Rowman and Littlefield, 2001), 11; Claude-Adrien Helvétius's treatise, *De l'esprit* (Paris: Durand, 1758), which we have cited frequently in the preceding chapters, was an effort to explain human diversity and the development of the human mind according to Locke's principles.

6. Voltaire, *Essai sur les moeurs et l'esprit des nations* (Paris: Garnier Frères, 1963), 2:810.

7. Guillaume-Thomas Raynal, *Histoire philosophique et politique des établissements et du commerce des Européens dans les deux Indes* (Amsterdam, 1770), 4:136.

8. For a discussion of the use of Enlightenment universalism to critique slavery, see Richard Popkin, "Condorcet, Abolitionist," in *Condorcet Studies I*, ed. Leonora Cohen Rosenfield (Atlantic Heights, NJ: Humanities Press, 1997), 35–47; and Alyssa Goldstein Sepinwall, *The Abbé Grégoire and the French Revolution: The Making of Modern Universalism* (Berkeley, CA: University of California Press, 2005). For a documentary history of the Société des Amis des Noirs, in which Condorcet and Grégoire both played leading roles, see Marcel Dorigny and Bernard Gainot, *La Société des Amis des Noirs, 1788–1799. Contribution à l'histoire de l'esclavage* (Paris: UNESCO, 1998). See also Lynn Hunt, *Inventing Human Rights: A History* (New York: Norton, 2008).

9. Edward Said, *Orientalism* (New York: Vintage, 1979); Michael Keevak, *The Story of a Stele: China's Nestorian Monument and its Reception in the West, 1625–1916* (Hong Kong: Hong Kong University Press, 2008), 17.

10. Muthu, *Enlightenment*, 279.

11. For the classical roots of Rousseau's "cultural primitivism," see Arthur Lovejoy, and George Boas, *Primitivism and Related Ideas in Antiquity* (New York: Octagon Books, 1965 [1935]).

12. Harris, *The Rise*, 83.

13. For the shift in French scientific and scholarly discourses on race from the eighteenth to the nineteenth century, see George W. Stocking, Jr., "French Anthopology in 1800," in *Race, Culture, and Evolution: Essays in the History of Anthropology* (Chicago, IL: The University of Chicago Press, 1982), 13–41.

14. On this point, see Colin Kidd, *The Forging of Races: Race and Scripture in the Protestant Atlantic World, 1600–2000* (Cambridge and New York: Cambridge University Press, 2006), especially Chapters 2 and 5.

15. For Clemenceau's defense of France's Revolutionary legacy in the early days of the Third Republic, see Jeremy Jennings, *Revolution and the Republic: A History of Political Thought in France since the Eighteenth Century* (Oxford and New York: Oxford University Press, 2011), 287.

Bibliography

Archival Sources:

Archives Nationales d'Outre-Mer (ANOM), Aix-en Provence

Periodicals:

Correspondance littéraire
Histoire de l'Académie Royale des Sciences
Journal des Sçavans
Mémoires de l'Académie des Inscriptions et Belles-Lettres
Mémoires de Trévoux

Primary Sources:

Adanson, Michel. *Voyage au Sénégal*. 1757. Edited by Denis Reynaud and Jean Schmidt. Saint-Etienne: Publications de l'Université de Saint-Etienne, 1996.

Anquetil-Duperron, Abraham-Hyacinthe. *Législation orientale*. Amsterdam: Marc Michel Rey, 1778.

———. *Voyage en Inde, 1754–1762: Relation du voyage en préliminaire à la traduction du Zend-Avesta*, 1771. Cahors: Maisonneuve et Larose, 1997.

———. *Zend-Avesta, ouvrage de Zoroastre*. Paris: Tilliard, 1771.

Argens, Jean-Baptiste du Boyer, marquis d'. *Lettres Chinoises, ou correspondance philosophique, historique, et critique, entre un Chinois voyageur à Paris et ses correspondans à la Chine, en Moscovie, en Perse et au Japon*. The Hague: Pierre Paupie, 1740.

Bernier, François. *Evénemens particuliers, ou ce qui s'est passé de plus considérable après la guerre pendant cinq ans, ou environ, dans les Etats du Grand Mogol*. Paris: Claude Barbin, 1670.

———. "Une nouvelle division de la Terre." *Journal des Sçavans* 1684, 133–140.

Blumenbach, Johann Friedrich. *On the Natural Variations of Mankind*. 1795. Translated by Thomas Bendyshe. New York: Bergman, 1969.

Bougainville, Louis-Antoine de. *Écrits sur le Canada: Mémoires—Journal— Lettres*, edited by Etienne Taillemite. Sillery: Septentrion, 2003.

———. *Voyage autour du monde*. 1771. Paris: Gallimard, 1982.

Boulainvilliers, Henri de. *La Vie de Mahomed.* London, 1730.

Boulanger, Nicolas-Antoine. *Le christianisme dévoilé, ou examen des principes et des effets de la Religion chrétienne.* London, 1766.

———. *Recherches sur l'origine du despotisme oriental.* London, 1763.

Brosses, Charles de. *Du culte des dieux fétiches.* Paris, 1760.

———. *Histoire des navigations aux terres australes.* Paris: Durand, 1756.

Buffon, Georges-Louis Leclerc, comte de. *Histoire naturelle générale et particulière.* Paris: Imprimerie Royale, 1750–1804.

Chardin, Jean. *Sir John Chardin's Travels in Persia,* edited by Sir Percy Sykes, 1686. London: The Argonaut Press, 1927.

Charlevoix, Pierre-François-Xavier de. *Histoire de la Nouvelle France.* Paris, 1744.

Condorcet, Jean-Antoine-Nicolas de Caritat, marquis de. *Esquisse d'un tableau historique des progrès de l'esprit humain.* 1793. Paris: Flammarion, 1988.

———. (Pasteur Schwartz). *Réflexions sur l'esclavage des nègres.* Neufchâtel: Société Typographique, 1781.

Dégerando, Joseph-Marie. *The Observation of Savage Peoples.* 1800. Translated by F. C. T. Moore. Berkeley, CA: University of California Press, 1969.

de la Vega, Garcilaso. *Comentarios reales.* 1609. Buenos Aires: Espasa-Calpe, 1987.

Demanet, abbé. *Nouvelle histoire de l'Afrique française.* Paris: La Veuve Duchesne, 1767.

Diderot, Denis, ed. Laurent Versini. *Diderot. Tome V: Correspondance.* Paris: Robert Laffont, 1997.

———. "Supplement to the Voyage of Bougainville." 1772. In *Diderot: Political Writings,* translated and edited by John Hope Mason and Robert Wokler.. Cambridge: Cambridge University Press, 1992.

Du Bos, abbé Jean-Baptiste. *Refléxions critiques sur la peinture et la poésie.* n.d.

Du Halde, Jean-Baptiste. *Description géographique, historique, chronologique, politique, et physique de l'Empire de la Chine et de la Tartarie chinoise.* Paris: P. G. Le Mercier, 1735.

Fourmont, Etienne. *Réflexions sur l'origine, l'histoire, et la succession des Anciens Peuples, Chaldéens, Hébreux, Phéniciens, Egyptiens, Grecs, etc., jusqu'au tems de Cyrus.* Paris: De Bure, 1747.

Girod de Chantrans, Justin. *Voyage d'un Suisse dans les colonies d'Amérique.* 1785. Edited by Pierre Pluchon. Paris: Librairie Jules Tallandier, 1980.

Graffigny, Françoise de. *Lettres d'une Péruvienne.* 1747.

Grotius, Hugo. *On the Origin of the Native Races of America.* 1642. Edinburg: Bibliotheca Curiosa, 1884.

Guignes, Chrétien-Louis-Joseph de. *Réflexions sur les anciennes observations astronomiques des Chinois, et sur l'état de leur empire dans les temps les plus reculés, lues a l'Institut de France.* n.d.

Guignes, Joseph de. *Histoire générale des Huns, des Turcs, des Mogols, et des autres Tartares occidentaux.* Paris: Desaint et Saillant, 1756.

———. *Mémoire dans lequel on prouve, que les chinois sont une colonie égyptienne, lu dans l'Assemblée publique de l'Académie Royale des Inscriptions et Belles Lettres, le 14 novembre 1758.*

Helvétius, Claude-Adrien. *De l'esprit.* Paris: Durand, 1758.

Herbelot, Barthelémy d'. *Bibliothèque orientale*. Paris: Compagnie des Libraires, 1697.

Hilliard d'Auberteuil, Michel-René. *Considérations sur l'Etat présent de la colonie française de Saint-Domingue*. Paris: Grangé, 1776.

Huet, Pierre-Daniel. *Histoire du commerce et de la navigation des anciens*. Lyon: Benoit Duplain, 1763.

Kircher, Athanasius. *China Illustrata*. 1667. Translated by Charles Van Tuyl. Muskogee, OK: Indian University Press, 1987.

La Condamine, Charles-Marie de. *Relation abrégée d'un voyage fait dans l'intérieur de l'Amérique Méridionale, depuis la côte de la Mer du Sud, jusqu'aux Côtes de Brésil et de la Guyane*. 1745. Maastricht: Dugour & Roux, 1778.

Lafitau, Joseph-François. *Mœurs des sauvages amériquains, comparés aux mœurs des premiers temps*. Paris: Saugrain, 1724.

Lahontan, Louis-Armand Lom d'Arce, baron de. *Dialogues de Monsieur le Baron de Lahontan et d'un Sauvage, dans l'Amérique*. Amsterdam: Veuve de Boeteman, 1704.

———. *Mémoires de l'Amérique Septentrionale, ou la suite des voyages de M. le Baron de Lahontan*. The Hague: Frères l'Honoré, 1703.

———. *Nouveaux voyages de M. le Baron de Lahontan dans l'Amérique Septentrionale*. The Hague: Frères l'Honoré, 1703.

———. Réal Ouellet and Alain Beaulieu, eds. *Lahontan: Oeuvres complètes*. Montreal: Presses Universitaires de Montreal, 1990.

La Pérouse, Jean-François de Galaup de. *Voyage de La Pérouse autour du monde*. Paris: Imprimérie de la République, 1797.

La Peyrère, Isaac. *Lettre de la Peyrère a Philotime, dans laquelle il expose les raisons qui l'ont obligé a abjurer la secte de Calvin qu'il professait, et le Livre des Preadamites qu'il avait mis au jour*. Paris: Augustin Courbé, 1668.

———. *Men before Adam, or a Discourse upon the Twelfth, Thirteenth, and Fourteenth Verses of the Fifth Chapter of the Epistle of the Apostle Paul to the Romans, by Which Are Proved That the First Men Were Created before Adam*. London, 1656.

———. *Relation du Groenland*. Paris: Thomas Jolly, 1663.

———. *A Theological System, upon that Presupposition That Men Were before Adam*. London, 1655.

Leroux-Deshautesrayes, Michel-Ange-André. *Doutes sur la Dissertation de M. de Guignes, qui a pour titre: Memoire dans lequel on prouve que les Chinois sont une colonie Egyptienne, proposés a Messieurs de l'Académie Royale des Belles Lettres*. Paris: Laurent Prault, 1759.

Mairan, Dortous de. *Lettres au R.P. Parrenin, Jésuite, Missionnaire à Pékin, concernant diverses questions sur la Chine*. Paris: Imprimerie Royale, 1770.

Malfert, R. P. Auguste. "Mémoire sur l'Origine des Nègres et des Américains." *Mémoires de Trévoux* (1733), 1927–1977.

Malouet, Pierre-Victor. *Mémoires de Malouet*. Paris: Plon, 1874.

———. *Mémoire sur l'esclavage des nègres*. Neufchâtel, 1788.

Marmontel, Jean-François. *Les Incas, ou la destruction de l'empire du Pérou*. 1777. Tours: André Mame et Cie, 1847.

Maupertuis, Pierre Moreau de. *Essai de cosmologie, système de la nature. Réponse aux objections de M. Diderot*. 1750. Paris: J. Vrin, 1984.

Maupertuis, Pierre Moreau de. *Lettre sur le progrès des sciences*. 1752.
———. *Vénus physique*. 1745.
Mercier, Louis-Sebastien. *L'an 2440, rêve s'il en fût jamais*. n.p., 1786.
Montaigne, Michel de. *Essais*. 1580. Paris: Bibliothèque de la Pléiade, 1950.
Montesquieu, Charles Sécondat de. *Lettres persanes*. 1721. Edited by Jacques Roger. Paris: Garnier-Flammarion, 1964.
———. *The Spirit of the Laws*. 1749. Translated by Anne Cohler. Cambridge: Cambridge University Press, 1989.
Moreau de Saint-Méry, Médéric-Louis-Élie. *Description topographique, physique, civile, politique, et historique de la partie française de d'Isle Saint-Domingue*. 1797. Edited by Blanche Maurel and Etienne Taillemite. Paris: Société de l'Histoire des Colonies Françaises, 1958.
Palissot, Charles. *Les Philosophes*. Paris: Duchesne, 1760.
Pauw, Cornelius de. *Défense des Recherches Philosophiques sur les Américains*. Berlin: Georges Jacques Decker, 1770.
———. *Recherches Philosophiques sur les Américains*. London, 1770.
———. *Recherches philosophiques sur les Egyptiens et les Chinois*. London: Thomas Johnson, 1774.
Pernety, Dom Antoine-Joseph. *Dissertation sur l'Amérique et les Américains, contre les recherches philosophiques de M. de Pauw*. Berlin, 1770.
———. *Histoire d'un voyage aux Isles Malouines, fait en 1763 et 1764, avec des observations sur le détroit de Magellan et sur les Patagons*. Paris: Saillant et Nyon, 1770.
Pezron, Paul-Yves. *L'Antiquité des Temps rétablie et défendue, contre les Juifs et les Nouveaux Chronologistes*. Paris: Veuve d'Edme Martin, 1687.
Poivre, Pierre. *Voyages d'un philosophe, ou observations sur les mœurs et les arts des peuples de l'Afrique, de l'Asie, et de l'Amérique*. Yverdon, 1768.
Quesnay, François. "Despotisme de la Chine." 1767. In *François Quesnay : Œuvres Economiques Complètes et Autres Textes*, edited by Christine Théré, Loïc Charles, et Jean-Claude Perrot. Paris: Institut National d'Etudes Démographiques, 2005.
Raynal, abbé Guillaume-Thomas. *Essai sur l'administration de Saint-Domingue*. 1785.
———. *Histoire philosophique et politique des établissements et du commerce des Européens dans les deux Indes*. Amsterdam, 1770.
Rousseau, Jean-Jacques. *Du contrat social*. 1762. Paris: Union Générale d'Editions, 1963.
———. *The First and Second Discourses*. 1750, 1755. Translated by Roger D. Masters. Boston, MA: Bedford St. Martin's, 1964.
Semedo, Alvarez. *The History of that Great and Renowned Monarchy of China*. London, 1655.
Tott, François de. *Memoirs of Baron de Tott*. 1785. Translated by John E. Woods. New York: Arno Press, 1973.
Tournemine. "Remarques du Père Tournemine Jésuite sur le mémoire touchant l'origine des Nègres et des Américains, inséré dans ce Journal au mois de Novembre 1733." *Mémoires de Trévoux* (1734), 620–630.
Turgot, Anne-Robert-Jacques. *Oeuvres*. Edited by Gustave Schelle. Paris: Felix Alcan, 1913.

Volney, Constantin-François de. 1791. *Les Ruines, ou Méditation sur les Révolutions des Empires*. Paris: Decembre-Alonnier, 1869.

———. *Voyage en Syrie et en Egypte, pendant les années 1783, 1784, et 1785*. Paris: Volland, 1787.

Voltaire,. *The Age of Louis XIV*. 1751. Translated by Martyn Pollack. London: J. M. Dent, 1961.

———. *Alzire, ou les Américains*. Paris: Jean-Baptiste-Claude Bauche, 1736.

———. "Candide, or Optimism." 1759. In *The Portable Voltaire*, edited by Ben Ray Redman. New York: The Viking Portable Library, 1977.

———. *Essai sur les moeurs et l'esprit des nations*. 1756. Paris: Garnier Frères, 1963.

———. *Le fanatisme, ou Mahomet le prophète*. Amsterdam: Estienne Ledet et Cie, 1753.

———. *Lettres chinoises, indiennes, et tartares, à M. de Paw, par un Bénédictin*. London, 1776.

———. *L'Orphelin de la Chine*. 1755. *Théatre classique des Français*. Paris, 1831.

———. *Traité de Métaphysique (1734), Reproduced from the Kehl Text*. 1734. Manchester: Manchester University Press, 1937.

———. *Voltaire: Correspondance choisie*. Edited by Jacqueline Hellegouarch. Librairie Générale Française, 1990.

———. *Zaïre*. 1732. *Œuvres complètes de Voltaire*, edited by Louis Moland. Paris, 1877.

Wimpffen, Alexandre-Stanislas de. *Haïti au XVIIIe siècle: Richesse et esclavage dans une colonie française*. 1797. Edited by Pierre Pluchon. Paris: Editions Karthala, 1993.

Secondary Sources:

Adams, Percy G. *Travelers and Travel Liars, 1660–1800*. Berkeley, CA: University of California Press, 1962.

Agnani, Sunil. "Doux commerce, douce colonisation: Diderot and the Two Indies of the French Enlightenment." In *The Anthropology of the Enlightenment*, edited by Larry Wolff and Marco Cipollini, 65–84. Stanford, CA: Stanford University Press, 2007.

Badir, Magdy Gabriel. *Voltaire et l'Islam (Studies on Voltaire and the Eighteenth Century), Vol. CXXV*. Oxford: Voltaire Foundation, 1974.

Baker, Keith Michael, and Peter Hanns Reill, eds. *What's Left of Enlightenment: A Postmodern Question*. Stanford, CA: Stanford University Press, 2001.

Ballantyne, Tony, ed. *Science, Empire, and the European Exploration of the Pacific*. Aldershot, UK: Ashgate, 2004.

Barret-Kriegel, Blandine. *Les académies de l'histoire*. Paris: Presses Universitaires de France, 1998.

Baum, Bruce. *The Rise and Fall of the Caucasian Race: A Political History of Racial Identity*. New York: New York University Press, 2006.

Beaglehole, J. C. "Eighteenth Century Science and the Voyages of Discovery." In *Science, Empire, and the European Exploration of the Pacific*, edited by Tony Ballantyne, 75–91. Aldershot, UK: Ashgate, 2004.

Beaulieu, Alain. *Convertir les fils de Caïn: Jésuites et Amérindiens nomades en Nouvelle-France, 1632–1642.* Québec: Nuit Blanche, 1990.

Becker, C. and V. Martin, eds. "Mémoires d'Adanson sur le Sénégal et l'île de Gorée." *Bulletin de l'Institut fondamental de l'Afrique noire* 42:4 (1980), 722–799.

Benot, Yves. *Diderot, de l'athéisme à l'anticolonialisme.* Paris: François Maspero, 1981.

Bindman, David. *Ape to Apollo: Aesthetics and the Idea of Race in the Eighteenth Century.* Ithaca: Cornell University Press, 2002.

Boucher, Philip P. *France and the American Tropics to 1700: Tropics of Discontent?* Baltimore, MD: Johns Hopkins University Press, 2008.

Boulle, Pierre. "François Bernier and the Origins of the Modern Concept of Race." In *The Color of Liberty: Histories of Race in France,* edited by Sue Peabody and Tyler Stovall, 11–27. Durham, NC: Duke University Press, 2003.

———. *Race et esclavage dans la France de l'Ancien Régime.* Paris: Perrin, 2007.

Brockey, Liam Matthew. *Journey to the East: The Jesuit Mission to China, 1579–1724.* Cambridge, MA: Harvard University Press, 2007.

Brumfitt, J. H. *Voltaire, Historian.* Westport, CT: Greenwood Press, 1985.

Carey, Daniel, and Lynn Festa, eds. *The Postcolonial Enlightenment: Eighteenth-Century Colonialism and Postcolonial Theory.* Oxford and New York: Oxford University Press, 2009.

Cassirer, Ernst. *The Philosophy of the Enlightenment.* 1932. Translated by Fritz Koellns and James Pettegrove. Boston: Beacon Press, 1955.

Certeau, Michel de. "Writing versus Time: History and Anthropology in the Works of Lafitau." *Yale French Studies* 59 (1980), 37–64.

Chevalier, Auguste. *Michel Adanson: Voyageur, naturaliste, et philosophe.* Paris: Larose, 1934.

Chinard, Gilbert. *L'Amérique et le rêve exotique dans la littérature française au XVIIe et au XVIIIe siècle.* Paris: Hachette, 1913.

Church, Henry Ward. "Corneille de Pauw and the Controversy over his Recherches Philosophiques sur les Américains." *Proceedings of the Modern Language Association* 51:1 (1936), 178–206.

Çirakman, Asli. "From Tyranny to Despotism: The Enlightenment's Unenlightened Image of the Turks." *International Journal of Middle East Studies* 33:1 (2001), 49–68.

Clarke, J. J. *Oriental Enlightenment: The Encounter between Asian and Western Thought.* London: Routledge, 1997.

Coller, Ian. "East of Enlightenment: Regulating Cosmopolitanism between Istanbul and Paris in the Eighteenth Century." *Journal of World History* 21:3 (2010), 447–470.

Collier, Simon. "Mercier's Enlightenment Utopia: Progress and Social Ideals." In *The Enlightenment and Its Shadows,* edited by Peter Hulme and Ludmilla Jordanova, 84–100. London: Routledge, 1990.

Corsi, Pietro. *The Age of Lamarck: Evolutionary Theories in France, 1790–1830.* Translated by Jonathan Mandelbaum. Berkeley, CA: University of California Press, 1988.

Cranston, Maurice. *The Noble Savage: Jean-Jacques Rousseau, 1754–1762.* Chicago, IL: University of Chicago Press, 1991.

Cultru, Prosper. *Un empereur de Madagascar au XVIIIe siècle: Benyowszky.* Paris: Augustin Challanel, 1906.

Curran, Brian. *The Egyptian Renaissance: The Afterlife of Ancient Egypt in Early Modern Italy.* Chicago, IL: University of Chicago Press, 2007.

Curtis, D. E. "Pierre Bayle and the Expansion of Time." *Australian Journal of French Studies* 13:3 (1976), 197–212.

Dale, Stephen F. *The Muslim Empires of the Ottomans, Safavids, and Mughals.* Cambridge and New York: Cambridge University Press, 2010.

Darnton, Robert. *The Forbidden Best-Sellers of Pre-Revolutionary France.* New York: Norton, 1996.

——. *The Great Cat Massacre and Other Episodes in French Cultural History.* New York: Vintage, 1985.

——. *The Literary Underground of the Old Regime.* Cambridge, MA: Harvard University Press, 1982.

David, Madeleine V. "Le Président de Brosses historien des religions et philosophe." In *Charles de Brosses, 1777–1977: Actes du colloque organisé à Dijon du 3 au 7 mail 1977*, edited by Jean-Claude Garreta. Geneva: Slatkine, 1981.

De Camp, Lyon Sprague. *Lost Continents: The Atlantis Theme in History, Science, and Literature.* New York: Dover Publications, 1970.

Demarchi, Franco, and Riccardo Scartezzini, eds. *Martino Martini: A Humanist and Scientist in Seventeenth Century China.* Trento: Università degli Studi di Trento, 1996.

Deschamps, Léon. *Histoire de la question coloniale en France.* Paris: Plon Nourrit, 1891.

Dew, Nicholas. *Orientalism in Louis XIV's France.* Oxford and New York: Oxford University Press, 2009.

Diop, David. "La mise à l'épreuve d'un *régime de véridiction* sur 'la paresse et la négligence des Nègres' dans le *Voyage au Sénégal* d'Adanson." In *L'Afrique du siècle des Lumières: savoirs et représentations*, edited by Catherine Gallouët, et al. Oxford: Voltaire Foundation, 2009.

Dorigny, Marcel, and Bernard Gainot. *La Société des Amis des Noirs, 1788–1799. Contribution à l'histoire de l'esclavage.* Paris: UNESCO, 1998.

Droixhe, Daniel. "Le primitivisme linguistique de Turgot." In *Primitivisme et mythes des origines dans la France des Lumières, 1680–1820*, edited by Chantal Grell and Christian Michel, 59–87. Paris: Presses de l'Université de Paris—Sorbonne, 1989.

Dubois, Laurent. *A Colony of Citizens: Revolution and Slave Emancipation in the French Caribbean, 1787–1804.* Chapel Hill, NC: University of North Carolina Press, 2004.

——. "An Enslaved Enlightenment: Rethinking the Intellectual History of the French Atlantic." *Social History* 31:1 (2006), 1–14.

Duchet, Michèle. *Anthropologie et histoire au siècle des Lumières.* Paris: François Maspéro, 1971.

——. *Diderot et l'Histoire des deux Indes, ou l'écriture fragmentaire.* Paris: A. G. Nizet, 1978.

256   *Bibliography*

Duchet, Michèle. *Le partage des savoirs: discours historique et discours ethnologique*. Paris: Editions La Découverte, 1985.
Dunmore, John. *Pacific Explorer: The Life of Jean-François de La Pérouse*. Annapolis, MD: Naval Institute Press, 1985.
Duviols, Jean-Paul. *L'Amérique espagnole vue et rêvée: Les livres de voyages de Christophe Colomb à Bougainville*. Paris: Editions Promodis, 1985.
Edelstein, Dan. "Hyperborean Atlantis: Jean-Sylvain Bailly, Madame Blavatsky, and the Nazi Myth." *Studies in Eighteenth-Century Culture* 35 (2006), 267–291.
Ehrard, Jean. *Lumières et esclavage: L'esclavage colonial et l'opinion publique en France au XVIIIe siècle*. Brussels: André Versaille, 2008.
Elisseeff-Poisle, Danielle. *Nicolas Fréret (1688–1749): Réflexions d'un humaniste du XVIIIe siècle sur la Chine*. Paris: Presses Universitaires de France, 1978.
Ellingson, Ter. *The Myth of the Noble Savage*. Berkeley, CA: University of California Press, 2001.
Epstein, David. "The Kourou Expedition to Guiana: The Genesis of a Black Legend." *Boletín de Estudios latinoamericanos y del Caribe* 37 (1984), 85–97.
Eriksson, Gunnar. *The Atlantic Vision: Olaus Rudbeck and Baroque Science*. Canton, MA: Science History Publications, 1994.
Eze, Emmanuel Chukwudi. *Race and the Enlightenment*. Malden, MA: Blackwell, 1997.
Fairchild, Hoxie Neale. *The Noble Savage: A Study in Romantic Naturalism*. New York: Russell & Russell, 1961 [1928].
Farge, Arlette. *Subversive Words: Public Opinion in Eighteenth-Century France*. University Park, PA: Pennsylvania State University Press, 1995.
Feest, Christian. "Father Lafitau as Ethnographer of the Iroquois." *European Review of Native American Studies* 15:2 (2001), 19–25.
Fenton, William N. "J. F. Lafitau, Precursor of Scientific Anthropology." *Southwestern Journal of Anthropology* 25:2 (1969), 173–187.
Feugère, Anatole. *Un précurseur de la Révolution: l'abbé Raynal, 1713–1796*. Geneva: Slatkine Reprints, 1970 [1922].
Findlen, Paula, ed. *Athanasius Kircher: The Last Man Who Knew Everything*. New York: Routledge, 2004.
Florenne, Yves. *Le Président de Brosses*. Paris: Mercure de France, 1964.
Foucault, Michel. *Discipline and Punish: The Birth of the Prison*. Translated by Alan Sheridan. New York: Vintage, 1995.
Fox, Christopher, Roy Porter, and Robert Wokler. *Inventing Human Science: Eighteenth Century Domains*. Berkeley and Los Angeles: University of California Press, 1995.
Fox-Genovese, Elizabeth. *The Origins of Physiocracy: Economic Revolution and Social Order in Eighteenth-Century France*. Ithaca, NY: Cornell University Press, 1976.
Fredrickson, George M. *Racism: A Short History*. Princeton, NJ: Princeton University Press, 2002.
Frostin, Charles. *Les révoltes blanches à Saint-Domingue au XVIIe et XVIIIe siècles*. Paris: Editions de l'Ecole, 1975.
Gallouët, Catherine, David M. Diop, Michèle Bocquillon, and Gérard Lahouati, eds. *L'Afrique du siècle des Lumières: savoirs et représentations*. Oxford: Voltaire Foundation, 2009.

Garraway, Doris. *The Libertine Colony: Creolization in the Early French Caribbean.* Durham, NC: Duke University Press, 2005.

Garreta, Jean-Claude, ed. *Charles de Brosses, 1777–1977. Actes du colloque organisé à Dijon du 3 au 7 mai 1977.* Geneva: Slatkine, 1981.

Garrigus, John. *Before Haiti: Race and Citizenship in French Saint-Domingue.* New York: Palgrave Macmillan, 2006.

———. "Redrawing the Colour Line: Gender and the Social Construction of Race in Pre-Revolutionary Haiti." *Journal of Caribbean History* 30:1–2 (1996), 28–50.

Gay, Peter. *The Enlightenment: An Interpretation.* New York: Knopf, 1967.

———. *The Party of Humanity.* New York: Norton, 1971.

Gerbi, Antonello. *The Dispute of the New World: The History of a Polemic, 1750–1900.* Translated by Jeremy Moyle Pittsburgh, PA: University of Pittsburgh Press, 1973.

Ghachem, Malick. *Sovereignty and Slavery in the Age of Revolution: Haitian Variations on a Metropolitan Theme.* Stanford University Dissertation, 2001.

Gilroy, Paul. *The Black Atlantic: Modernity and Double Consciousness.* Cambridge: Harvard University Press, 1993.

Gliozzi, Giuliano. *Adam et le Nouveau Monde.* Lecques: Théétète, 2000.

———. "Rousseau: Mythe du bon sauvage ou critique du mythe des origines?" In *Primitivisme et mythes des origines dans la France des Lumières, 1680–1820,* edited by Chantal Grell and Christian Michel, 193–203. Paris: Presses de l'Université de Paris-Sorbonne, 1989.

Göçek, Fatma. *East Encounters West: France and the Ottoman Empire in the Eighteenth Century.* Oxford and New York: Oxford University Press, 1987.

Gordon, Daniel. "On the Supposed Obsolescence of the French Enlightenment." In *Postmodernism and the Enlightenment: New Perspectives in Eighteenth-Century French History,* edited by Daniel Gordon, 201–221. New York: Routledge, 2001.

———. *Postmodernism and the Enlightenment: New Perspectives in Eighteenth-Century French History.* New York: Routledge, 2001.

Gossiaux, P. P. "De Brosses: le Fétichisme, de la démonologie à la linguistique." In *Charles de Brosses, 1777–1977. Actes du colloque organisé à Dijon du 3 au 7 mai 1977,* edited by Jean-Claude Garreta, 167–185. Geneva: Slatkine, 1981.

Gould, Stephen Jay. *The Mismeasure of Man.* New York: Norton, 1996 [1981].

Grafton, Anthony. "Joseph Scaliger and Historical Chronology: The Rise and Fall of a Discipline." *History and Theory* 14:2 (1975), 156–185.

———. "Kircher's Chronology." In *Athanasius Kircher: The Last Man Who Knew Everything,* edited by Paula Findlen, 171–187. New York: Routledge, 2004.

Grafton, Anthony, April Shelford, and Nancy Siraisi. *New Worlds, Ancient Texts: The Power of Tradition and the Shock of Discovery.* Cambridge: Harvard University Press, 1992.

Gray, John. *Enlightenment's Wake: Politics and Culture at the Close of the Modern Age.* London and New York: Routledge, 1995.

Grell, Chantal. "Hérodote et la Bible: Tradition chrétienne et histoire ancienne dans la France moderne (XVI-XVIIIe siècles)." *Historiographie* 7 (1985), 60–91.

Grell, Chantal. *L'Histoire entre érudition et philosophie: Etude sur la connaissance historique à l'age des Lumières.* Paris: Presses Universitaires de France, 1993.

Grell, Chantal, and Christian Michel, eds. *Primitivisme et mythes des origines dans la France des Lumières, 1680–1820.* Paris: Presses de l'Université de Paris—Sorbonne, 1989.

Guilderson, Hugh L. *From the State of Nature to the Empire of Reason: Civilization in Buffon, Mirabeau, and Raynal.* Boston College Dissertation, 1994.

Guy, Basil. *The French Image of China before and after Voltaire.* Geneva: Publications de l'Institut et Musée Voltaire, 1963.

Habermas, Jürgen. *The Philosophical Discourse of Modernity.* Cambridge, MA: MIT Press, 1987.

Hadidi, Djavad. *Voltaire et l'Islam.* Paris: Publications Orientalistes de France, 1974.

Harris, Marvin. *The Rise of Anthropological Theory.* Lanham, MD: Rowman & Littlefield, 2001.

Harvey, David. *The Condition of Postmodernity: An Enquiry into the Origins of Cultural Change.* Oxford: Blackwell, 1990.

Harvey, David Allen. "Living Antiquity: Lafitau's *Moeurs des sauvages amériquains* and the Religious Roots of the Enlightenment Science of Man." *Proceedings of the Western Society for French History* 36 (2008), 75–92.

———. "The Noble Savage and the Savage Noble: Philosophy and Ethnography in the *Voyages* of the Baron de Lahontan." *French Colonial History* 11 (2010), 161–191.

Hazard, Paul. *The European Mind, 1680–1715.* Cleveland, OH: Meridian Books, 1963.

Headrick, Daniel. *The Tools of Empire: Technology and European Imperialism in the Nineteenth Century.* Oxford: Oxford University Press, 1981.

Hertzberg, Arthur. *The French Enlightenment and the Jews.* New York: Columbia University Press, 1968.

Hodgen, Margaret T. *Early Anthropology in the Sixteenth and Seventeenth Centuries.* Philadelphia, PA: University of Pennsylvania Press, 1971.

Hollinger, David. "The Enlightenment and the Genealogy of Cultural Conflict in the United States." In *What's Left of Enlightenment? A Postmodern Question,* edited by Keith Michael Baker and Peter Hanns Reill, 7–18. Stanford, CA: Stanford University Press, 2001.

Hunt, Lynn. *Inventing Human Rights: A History.* New York: Norton, 2008.

Hunt, Lynn, Margaret Jacob, and Wijnand Mijnhardt. *The Book That Changed Europe: Picart & Bernard's Religious Ceremonies of the World.* Cambridge, MA: Harvard University Press, 2010.

Huxley, Robert. *The Great Naturalists.* London: Thames and Hudson, 2007.

Iacono, Alfonso M. "The American Indians and the Ancients of Europe: The Idea of Comparison and the Construction of Historical Time in the 18th Century." In *The Classical Tradition and the Americas,* edited by Wolfgang Haase and Mayer Reinhold. New York: Walter de Gruyter, 1994.

Iliffe, Rob. "'Aplatisseur du monde et de Cassini': Maupertuis, Precision Measurement, and the Shape of the Earth in the 1730s." *History of Science* 31:4 (1993), 335–375.

Imbruglia, Girolamo. "Da Raynal a Burke. Il tradizionalismo philosophique di Malouet e il 1789." *Studi Settecenteschi* 10 (1987), 85–119.

Irwin, Robert. *Dangerous Knowledge: Orientalism and Its Discontents.* Woodstock, NY: The Overlook Press, 2008.

Isaac, Benjamin. *The Invention of Racism in Classical Antiquity.* Princeton, NJ: Princeton University Press, 2004.

Israel, Jonathan. *Radical Enlightenment: Philosophy and the Making of Modernity, 1650–1750.* Oxford and New York: Oxford University Press, 2001.

Iversen, Erik. *The Myth of Egypt and its Hieroglyphs in European Tradition.* Princeton, NJ: Princeton University Press, 1993 [1961].

Jennings, Jeremy. *Revolution and the Republic: A History of Political Thought in France Since the Eighteenth Century.* Oxford and New York: Oxford University Press, 2011.

Jimack, Peter, and Jenny Mander. "Reuniting the World: The Pacific in Raynal's *Histoire des Deux Indes*." *Eighteenth-Century Studies* 41:2 (2008), 189–202.

Jones, Tom. "The French Expedition to Lapland." *Terrae incognitae* 2 (1970), 15–24.

Kaiser, Thomas. "The Evil Empire? The Debate on Turkish Despotism in Eighteenth-Century French Political Culture." *The Journal of Modern History* 72:1 (2000), 6–34.

Keevak, Michael. *The Story of a Stele: China's Nestorian Monument and its Reception in the West, 1625–1916.* Hong Kong: Hong Kong University Press, 2008.

Kellman, Jordan. *Discovery and Enlightenment at Sea: Maritime Exploration and Observation in the Eighteenth-Century French Scientific Community.* Princeton University Dissertation, 1998.

Kennedy, J. H. *Jesuit and Savage in New France.* Hamden, CT: Archon Books, 1971.

Kidd, Colin. *The Forging of Races: Race and Scripture in the Protestant Atlantic World, 1600–2000.* Cambridge and New York: Cambridge University Press, 2006.

King, David. *Finding Atlantis: A True Story of Genius, Madness, and an Extraordinary Quest for a Lost World.* New York: Harmony Books, 2005.

King, Stewart. *Blue Coat or Powdered Wig: Free People of Color in Pre-Revolutionary Saint-Domingue.* Athens, GA: University of Georgia Press, 2001.

Krist, Markus. "Kultur, Zeit, und Anthropologie in J. F. Lafitaus Moeurs des sauvages amériquains (1724)." *Romanistische Zeitschrift für Literaturgeschichte* 19:1–2 (1995), 21–41.

La Condamine, Pierre de. "Les aventures extraordinaires de Jean et Isabelle Godin des Odonais." *Miroir de l'histoire* 99 (1958), 1313–1322.

Laming-Emperaire, Annette. *Le problème des origines américaines: Théories, hypothèses, documents.* Ann Arbor: UMI, 1980.

Lanctot, Gustave, ed. *Collection Oakes: Nouveaux Documents de Lahontan sur le Canada et Terre-Neuve.* Ottawa: J. P. Patenaude, 1940.

Lanson, Gustave. *Voltaire,* translated by Robert A. Wagoner. New York: John Wiley and Sons, 1960.

Laurens, Henry. *Aux sources de l'orientalisme: La Bibliothèque Orientale de Barthélemy d'Herbelot.* Paris: Maisonneuve et Larose, 1978.

Laurens, Henry. *Les origines intellectuelles de l'expédition d'Egypte: L'Orientalisme islamisant en France (1698–1798).* Paris and Istanbul: Editions Isis, 1987.

Leoni, Sylviane. *Charles de Brosses et le voyage lettré au XVIIIe siècle. Colloque de Dijon, 3–4 octobre 2002.* Dijon: Editions Universitaires de Dijon, 2004.

Leung, Cécile. "Etienne Fourmont (1683–1745): The Birth of Sinology in the Context of the Institutions of Learning in Eighteenth-Century France." *Sino-Western Cultural Relations* 17 (1995), 39–56.

Liebersohn, Harry. *The Travelers' World: Europe to the Pacific.* Cambridge, MA: Harvard University Press, 2006.

Livingstone, David. "The Pre-Adamite Theory and the Marriage of Science and Religion." *Transactions of the American Philosophical Society* 82:3 (1992).

Livingstone, David, and Charles Withers, eds. *Geography and the Enlightenment.* Chicago, IL: University of Chicago Press, 1999.

Lokke, Carl Ludwig. *France and the Colonial Question: A Study of Contemporary French Opinion, 1763–1801.* 1932. New York: AMS, 1968.

Lovejoy, Arthur, and George Boas. *Primitivism and Related Ideas in Antiquity.* New York: Octagon Books, 1965 [1935].

Lowe, Lisa. *Critical Terrains: French and British Orientalisms.* Ithaca, NY: Cornell University Press, 1991.

Lusebrink, Hans-Jürgen, and Manfred Tietz, eds. *Lectures de Raynal: L'Histoire des deux Indes en Europe et en Amérique au XVIIIe siècle.* Oxford: Voltaire Foundation, 1991.

MacCormack, Sabine. "Limits of Understanding: Perceptions of Greco-Roman and Amerindian Paganism in Early Modern Europe." In *America in European Consciousness, 1493–1750,* edited by Karen Ordahl Kupperman. Chapel Hill, NC: University of North Carolina Press, 1995.

Mackerras, Colin. *Western Images of China.* Oxford: Oxford University Press, 1999.

Manuel, Frank. *The Eighteenth Century Confronts the Gods.* New York: Athenaeum, 1967.

Marcil, Yasmine. "La presse et le compte rendu de récits de voyage scientifique; le cas de la querelle entre Bouguer et La Condamine." *Science et techniques en perspective* 3:2 (1999), 285–304.

Marshall, P. J. and Glyndwr Williams. *The Great Map of Mankind: Perceptions of New Worlds in the Age of Enlightenment.* Cambridge, MA: Harvard University Press, 1982.

Mathur, Mary E. Fleming. "The Iroquois in Ethnography...A Time-Space Concept." *The Indian Historian* 2:3 (1969), 12–18.

Matsuda, Matt. *Empire of Love: Histories of France and the Pacific.* New York and Oxford: Oxford University Press, 2005.

McGregor, Gaile. *The Noble Savage in the New World Garden: Notes Toward a Syntactics of Place.* Toronto: University of Toronto Press, 1988.

Meek, Ronald L. *Social Science and the Ignoble Savage.* Cambridge: Cambridge University Press, 1976.

Mercier, Roger. "L'Amérique et les Américains dans l'*Histoire des deux Indes* de l'abbé Raynal." *Revue française d'histoire d'outre-mer* 65:3 (1978), 309–324.

———. "Les Français en Amérique du Sud dans le XVIIIe siècle: La Mission de l'Académie des Sciences, 1735–1745." *Revue Française d'Outre-Mer* 56:205 (September 1969), 327–374.

Moscovici, Claudia. "An Ethics of Cultural Exchange: Diderot's *Supplément au Voyage de Bougainville.*" *Clio* 30:3 (2001), 289–307.

Mosse, George. *Toward the Final Solution: A History of European Racism.* New York: Howard Fertig, 1978.

Motsch, Andreas. *Lafitau et l'émergence du discours ethnographique.* Sillery, PQ: Septentrion, 2001.

Murray, James C. *Spanish Chronicles of the Indies: Sixteenth Century.* New York: Twayne, 1994.

Muthu, Sankar. *Enlightenment against Empire.* Princeton, NJ: Princeton University Press, 2003.

Nelles, Paul. "Du savant au missionnaire: La doctrine, les moeurs, et l'écriture de l'histoire chez les jésuites." *XVIIe siècle* 237:4 (2007), 669–689.

Nelson, William Max. "Making Men: Enlightenment Ideas of Racial Engineering." *American Historical Review* 115:5 (December 2010), 1364–1394.

Nirenberg, David. "Was There Race Before Modernity? The Example of 'Jewish' Blood in Late Medieval Spain." In *The Origins of Racism in the West,* edited by Miriam Eliav-Feldon, et al., 232–264. Cambridge and New York: Cambridge University Press, 2009,.

Nussbaum, Felicity, ed. *The Global Eighteenth Century.* Baltimore, MD: Johns Hopkins University Press, 2003.

O'Brien, Karen. *Narratives of Enlightenment: Cosmopolitan History from Voltaire to Gibbon.* Cambridge: Cambridge University Press, 1997.

———. "The Return of the Enlightenment." *American Historical Review* 115:5 (December 2010), 1426–1435.

Ogle, Gene. "'The Eternal Power of Reason' and 'The Superiority of Whites': Hilliard d'Auberteuil's Colonial Enlightenment." *French Colonial History* 3 (2003), 35–50.

Outram, Dorinda. *The Enlightenment.* Cambridge: Cambridge University Press, 2005.

Pagden, Anthony. *European Encounters with the New World: From Renaissance to Romanticism.* New Haven, CT: Yale University Press, 1993.

———. *The Fall of Natural Man: The American Indian and the Origins of Comparative Ethnology.* Cambridge: Cambridge University Press, 1982.

———. *Lords of All the World: Ideologies of Empire in Spain, Britain, and France, c. 1500–1800.* New Haven, CT: Yale University Press, 1995.

Pagliaro, Harold, ed. *Racism in the Eighteenth Century.* Cleveland, OH: Case Western Reserve University Press, 1973.

Peabody, Sue. *"There Are No Slaves in France": The Political Culture of Race and Slavery in the Ancien Regime.* Oxford: Oxford University Press, 1996.

Peabody, Sue, and Tyler Stovall, eds. *The Color of Liberty: Histories of Race in France.* Durham, NC: Duke University Press, 2003.

Pinot, Virgile. *La Chine et la formation de l'esprit philosophique en France, 1640–1740.* 1932. Geneva: Slatkine Reprints, 1971.

Pioffet, Marie-Christine. "Le Scythe et l'Amérindien: Esquisse d'une ethnologie comparée dans les textes de la Nouvelle-France." *Etudes canadiennes* 56 (2004), 207–221.

Pocock, J. G. A. *Barbarism and Religion, Vol. II: Narratives of Civil Government.* Cambridge: Cambridge University Press, 1999.

Poliakov, Leon. *The Aryan Myth: A History of Nationalist and Racist Ideas in Europe.* New York: Basic Books, 1971.

Pomeau, René. "Voyages et lumières dans la littérature française du XVIIIe siècle." *Studies on Voltaire and the Eighteenth Century* 57 (1967), 1269–1289.

Popkin, Jeremy. *News and Politics in the Age of Revolution: Jean de Luzac's Gazette de Leyde.* Ithaca, NY: Cornell University Press, 1989.

Popkin, Richard. "Condorcet, Abolitionist." In *Condorcet Studies I,* edited by Leonora Cohen Rosenfeld, 35–47. Highlands, NJ: Humanities Press, 1997,.

———. "The Philosophical Basis of Eighteenth-Century Racism." In *Racism in the Eighteenth Century,* edited by Harold Pagliaro, 245–262. Cleveland, OH: Case Western Reserve University Press, 1973.

Pouloin, Claudine. "La connaissance du passé et la vulgarisation du débat sur les Chronologies dans l'Encyclopédie." *Revue d'histoire des sciences* 44:3 (1991), 393–411.

———. *Le temps des origines: L'Eden, le Déluge, et les 'temps reculés' de Pascal à l'Encyclopédie.* Paris: Honoré Champion, 1998.

Ranum, Orest. *Artisans of Glory: Writers and Historical Thought in Seventeenth-Century France.* Chapel Hill, NC: University of North Carolina Press, 1980.

Raphanaud, Gaston. *Le Baron Malouet, ses idées, son œuvre.* Paris: A. Michalon, 1907.

Roberts, Kathleen Glenister. *Alterity and Narrative: Stories and the Negotiation of Western Identities.* Albany, NY: State University of New York Press, 2007.

Roelens, Maurice. "Lahontan dans *l'Encyclopédie* et ses suites." In *Recherches nouvelles sur quelques écrivains des Lumières,* edited by Jacques Proust, 163–200. Geneva: Droz, 1972.

Roger, Jacques. *Buffon, un philosophe au Jardin du Roi.* Paris: Fayard, 1989.

———. *Les sciences de la vie dans la pensée française du XVIIIe siècle.* Paris: Armand Colin, 1963.

Rossi, Paolo. *The Dark Abyss of Time: The History of the Earth and the History of Nations from Hooke to Vico.* Translated by Lydia Cochrane. Chicago, IL: University of Chicago Press, 1984.

Rothschild, Emma. "A Horrible Tragedy in the French Atlantic." *Past and Present* 192 (August 2006), 67–108.

Roy, Joseph-Edmond. *Le Baron de Lahontan.* Montreal: Editions Elysée, 1974.

Rupp-Eisenreich, Britta, ed. *Histoires de l'Anthropologie (XVIe-XIXe siècles).* Paris: Klincksieck, 1984.

Ryan, Michael. "Assimilating New Worlds in the Sixteenth and Seventeenth Centuries." *Comparative Studies in Society and History* 23:4 (1981), 519–538.

Ryan, Tom. "'Le Président des Terres Australes': Charles de Brosses and the French Enlightenment Beginnings of Oceanic Anthropology." In

Science, Empire, and the European Exploration of the Pacific, edited by Tony Ballantyne, 247–276. Aldershot, UK: Ashgate, 2004.

Sadrin, Paul. *Nicolas-Antoine Boulanger (1722–1759) ou avant nous le déluge.* Oxford: Voltaire Foundation, 1986.

Safier, Neil. *Measuring the New World: Enlightenment Science and South America.* Chicago, IL: University of Chicago Press, 2008.

Said, Edward. *Orientalism.* New York: Vintage, 1979.

Sala-Molins, Louis. *Dark Side of the Light: Slavery and the French Enlightenment,* translated by John Conteh-Morgan. Minneapolis, MN: University of Minnesota Press, 2006.

Sandler, Iris. "Pierre-Louis Moreau de Maupertuis: A Precursor of Mendel?" *Journal of the History of Biology* 16:1 (1983), 101–136.

Schaub, Diana J. *Erotic Liberalism: Women and Revolution in Montesquieu's Persian Letters.* Boston, MA: Rowman and Littlefield, 1995.

Schechter, Ronald. *Obstinate Hebrews: Representations of Jews in France, 1715–1815.* Berkeley, CA: University of California Press, 2003.

Schmidt, James. "What Enlightenment Project?" *Political Theory* 28:6 (2000), 734–757.

Schwab, Raymond. *La Renaissance orientale.* Paris: Payot, 1950.

Sepinwall, Alyssa Goldstein. *The Abbé Grégoire and the French Revolution: The Making of Modern Universalism.* Berkeley, CA: University of California Press, 2005.

Shelford, April G. *Transforming the Republic of Letters: Pierre-Daniel Huet and European Intellectual Life, 1650–1720.* Rochester, NY: University of Rochester Press, 2007.

Shklar, Judith N. "Politics and the Intellect." In *Political Thought and Political Thinkers,* edited by Stanley Hoffmann, 94–104. Chicago, IL: The University of Chicago Press, 1998.

Sloan, Philip. "The Idea of Racial Degeneracy in Buffon's *Histoire naturelle.*" In *Racism in the Eighteenth Century,* edited by Harold Pagliaro, 293–321. Cleveland, OH: Case Western Reserve University, 1973.

Smith, Bernard. *European Vision and the South Pacific, 1768–1850.* Oxford: Oxford University Press, 1960.

Spence, Jonathan. *Emperor of China: Self Portrait of K'ang-Hsi.* New York: Vintage, 1988.

Stocking, George W., Jr. "French Anthopology in 1800." In *Race, Culture, and Evolution: Essays in the History of Anthropology.* Chicago, IL: The University of Chicago Press, 1982, 13–41.

Terrall, Mary. *The Man Who Flattened the Earth: Maupertuis and the Sciences in the Enlightenment.* Chicago, IL: University of Chicago Press, 2002.

Todorov, Tzvetan. *On Human Diversity: Nationalism, Racism, and Exoticism in French Thought.* Cambridge, MA: Harvard University Press, 1993.

Trousson, Raymond. *Denis Diderot, ou le vrai Prométhée.* Paris: Taillandier, 2005.

———. *Jean-Jacques Rousseau.* Paris: Taillandier, 2003.

———. *Voyages aux pays de nulle part: histoire littéraire de la pensée utopique.* Brussels: Editions de l'Université de Bruxelles, 1999.

Venturi, Franco. "Oriental Despotism," *Journal of the History of Ideas* 24:1 (1963), 133–142.

Vidal-Naquet, Pierre. *The Atlantis Story: A Short History of Plato's Myth*, translated by Janet Lloyd. Exeter, UK: University of Exeter Press, 2007.

Vogel, Ursula. "The Skeptical Enlightenment: Philosopher Travellers Look Back at Europe." In *The Enlightenment and Modernity*, edited by Norman Geras and Robert Wokler, 3–24. Basingstroke and London: Macmillan, 2000.

Vyverberg, Henry. *Human Nature, Cultural Diversity, and the French Enlightenment*. New York: Oxford University Press, 1989.

Wade, Ira Owen. *The Intellectual Origins of Voltaire*. Princeton, NJ: Princeton University Press, 1969.

———. *Voltaire and Madame du Châtelet: An Essay on the Intellectual Activity at Cirey*. New York: Octagon Books, 1967.

Walker, D. P. *The Ancient Theology: Studies in Christian Platonism from the Fifteenth to the Eighteenth Century*. Ithaca, NY: Cornell University Press, 1972.

Weber, David J. *Bárbaros: Spaniards and Their Savages in the Age of Enlightenment*. New Haven, CT: Yale University Press, 2005.

Wolff, Larry, and Marco Cipolloni, eds. *The Anthropology of the Enlightenment*. Stanford, CA: Stanford University Press, 2007.

Wolin, Richard. *The Seduction of Unreason: The Intellectual Romance with Fascism from Nietzsche to Postmodernism*. Princeton, NJ: Princeton University Press, 2004.

Wolpe, Hans. *Raynal et sa machine de guerre: L'Histoire des deux Indes et ses perfectionnements*. Stanford, CA: Stanford University Press, 1957.

Wuthnow, Robert. *Communities of Discourse: Ideology and Social Structure in the Reformation, the Enlightenment, and European Socialism*. Cambridge, MA: Harvard University Press, 1989.

Young, David. "Montesquieu's View of Despotism and His Use of Travel Literature." *The Review of Politics* 40:3 (1978), 392–405.

Index